AF600058

THE CATHOLIC UNIVERSITY OF AMERICA
CANON LAW STUDIES
NO. 215

THE ELECTION OF BISHOPS IN THE LETTERS OF GREGORY THE GREAT

WITH AN APPENDIX ON THE PALLIUM

BY

JOHN ALBERT EIDENSCHINK, O.S.B., B.A., J.C.L.
Monk of St. John's Abbey, Collegeville, Minnesota

A DISSERTATION

Submitted to the Faculty of the School of Canon Law of the Catholic University of America in Partial Fulfillment of the Requirements for the Degree of Doctor of Canon Law

THE CATHOLIC UNIVERSITY OF AMERICA PRESS
WASHINGTON, D.C.
1945

Nihil Obstat:

CLEMENS V. BASTNAGEL, J.U.D.
Censor Deputatus
Washingtonii, die 7 *maii* 1945.

Imprimi Potest:

✠ALCUINUS DEUTSCH, O.S.B.
Abbas Sancti Joannis Baptistae
Abbatia Sancti Joannis Baptistae, die 10 *maii* 1945.

Imprimatur:

✠JOSEPHUS F. BUSCH, D.D.
Episcopus Sancti Clodoaldi
Sancti Clodoaldi, die 14 *maii* 1945.

Printed in the United States of America

St. John's University Press
Collegeville, Minnesota

REVERENDISSIMO ET AMPLISSIMO DOMINO
ABBATI ALCUINO DEUTSCH
NECNON REVERENDIS PATRIBUS ET
VENERABILIBUS FRATRIBUS
ABBATIAE S. IOANNIS BAPTISTAE
HOC OPUSCULUM HUMILITER DICAT AUCTOR

TABLE OF CONTENTS

APPENDIX

FOREWORD

Pope Gregory the Great (590-604) has rightly been considered by all students of history as one of the most notable figures who have made their influence felt upon their own and upon succeeding generations. To the students of ecclesiastical history Gregory the Great is one of the Fathers, one of the four great Doctors of the Western Church; his life and works must therefore ever remain the subjects of careful study as they have been throughout the centuries, even from his own day.

Among the many writings of this great Pope, his letters occupy a very important position, particularly for the student of the history of canonical institutes. For his letters are not merely personal letters, read because of sentimental interest; they are, for the most part, records of the activities of a Pope whose personal interest, in a trying period of history, embraced the welfare of the entire Church of his day, and was manifested in the letters written upon all matters of discipline, great and small. His letters picture for posterity the status of the Church and its canonical institutes as these existed at the end of the sixth century.

Some eight hundred and fifty letters of St. Gregory have been preserved. These have formed the basis for the present study, which concerns itself with the election of bishops at the end of the sixth century as outlined in the letters of Pope Gregory. For the proper understanding of Gregory's letters a clear picture of the organization of the Church during his pontificate is necessary: a brief historical sketch of the growth of the patriarchates and of metropolitan provinces has, therefore, been given in the first chapter. Particular attention was paid to the Western patriarchate because the majority of Gregory's letters deal with conditions there. The second chapter gives the story of the various elections of bishops with which Gregory dealt. An attempt has been made in the third chapter to identify the sources which Gregory may have used in listing the qualities required of a candidate for the episcopacy. In the fourth chapter important points of law relative to the election of bishops as illustrated in Gregory's letters are considered. Of special interest is the fact that at times the pallium was granted in connection with the papal approval and ratification of an episcopal election and consecration. Because of the importance of this ecclesiastical vestment and of the uncertainties of its origin and early use, an appendix has been devoted to the pallium: its origin and early use and its use at the end of the sixth century as depicted in the letters of St. Gregory.

In order that the letters of Gregory the Great might be correctly interpreted in the light of preceding history, constant reference has been made to earlier source materials, and the historical development of the various subjects treated has been briefly indicated. Throughout the study reference has been made to the formulas of the *Liber Diurnus*; these have been compared with the letters of Pope Gregory in an effort to ascertain whether his letters were used to form the formulas of the *Liber Diurnus*, or whether the formulas of the *Liber Diurnus* were used by the Pope in the formation of his letters.

It is a pleasure to give expression here to my gratitude to the members of the Faculty of the School of Canon Law for their guidance and encouragement, and to the Librarians of the Catholic University for their unfailing courtesy.

For the opportunity of advanced studies at the Catholic University of America the writer wishes to express his sincere thanks to his religious superior, the Right Reverend Alcuin Deutsch, O.S.B., Abbot of St. John's Abbey. To all, confreres, relatives and friends, who have by their prayers, advice and encouragement contributed to the completion of this study, the writer is deeply grateful.

UT IN OMNIBUS GLORIFICETUR DEUS

CHAPTER I

THE ORGANIZATION OF THE CHURCH IN 590

SECTION I. THE FIVE PATRIARCHATES

In order properly to understand the differences in the matter of the Pope's relation to the election and confirmation of bishops in various parts of the world, it is necessary to present first a brief account of the organization of the Church at the accession of Gregory the Great in the year 590.[1] The

[1] The early biographies of Gregory the Great, listed in chronological order, are as follows: 1. that of Gregory of Tours (†594) in his *Historia Francorum,* x, c. 1—*Monumenta Germaniae Historica* [=*MGH*], Scriptorum Rerum Merovingicarum Tomus I, *Gregorii Turonensis Opera,* Arndt and Krusch (Hannoverae: Impensis Bibliopolii, 1885), V, 406-409. 2. That of the author of the *Liber Pontificalis*—Duchesne, *Le Liber Pontificalis* (2 vols., Paris, 1886), I, 312; the edition of Duchesne, in preference to that of Mommsen [*MGH,* Gestorum Pontificum Romanorum I, *Libri Pontificalis pars prior* (Berolini: Apud Weidmannos, 1898)], will be used throughout this work and will be cited hereafter as *Liber Pontificalis.* 3. That of an unknown monk of Whitby, written about the year 713—Gasquet, *A Life of Pope St. Gregory the Great written by a Monk of the Monastery of Whitby* (printed from MS St. Gallen, 567, Westminster: Art and Book Company, 1904). 4. That of St. Bede in his *Historia Ecclesiastica,* Lib. ii, c. 1—Plummer, *Venerabilis Bedae Opera Historica* (2 vols., Oxonii, E Typographeo Clarendoniano, 1896), I, 73-81; II, 67-73, 389-391. 5. The more complete biographies written by Paul the Deacon (toward the end of the eighth century) and by John the Deacon (in the year 872 at the request of Pope John VIII). These biographies have been frequently edited; the edition of the Maurists [Volume XV of *Sancti Gregorii Papae I. Cognomento Magni Opera Omnia* (17 vols., Venetiis, 1768-1776)] has been reproduced in Migne, *Patrologiae Cursus Completus, Series Latina* (221 vols., Parisiis, 1844-1864), LXXV. Abbreviated hereafter as *PL.* A critical edition of the *Vita* by Paul the Deacon has been published by Grisar, "Die Gregorbiographie des Paulus Diaconus in ihrer ursprünglichen Gestalt," *Zeitschrift für katholische Theologie,* XI (1887), 158-173. Hereafter abbreviated *ZKT.*

An account of the more modern biographies is given by F. Homes Dudden in the preface to his *Gregory the Great, His Place in History and Thought* (2 vols., London: Longmans, Green and Co., 1905), I, viii-xv. Yet more recent biographies are the following: Howorth, *Gregory the Great* (London: John Murray, 1912); Snow, *St. Gregory the Great* (2. ed., New

primacy of the Pope over the entire Church at this period of history was unquestioned, and Gregory the Great made frequent use of his rights as successor of St. Peter.[2]

York: Benziger Brothers, 1924)—a merely popular work; Batiffol, *Saint Gregory the Great* (translated from the French by John L. Stoddard, New York: Benziger Brothers, 1929)—a more scholarly work. A recent critical study is that of Caspar, *Geschichte des Papsttums von der Anfängen bis zur Höhe der Weltherrschaft* (2 vols., Tübingen: Verlag von J.C.B. Mohr, 1930-1933), II, 306-514; abbreviated hereafter as *Geschichte des Papsttums*. Caspar's work has been rather severely criticized by Stein, "La période byzantine de la papauté," *Catholic Historical Review*, XXX (1935), 129-163; hereafter abbreviated *CHR*. While admitting that the two volumes are great examples of German scholarship, Stein states that the work is "intégralement protestante." He continues: "Il va sans dire qu'il n'est guère possible à un historien imbue d'esprit protestant et bismarckien de raconter avec justesse et avec justice la vraie histoire de ce qui est l'institution suprême de l'église catholique."—*art. cit.*, p. 129. Throughout his review Stein points out various errors into which Caspar has fallen; these will be noted when necessary. A wholly favorable review of Caspar's second volume is that by Baethgen, *Zeitschrift der Savigny-Stiftung für Rechtsgeschichte*, Kan. Abt., XXIV (1935), 344-355; abbreviated hereafter *ZSS*.

The letters of Gregory the Great will be cited throughout this work from the edition of Ewald and Hartmann in *MGH*, Epistolarum Tomi I et II, *Gregorii I Papae Registrum Epistolarum* (Berolini: Apud Weidmannos, 1891-1899). Ewald's conclusions (upon which Hartmann relied in completing the work after Ewald's death) regarding the *MSS* containing Gregory's letters were attacked by Peitz in 1917: *Das Register Gregors I.* (Ergänzungshefte zu den *Stimmen der Zeit*, zweite Reihe, Forschungen, 2. Heft, Freiburg im Breisgau, 1917). Peitz' conclusions have been emphatically rejected in favor of those of Ewald by the following: Tangl, "Gregor-Register und Liber Diurnus," *Neues Archiv der Gesellschaft für ältere deutsche Geschichtskunde*, XLI (1917), 741-752; cited hereafter *Neues Archiv*; Posner, "Das Register Gregors I.," *Neues Archiv*, XLIII (1922), 243-315.

[2] Though Dudden expressly admits this (*Gregory the Great*, II, 226), he frequently seeks to minimize Gregory's acts of authority. Cf. *op. cit.*, I, 434, 454, 476; II, 225-228. On the latter pages he ascribes to Gregory the origin of a "divided principality and triple See" theory relative to the position of Rome, Alexandria and Antioch as "conjointly representing the See of the Prince of the Apostles and sharing equally in the primacy that belonged to it as such." A careful reading of the texts of Gregory's letters in their historical setting will suffice to show that their meaning has been distorted by Dudden. Cf. *Epp.* v, 42; vi, 58; vii, 37; viii, 2. 28; x, 14; xiii, 44; Batiffol, *Saint Gregory the Great*, pp. 230-234; Fliche-Martin, *Histoire de l'Église* (7 vols., Paris: Bloud et Gay, 1935-1940), V, 61f; hereafter cited as *Histoire*.

In the West in 590 the Pope was recognized as the sole patriarch, whereas the East was divided into four patriarchates, those of Constantinople, Alexandria, Antioch and Jerusalam. The doctrine of the five patriarchates dominates the sixth century, and was clearly expressed by Justinian in his Novels.[3] The doctrine of patriarchates may be said to have been officially recognized at the Council of Nicaea (325), even though the Council did not use the word "patriarch."[4]

As is well known, the third canon of the I Council of Constantinople (381) granted to Constantinople a primacy of honor second only to that of Rome, for Constantinople is, as the canon states, "new Rome."[5] Canon 3 remained a dead letter for the time being, and it was never accepted at Rome.[6]

---

[3] Cf. N. (109); (123, 3); (131, 2). Cf. also Fliche-Martin, *Histoire*, IV, 536; Maassen, *Der Primat des Bischofs von Rom und die alten Patriarchalkirchen* (Bonn: Henry und Cohen, 1853), p. 113f. Cited hereafter as *Primat*. Laws referring to the Church were directed by Justinian to the five patriarchs, who were to inform their metropolitans of them; these were in turn to bring them to the attention of their bishops. Cf. N. (5); Duchesne, *L'Église au VIe siècle* (Paris: E. de Boccard, 1925), p. 265. Cited hereafter as *L'Église*.

[4] Cf. canons 6, 7—Bruns, *Canones Apostolorum et Conciliorum Saeculorum IV. V. VI. VII.* (2 vols., Berolini: Typis et sumptibus G. Reimeri, 1839), I, 15f; cited hereafter as *Canones*; Turner, *Ecclesiae Occidentalis Monumenta Iuris Antiquissima* (2 vols. in 5 parts, Oxonii: E Typographo Clarendoniano, 1899-1930), I, ii, 120f; cited hereafter as Turner; Maassen, *Primat*, pp. 13-17; 44; 86-100; Hefele-Leclercq, *Histoire des Conciles* (10 vols. in 19, Paris: Letouzey et Ané, 1907-1938), I, 552-559; 1182-1202; 569; Chapman, *Studies on the Early Papacy* (New York: Benziger Brothers, 1928), p. 14; cited hereafter as *Papacy*; Leclercq, "Episcopat," *Dictionnaire d'archéologie chrétienne et de liturgie* (14 vols. in 27, Paris: Librairie Letouzey et Ané, 1907—), V, 235. Abbreviated hereafter *DACL*.

[5] Bruns, *Canones*, I, 21.

[6] Cf. Duchesne, *Origines du culte chrétien* (5. ed., Paris: Anciennes Maisons Thorin et Frontemoing, 1920), pp. 24-26; the fifth edition will be used throughout this work and will be cited as *Origines*. Cf. also Hefele-Leclercq, *Histoire des Conciles*, II, 1260-1270; Chapman, *Papacy*, pp. 18-20. Whether Rome ever protested against this canon depends on the authenticity of the *decretum Gelasianum*; cf. Chapman, "On the Decretum Gelasianum," *Revue bénédictine*, XXX (1913), 187-207; 315-333; *Papacy*, p. 20, note 2. Chapman's defense of the authenticity of the *decretum* was directed against the conclusions of Ernst von Dobschütz's masterly work: "Das Decretum Gelasianum de libris recipiendis et non recipiendis in

Despite Rome's failure to accept Constantinople's position as the "second see," the bishops of Constantinople began to extend their jurisdiction over the civil dioceses of Asia, Pontus and Thrace, and this jurisdiction was guaranteed to Constantinople by the Council of Chalcedon in 451; Jerusalem was also recognized as a patriarchate.[7] Pope Leo I (440-461) insisted on protecting the prerogatives of Alexandria and Antioch over against the pretensions of Constantinople. While he joyfully approved the questions of faith that had been decreed at Chalcedon, he declared as null those things "quae ad explendum episcopi Constantinopolitani vanitatem contra leges Nicaenas acta sunt."[8]

---

kritischem Text," *Texte und Untersuchungen zur Geschichte der altchristlichen Literatur*, hrsg. v. Adolf Harnack und Carl Schmidt (XXXVIII, Heft 4, Leipzig: J. C. Hinrichs'sche Buchhandlung, 1912). Dobschütz concludes that the first three chapters of the *decretum* come from a synod held under Pope Damasus (366-384); the last two are the work of a private individual and not of Pope Gelasius. Cf. *op. cit.*, pp. 3-11, VI. It is with the latter conclusion that Chapman disagrees. Thiel gives only the last three chapters given by Dobschütz; cf. *Epistolae Romanorum Pontificum Genuinae a S. Hilario* (461-468) *usque ad Pelagium* (556-561) (Brunsbergae, 1868), pp. 454ff.; 44-53; hereafter cited as *Epistolae*. Thiel's conclusions were accepted by Jaffé-Kaltenbrunner; cf. *Regesta Pontificum Romanorum ab condita Ecclesia ad annum post Christum natum MCXCVIII* (2. ed. correctam et auctam auspiciis Gulielmi Wattenbach curaverunt S. Loewenfeld, F. Kaltenbrunner, P. Ewald, 2 vols. in 1, Lipsiae, 1885-1888), nn. 251, 700. Hereafter abbreviated JK, JE, JL and number; where no number is given the citation will be Jaffé, plus volume and page. The more common opinion today is that the first two chapters of the *decretum* are the work of Pope Damasus; the third chapter contains an authentic decree of the year 382; the fourth and fifth chapters are the work of a private individual and were added to the original some time after Pope Pelagius I (556-561). Cf. Caspar, *Geschichte des Papsttums*, II, 773f.; Höpfl-Gut, *Introductio Generalis in Sacram Scripturam* (4. ed., Romae; Editiones Comm. A. Arnodo, 1940), p. 169; Ziegler, "Pope Gelasius and his Teaching on the Relation of Church and State," *CHR*, XXVII (1941-1942), 417-418. The latter holds that the addition was made "in or near the time of Gelasius (492-496)" rather than after the time of Pope Pelagius I (556-561).

[7] Cf. canons 9, 17, 28—Bruns, *Canones*, I, 28, 30, 32; Chapman, *Papacy*, p. 23; Duchesne, *Origines*, p. 26f.; Leclercq, "Patriarcat," *DACL*, XIII, 2478f.

[8] JK, 490. Cf. also JK, 481-484, 495; Anonymous, "Rome et le 28e

During the Acacian schism (484-519), the patriarch Acacius and his successors consolidated their position in reference to the 28th canon of Chalcedon. Pope Hormisdas (415-523) and the Emperor Justin 1 (518-527) strove successfully for the reunion of the patriarch of Constantinople with Rome; their efforts were crowned with success in 519.[9] Eight years later Justinian became Emperor (527-565), and there is no further protest on the part of the Popes regarding the position of Constantinople as one of the eastern patriarchates. Gregory the Great listed the patriarch of Constantinople first in the inscription of his synodical letter;[10] he strove unsuccessfully, however, to forbid the patriarchs of Constantinople to use the title "ecumenical bishop."[11]

---

canon de Chalcédoine," *Bessarione*, II (1897-1898), 215-224; Anonymous, "Le 28e canon de Chalcédoine," *Bessarione*, I (1897), 875-885. Undoubtedly Gregory the Great refers to canon 28 when he says: "...sicut Chalcedonensis synodus in uno loco ab ecclesia Constantinopolitana falsata est..." —*Ep.* vi, 14. Cf. Hartmann's note 3 *ibid.*; Caspar, *Geschichte des Papsttums*, II, 448, note 4. Constantinople continued to use the jurisdiction granted it by the Council of Chalcedon; cf. JK, 584, 585, 586; Thiel, *Epistolae*, p. 205f.

[9] For the beginning of the schism, cf. JK, 599, 600; Thiel, *Epistolae*, p. 243. For the healing of the schism, cf. JK, 819-820; Thiel, *Epistolae*, pp. 877, 879; Guenther, *Epistulae Imperatorum Pontificum Aliorum inde ab a. CCCLXVII usque ad a. DLIII datae Avellana quae dicitur collectio, Corpus Scriptorum Ecclesiasticorum* Latinorum, XXXV (Vindobonae: F. Tempesky, 1895-1899), Nos. 168, 169. Hereafter cited *Avellana*, plus number; the *Corpus Scriptorum* will be abbreviated *CSEL*. The *Collectio Avellana* could not have been made earlier than 553. For a time it was thought that the author of the collection was Dionysius Exiguus, but that theory is untenable. Cf. Guenther, "Avellana-Studien," *Sitzungsberichte der philosophisch-historischen Classe der kaiserlichen Akademie der Wissenschaften in Wien*, CXXXIV (1896), 2, 68ff. Many of the letters of the *Avellana*, from No. 105-170, deal with the papal and imperial efforts to heal the schism of Acacius. Cf. also Chapman, *Papacy*, pp. 24, 213-214; O'Sullivan-Burns, *Medieval Europe* (New York: F. S. Crofts & Company, 1943), p. 221f.

[10] *Ep.* i, 24.

[11] Cf. *Epp.* v, 37. 39. 41. 44. 45; vi, 58; vii, 4. 5. 6. 24. 28. 30. 31; viii, 29; ix, 156. 175; xiii, 43; Caspar, *Geschichte des Papsttums*, II, 452-465.

SECTION II. ECCLESIASTICAL PROVINCES AND METROPOLITANS

The fourth and fifth canons of the Council of Nicaea take for granted the existence of ecclesiastical provinces under the jurisdiction of a metropolitan, who had the right to confirm the election of bishops within the province and to preside at synods.[12] Although the Council of Nicaea accepted the boundaries of the civil province for the boundaries of the ecclesiastical province, the Church was not necessarily dependent upon the civil divisions. This was stated clearly in a letter of Pope Innocent I (402-417) and in the 12th canon of the Council of Chalcedon.[13]

SECTION III. THE WESTERN PATRIARCHATE

As by far the majority of Gregory's letters deal with ecclesiastical affairs in the West, it will suffice to consider briefly the growth of metropolitans in those parts of the ancient world that were subject to him as patriarch of the West. The extent of the western patriarchate was as follows: "it embraced the Prefecture of Italy, those of the two Gauls, and that of

[12] Cf. Bruns, *Canones*, I, 15; Turner, I, ii, 116f; Hefele-Leclercq, *Histoire des Conciles*, I, 539-552; Duchesne, *Origines*, p. 22f; Maassen, *Primat*, p. 7f. The latter notes that the first time the word "metropolitan" occurs was at the Council of Nicaea; it occurs frequently thereafter, especially in the Council of Antioch (341): cf. canons 9, 11, 13, 16, 19, 20—Bruns, *Canones*, I, 82-85; Turner, II, ii, 256-261; 266-269; 272-275; 282-283; 286-289; 290-293.

[13] Cf. JK, 310; Mansi, *Sacrorum Conciliorum Nova et Amplissima Collectio* (53 vols. in 60, Paris-Arnhem-Leipzig, 1901-1927), III, 1028; hereafter cited as Mansi; Bruns, *Canones*, I, 28; Maasen, *Primat*, p. 9; Schmitz, "Metropolitanverfassung und Provinzialsynode in Gallien während des fünften Jahrhunderts," *Archiv für katholisches Kirchenrecht*, LVII (1887), p. 5; abbreviated hereafter as *AKK*. Some have claimed that the 17th canon of Chalcedon contradicts the 12th canon; there is, however, no conflict, for the 17th does not refer to the division of a civil province. Cf. Schroeder, *Disciplinary Decrees of the General Councils, Text, Translation and Commentary* (St. Louis: Herder and Company, 1937), pp. 104, 116. Cited hereafter *Disciplinary Decrees*. Cf. also Caspar, *Geschichte des Papsttums*, II, 323; Sägmüller, *Lehrbuch des katholischen Kirchenrechts* (4. ed., 1 vol. in 4 parts, Freiburg im Breisgau: Herder, 1925-1934), p. 590. Cited hereafter as *Lehrbuch*.

Eastern Illyricum. The first Prefecture contained the three political dioceses of Italy, Western Illyricum and Africa; the second Prefecture included the diocese of Spain, of the *Septem Provinciae,* (i.e., Gaul, Belgium, *Germania prima* and *secunda,* etc.) and Britain. The third Prefecture was that of Illyricum Orientale, with the dioceses of Macedonia and Dacia, which since Theodosius I (379-395) had formed a portion of the Eastern Empire."[14]

1. THE FIRST PREFECTURE

Throughout the western patriarchate the development of ecclesiastical provinces and metropolitan sees was later than it was in the East.[15] Rome had, however, always maintained rather close watch over the episcopal sees of the surrounding territory, exercizing over them the powers of a metropolitan. The metropolitan province of the Pope included Italy as far north as Tuscany, comprising Campania, Tuscia, Umbria, Picenum Suburbicarium, Apulia, Calabria, Bruttium, Lucania, Samnium, Valeria, and the islands of Sicily, Sardinia and Corsica.[16]

In the north of Italy there were very few episcopal sees before the fourth century: Ravenna, Milan, Aquileia, Brescia and Verona. Milan was the only metropolitan see in northern Italy until the beginning of the fifth century, when Aquileia

---

[14] Grisar, *History of Rome and the Popes in the Middle Ages* (Authorized English translation edited by Luigi Cappadelta, 3 vols., London: Kegan Paul, Trench, Truebner and Co., Ltd., 1911-1913), I, 344. Cited hereafter as *History of Rome.*

[15] Cf. Maassen, *Primat,* pp. 12, 121f; Leclercq, "Episcopat," *DACL,* V, 234; Fliche-Martin, *Histoire,* II, 400-402.

[16] Cf. Maassen, *Primat,* p. 103; Hartmann, *Geschichte Italiens im Mittelalter,* (4 vols., Stuttgart-Gotha: Friederich Andreas Perthes, 1900-1915; 1st vol. re-edited in 1923), II, 161; cited hereafter as *Geschichte Italiens;* Fliche-Martin, *Histoire,* V, 39f. The latter note that Sardinia and Corsica were under Byzantine Africa for civil and military purposes, but yet belonged to the metropolitan jurisdiction of Rome and not to Carthage. Cf. *ibid.,* 212-214; also Diehl, *L'Afrique byzantine, Histoire de la domination byzantine en Afrique,* 533-709 (Paris: Ernest Leroux, Éditeur, 1896), p. 469f; cited hereafter as *L'Afrique byzantine.* It must also be noted that in the time of Gregory the Great the bishop of Cagliari in Sardinia was a metropolitan; cf. *Ep.* i, 47.

obtained metropolitan rights. A little later the province of Aemilia was detached from the jurisdiction of Milan and furnished a number of suffragan sees to the bishop of Ravenna, who, however, remained a suffragan of the Roman see, as he was consecrated at Rome and was obliged to attend the Roman synods.[17]

Besides Italy, the political dioceses of Western Illyricum and Africa were also included in the Prefecture of Italy. Originally, at the time of Constantine (306-337), all Illyricum belonged to the Western Empire. In 379 Gratian detached from the West the dioceses of Dacia and Macedonia, which became part of Theodosius' Eastern Empire, i.e., the former boundary was pushed further west so that the original Prefecture of Illyricum was divided into two parts, Eastern and Western, the line of division running from modern Kotos to a point west of the present Belgrade. Thus the provinces of Dalmatia and of Pannonia Secunda formed the eastern boundary of the western half of the Empire. In 437 Pannonia was transferred over to the jurisdiction of the Eastern Empire, coming under the jurisdiction of the Pretorian Prefect of Eastern Illyricum, who first resided at Sirmium, but moved to Thessalonica after the invasion of the Huns.[18]

Dalmatia or Western Illyricum, with its metropolitan see of Salona, was always subject to the Pope as patriarch of the West. Some claim that Pope Zosimus in 418 created Bishop Hesychius of Salona his vicar. No definite statement can be made as to the truth of this claim, but it is definite that none of Bishop Hesychius' successors at Salona had this honor,

---

[17] Cf. Duchesne, *Mémoire sur l'origine des diocèses épiscopaux dans l'ancienne Gaule* (Paris, 1890), p. 44f; cited hereafter as *Mémoire*; *idem*, *Origines*, pp. 32-38; Kirsch, *Kirchengeschichte* (4 vols., Freiburg im Breisgau; Herder, 1930-1933), I, 742; Grisar, *History of Rome*, I, 347. Further details concerning the creation of Ravenna as a metropolitan see are given in the appendix at note 37ff.

[18] Cf. Spinka, *A History of Christianity in the Balkans*, (Chicago: The American Society of Church History, 1933), p. 12; Duchesne, *Origines*, p. 42f. Dacia and Macedonia temporarily reverted to Western Illyricum from 380-395. Cf. Honig, "The So-Called 'Vicariate' of Illyricum," *Anglican Theological Review*, XXVI (1944), 91.

and at the time of Gregory the Great the bishop of Salona was metropolitan of Dalmatia but claimed no further honors.[19]

Africa had suffered much from the invasion of the Vandals under Genseric in 429, and under the Vandal kingdom until the reconquest of Africa for the Empire by Belisarius, Justinian's capable general, in 533-544.[20] Shortly after the reunion of Africa with the Empire, Justinian ordered that all ecclesiastical property held by the invaders was to be restored to the Church, that the Jews were not to hold Christian slaves, that the privileges of Carthage and other metropolitans, mentioned in the first book of his Code, were to remain unchanged.[21]

The African Church had a hierarchical organization different from other regions. At the time of St. Cyprian as bishop of Carthage (248-258) Africa was undivided, and the bishop of Carthage was recognized as the leading bishop. Early in the fourth century, Proconsular Africa and Numidia were recognized as distinct provinces, and the latter had its own primate, the bishop who had been first consecrated holding this title and office. By the year 403, Proconsular Africa, Numidia, Byzacene, Tripolitania, Mauretania Sitiphensis and Mauretania Caesariensis existed as independent provinces, each of which had its own primate.[22] The senior bishop accord-

---

[19] Cf. JK, 339; Zeiller, "Les rélations de l'ancienne église de Salone avec l'Église romaine," *Bessarione*, Series 2, IV (1903), 235-248; Zeiller, "Le chorévêque Eugraphus—Note sur le chorépiscopat en Occident au Ve siècle," *Revue d'histoire ecclésiastique*, VII (1906), 27-32; abbreviated hereafter *RHE*; Hartmann, *Geschichte Italiens*, II, 176f. Salona was destroyed by the barbarians shortly after the opening of the seventh century, and the Emperor bade the inhabitants to settle in Spalato. Cf. Doelger, *Regesten der Kaiserurkunden des oströmischen Reiches* (Corpus der griechischen Urkunden des Mittelalters und der Neueren Zeit, hrsg. von den Akademien der Wissenschaften in München und Wien, Reihe A. Abteilung I, i. Teil, Regesten von 565-1025) München und Berlin: Verlag R. Oldenbourg, 1924), n. 154. Cited hereafter *Regesten*.

[20] Cf. Diehl, *L'Afrique byzantine*, pp. 30-50.

[21] Cf. N. (37), "De Africana ecclesia." Justinian later again ordered the rights of Carthage and other metropolitans to be preserved. Cf. N. (131, 4).

[22] Cf. Batiffol, "Le *primae sedis episcopus* en Afrique," *Revue des sciences religieuses*, III (1923), 425-429; abbreviated hereafter *RSR*; Duchesne, *Origines*, 16-23.

ing to the time of consecration in each of the provinces was recognized as primate,[23] except in Proconsular Africa, where Carthage continued to hold the position of metropolitan of that province and of the whole of Africa. Provincial synods were held regularly under the presidency of the bishop of Carthage, though not necessarily in Carthage itself. Though Carthage continued to enjoy special honors, the provinces were in fact independent, each with its own primate. If Donatism had not been so widespread in Africa, and if Africa had not been so close to the Roman Church, both materially and in affection, Carthage might have developed into a patriarchate.[24]

2. THE SECOND PREFECTURE

The Second Prefecture included Spain, Gaul and Britain. There are extremely few records for the early history of Christian Spain. Yet it is known that during the first four centuries the hierarchy was firmly established.[25] While many authors state that the canons of Nicaea concerning the institution of ecclesiastical provinces and metropolitans had little or no

---

[23] Cf. canon 44 of III Carthage: "Aetate et ipsa promotione antiquissimus"—Bruns, *Canones*, I, 131; canon 89, *Statuta Concilii Africae*: "Deinde placuit, ut quicunque deinceps ab episcopis ordinantur per provincias Africanas, literas accipiant ab ordinatoribus suis manu eorum conscriptas, continentes consulem et diem, ut nulla altercatio de posterioribus vel anterioribus oriatur."—Bruns, *Canones*, I, 178. Cf. Batiffol, *op. cit.*, p. 429f.; Sägmüller, *Lehrbuch*, p. 598; Bingham, *The Antiquities of the Christian Church* (2 vols., London, 1865), II, 1039; Findlay, *Canonical Norms Governing the Deposition and Degradation of Clerics*, (Catholic University of America Canon Law Studies, No. 130, Washington, D.C.: Catholic University of America Press, 1941), p. 31.

[24] Cf. Chapman, *Papacy*, p. 12; Duchesne, *L'Église*, p. 648. In 566 Justin II (565-578) confirmed the right of the primate of Byzacene to send directly to the Emperor in Constantinople a bishop to make complaints in ecclesiastical affairs. Cf. Doelger, *Regesten*, n. 7. For the civil reorganization of the provinces and administration of Africa under the Emperor Maurice (582-602), cf. Diehl, *L'Afrique byzantine*, pp. 466-492; Fliche-Martin, *Histoire*, V, 211-214. The first mention of the African exarch occurs in July 591, in a letter of Gregory the Great; cf. *Ep.* i, 59.

[25] Cf. Garcia Villada, *Historia Eclesiástica de España* (3 vols. in 5, Madrid: Libreria Fernando Fe, 1929-1936), II, i, 185; Leclercq, "Espagne," *DACL*, V, 417f.

effect in the West, except perhaps in Africa,[26] Garcia Villada contends that metropolitans as heads of ecclesiastical provinces existed in Spain at least from the beginning of the fourth century.[27] In the beginning this dignity in each province was held by the oldest bishop according to ordination. Not long after, in accordance with the law of the Council of Antioch in 341,[28] the title was assigned to the capital city of each province.[29]

During the fifth and sixth centuries Spain suffered from various barbarian invasions. In 578 the Visigothic kingdom was firmly established in Spain with the capital city at Toledo. The pre-existing Roman system was for the most part maintained, and the division into provinces persisted, though the old Roman divisions were not always maintained. After the conversion of the Visigoths, which took place at the III Council of Toledo in 589, there were only five provinces and five metropolitans in the Iberian peninsula. To these must be added the province of Narbonne in Gaul, which at this time was still under the Visigothic kings of Spain.[30]

---

[26] Cf. e.g., Maassen, *Primat*, p. 12; Duchesne, *Origines*, p. 22f; Leclercq, "Episcopat," *DACL*, V, 234.

[27] Cf. *Historia Eclesiástica de España*, II, i, 200. The I Council of Toledo (400) decreed that all the canons of the Council of Nicaea were to be observed in Spain, and that anyone who presumed to act contrary to them was to be excommunicated. Cf. Bruns, *Canones*, I, 203.

[28] Canon 9—Bruns, *Canones*, I, 82; Turner, II, ii, 256-261.

[29] Cf. Garcia Villada, *op. cit.*, I, i, 206; II, i, 200f; Leclercq, "Espagne," *DACL*, V, 421. The 58th canon of Elvira, which speaks of the "prima cathedra episcopatus," has been variously interpreted: Batiffol maintains that it can only refer to Rome. Cf. "La *prima cathedra episcopatus* du concile d'Elvire," *Journal of Theological Studies*, XXIII (1921-1922), 263-270; hereafter abbreviated *JTSt.* Fliche-Martin, relying upon the studies of Jüllicher ("Die Synode von Elvira als Zeuge für den römischen Primat," *Zeitschrift für Kirchengeschichte*, XLII [1923], 44ff.) and Sybel ("Die Synode von Elvira," *ibid.*, 243ff.) maintain that it refers, not to Rome, but to the oldest bishop according to the time of ordination in each province. Cf. *Histoire*, II, 401, note 1.

[30] Cf. Garcia Villada, *Historia Eclesiástica de España*, II, i, 202, 207, 212-214; Ziegler, *Church and State in Visigothic Spain* (Washington, D.C.: Catholic University of America, 1930), pp. 7-35, 48f.

Gregory the Great became Pope one year after the conversion of the Visigoths. By way of anticipation it may be stated here that there is but one reference in his letters to an episcopal election in Spain. From *Ep.* xiii, 47, which deals mainly with the cases of two bishops who claimed to have been unjustly deposed, it is evident that the bishops of Spain were elected, presumably by the inhabitants of the diocese, and were consecrated, presumably by several bishops with the consent of others, for Gregory uses the expressions: "si electus fuerit;" "episcopi qui eum ordinaverunt vel ordinationi consentientes." He adds no further details about the election.

Gaul, like Spain, belonged to the Second Prefecture, and, also like Spain, suffered much from invasions and wars. The Frankish nation under King Clovis was converted to the Catholic Faith in 496. Yet Catholicism did not unite the kingdom, for, according to Frankish law, upon the death of the king the kingdom was divided among his sons. Thus the boundaries of the various Frankish kingdoms kept continually changing during the course of the sixth and seventh centuries.[31]

Neither the I Council of Arles (314) nor the Council of Valence (374) made any mention of metropolitans. In 410, however, the I Council of Turin granted Proculus of Marseilles the rights of a metropolitan for his lifetime, but refused those rights to the see itself, as it belonged to the province of Vienne, which the same Council more or less divided between the metropolitans of Vienne (the city) and Arles in order to establish peace.[32] Pope Zosimus (417-418) created Patroclus of Arles papal vicar, granting him special rights: that no bishop of Gaul was to travel without "litterae formatae" from him;

---

[31] Cf. Duchesne, *L'Église*, pp. 486-550; Boucharlat, *Les élections épiscopales sous les Mérovingiens* (Lyon: Imprimerie Waltener et Co., 1904), *passim*; cited hereafter as *Les élections épiscopales*. Cf. also Leclercq, "Gallicane, Église," *DACL*, VI, 395-399; 440.

[32] Canons 1 and 2—Bruns, *Canones*, II, 114; cf. Leclercq, "Gallicane, Église," *DACL*, VI, 440; Schmitz, "Metropolitanverfassung und Provincialzynode in Gallien während des fünften Jahrhunderts," *AKK*, LVII (1887), 5-8; Boucharlat, *op. cit.*, p. 121.

that he, as metropolitan, had the right to consecrate the bishops of the provinces of Vienne and Narbonne.[33] Yet the dispute between Arles and Vienne continued, and in 450 Pope Leo I definitely divided the province of Vienne between the two metropolitan sees; his division was confirmed by Pope Symmachus in 513, and the bishops of Arles continued to be appointed papal vicars.[34] The existence of the papal vicariate at Arles did not seriously interfere with the rights of the metropolitans in their own provinces.[35]

It must be borne in mind that during the century preceding the pontificate of Gregory the Great, and also during

---

[33] Cf. JK, 328, 333, 334, 340, 341; Grisar, "Rom und die fränkische Kirche vornehmlich im sechsten Jahrhundert," *ZKT*, XIV (1890), 449. For further information on the "litterae formatae," cf. Fabricius, "Die Litterae Formatae im Frühmittelalter," *Archiv für Urkundenforschung*, IX (1926), 39-86; 168-194.

[34] Cf. JK, 407, 450, 785, 913, 914, 918, 945, 946, 947; JE, 1374-1376; Grisar, *op. cit.*, pp. 450-472. Bishop Remigius of Rouen was not appointed papal vicar over Clovis' kingdom; the document upon which this claim is based is false. Cf. JK, †866; Thiel, *Epistolae*, pp. 123, 1004.

Duchesne (*Origines*, p. 40; *L'Église*, p. 530) maintains that the vicariate was an empty honor; his opinion has been accepted by Caspar (*Geschichte des Papsttums*, II, 495.) This is similar to the theory of Loening (*Geschichte des deutschen Kirchenrechts*, II, *Das Kirchenrecht im Reiche der Merowinger* [Strassbourg, 1878]) and Hauck (*Kirchengeschichte Deutschlands*, I [Leipzig, 1887]) who have sought to prove that the Frankish Church was a "national Church," almost entirely cut off from contact with Rome and almost independent of the Roman primacy. Duchesne, however, admits that the primacy was recognized in Gaul; cf. L'*Église*, p. 531f. Grisar correctly contends that Loening and Hauck have misinterpreted the historical facts and that the Roman primacy was always recognized in Gaul and the papal vicariate was more than an empty honor. Cf. "Rom und die fränkische Kirche vornehmlich im sechsten Jahrhundert," *ZKT*, XIV (1890), 447-487. Cf. also Vaes, "La papauté et l'Église franque à l'époque de Grégoire le Grand," *RHE*, VI (1905), 537-555; Fehr, "Der Primat des apostolischen Stuhles in der gallisch-fränkischen Kirche, *AKK*, XIX (1868), 365-402; Vacandard, "Les élections épiscopales sous les Mérovingiens," *Études de critique et d'histoire religieuse* (5. ed. Paris: Librairie Victor Lecoffre, 1913), I, 123-127. It was only in the later period of the Merovingian kingdom that actually all contact with Rome was interrupted because of the general turmoil that prevailed.

[35] Cf. Schmitz, "Die Rechte der Metropoliten und Bischöfe in Gallien vom vierten bis sechsten Jahrhundert," *AKK*, LXXII (1894), 3-49.

that pontificate, the Church in Gaul was in a peculiarly subservient position to the State, even though the primacy of the Pope was recognized. The Pope, his vicar, the metropolitans and the bishops all had to reckon with the royal will or with that of the royal favorites. Gregory's relations with the Church in Gaul will be considered later insofar as they pertain to the election and appointment of bishops.

Britain also belonged to the Prefecture of Gaul. However, as Gregory had no contacts with the Celtic Church, which flourished even after Britain had succumbed to the barbarian invasions, and as it was only during his reign that a hierarchy was reestablished in Britain, the establishment of metropolitans in that country will be considered later.

3. THE THIRD PREFECTURE

The third Prefecture under the Pope as patriarch of the West was that of Eastern Illyricum. It has already been noted that all Illyricum originally belonged to the Western Empire, that in 379 Dacia and Macedonia were transferred to the Eastern Empire, Illyricum being divided into two parts, and that in 437 Pannonia was transferred over to the Prefecture of Eastern Illyricum.[36]

Although politically Illyricum became a part of the Eastern Empire in 379, it remained subject to the Pope as patriarch of the West despite the efforts of the bishops of Constantinople, seconded by the emperors, to obtain control of those provinces. Perhaps it was in order to forestall these efforts that the Pope appointed the bishop of Thessalonica papal vicar.[37] Authors dispute as to the exact date when the

---

[36] Cf. *supra*, p. 8.

[37] Recently Honig has attempted to deny the existence of the papal vicariate at Thessalonica entirely. Cf. Honig, "The So-Called 'Vicariate' of Illyricum," *Anglican Theological Review*, XXVI (1944), 87-98. It would be beyond the scope of this thesis to refute each of the author's arguments one by one; suffice it to say that he has misinterpreted the canons to uphold his theory of the "democratic feature of the organization of early Christianity;" that he considers Theodosius' edict of 421 [C. Th. (16.2) 45] as "extremely valuable testimony of the fundamentally democratic structure of the Church as being still alive in the fifth century;" that he relies for some of his conclusions on Friedrich's rejection of the authenticity of some of the documents relating to the vicariate, though he seems un-

papal vicariate was established: Hefele-Leclercq maintain that Pope Damasus (366-384) appointed Bishop Acholius of Thessalonica his vicar;[38] Maassen maintains the same, adding that the arrangement was made more positive by Damasus' successor Siricius (384-399).[39] The opinion of Hinschius,[40] who holds that the vicariate at Thessalonica was established by Pope Innocent I (401-417), has been accepted and made more definite by Streichhan.[41] Up until the time of Pope Leo I (440-461), the bishops of Thessalonica were personally appointed papal vicars. Leo I linked the vicariate to the see itself in 444.[42]

---

aware that Friedrich's conclusions ("Ueber die Sammlung der Kirche von Thessalonich und das päpstliche Vikariat für Illyricum," *Sitzungsberichte der philosophisch-philologischen und historischen Classe der Akademie der Wissenschaften zu München*, [1891], 771-887) have been rejected by Streichhan ("Die Anfänge der Vikariates von Thessalonich," *ZSS*, XLIII, Kan. Abt. XII [1922], 330-384); that he so completely misunderstands the relation of the Pope to the emperor as to come to the conclusion that it doesn't matter if the papal letters referring to the bishop of Thessalonica's position are genuine or not; finally, that he fails to mention some of the important papal letters bearing on the problem. It may also be noted that Friedrich's conclusions have also been rejected by Duchesne, "L'Illyricum ecclésiastique," *Byzantinische Zeitschrift*, I (1892), 531-550; and by Nostiz-Rieneck, "Die päpstlichen Urkunden für Thessalonike und deren Kritik durch Prof. Friedrich," *ZKT*, XXI (1897), 1-50. Silva-Tarouca's edition of the *Collectio Thessalonicensis* is not available; the author, however, accepted the conclusions of Nostiz-Rieneck; cf. *Nuovi studi sulle antiche lettere dei papi* (Roma: Pontificia Università Gregoriana, 1932), pp. lff. This book is a reprint of several articles appearing under the same title in *Gregorianum*, XII (1931), 3-56; 349-425; 547-598.

[38] *Histoire des Conciles*, I, 565; cf. also Fliche-Martin, *Histoire*, IV, 537.

[39] Cf. *Primat*, p. 128; JK, 259.

[40] *Das Kirchenrecht der Katholiken und Protestanten in Deutschland* (6 vols., 1869-1895), Berlin: Verlag von I. Guttentag), I, 583. Cited hereafter *Kirchenrecht*.

[41] "Die Anfänge der Vikariates von Thessalonich," *ZSS*, XLIII (1922), 330-384. Cf. JK, 300; Caspar, *Geschichte des Papsttums*, I, 309f.; 601; 612.

[42] Cf. JK, 403, 404, 409, 411. Streichhan, *op. cit.*, pp. 381-384. Silva-Tarouca has demonstrated that certain of the letters of Leo I are spurious or at least suspect; he summarizes the concluding section of his article thus: "Epistolas [S. Leonis M.] in editione Balleriana (ML 54) numeris 43, 74, 111, 112, 113, 118, 120, 137, 141, [JK, 437, 456, 487, 488, 489, 494,

Even after Innocent I established the papal vicariate at Thessalonica, the bishops of Constantinople continued to press their claims in Illyricum, as is indicated in a law of Theodosius of the year 421.[43] The attempts of Constantinople were without effect, except during the Acacian schism, 484-519, when the bishop of Thessalonica abandoned the title of papal vicar and separated himself from Rome.[44] In 514, however, the great majority of the bishops of Illyricum were reunited with Rome and the papal vicariate continued.[45] In 531 the patriarch Epiphanius of Constantinople excommunicated and deposed Bishop Stephen of Larissa, one of the metropolitan sees subject to Thessalonica. Bishop Stephen appealed to Pope Boniface II (530-532), who, in a synod held at Rome, reaffirmed the Pope's special rights over Illyricum through his vicar.[46]

Shortly thereafter, Justinian "under pretense of wishing to enhance the importance of the city nearest his birthplace, Scupi (modern Skoplye), greatly enlarged and beautified it, and made it the capital of the prefecture by transferring to it the residence of the Praetorian Prefect from Thessalonica. In 535 (by Novella XI) he raised it to the rank of an autocephalous archbishopric, to which he gave the name Justiniana Prima. To this new see he granted great privileges and subjected to it the diocese of Dacia consisting of the provinces of Dacia Mediterranea and Dacia Ripensis, Moesia Superior,

---

496, 511, 516] indicatas, spurias, vel saltem suspectas—nn. 27, 36, 39, 47, 48, 49, 154, 157, 158 [JK, 422, 430, 433, 440, 441, 442, 530, 534, 533]—esse demonstratur."—"Nuovi studi sulle antiche lettere dei Papi," *Gregorianum*, XII (1931), 547. It may be noted that Silva-Tarouca did not call into question any of the letters of Pope Leo dealing with the vicariate at Thessalonica.

[43] Cf. C. Th. (16.2) 45. The same law was repeated in Justinian's Code: (1, 2) 6.

[44] Cf. *Avellana*, No. 101; Thiel, *Epistolae*, 383f.

[45] Cf. Scott, *The Eastern Churches and the Papacy*, London: Sheed and Ward, 1938), pp. 214-225; Fliche-Martin, *Histoire*, IV, 537.

[46] Cf. Jaffé, I, 112; Hefele-Leclercq, *Histoire des Conciles*, II, 1117-1119; Fliche-Martin, *Histoire*, IV, 537; Caspar, *Geschichte des Papsttums*, II, 206-209.

Dardania, Praevalis, Macedonia Secunda, and as much as remained of Pannonia Secunda."[47]

Pope Agapitus (535-536) protested against this act, but in vain.[48] Pope Vigilius (537-555) was able to obtain the following concession from Justinian: the metropolitan was to remain autocephalous, but was to act as papal vicar. Thus Illyricum had two papal vicariates: one in Thessalonica and another in Prima Justiniana.[49]

---

[47] Spinka, *A History of Christianity in the Balkans*, p. 13. Cf. Fliche-Martin, IV, 538; Novel (11): "De privilegiis archiepiscopi Primae Justinianae: Multis et variis modis nostram patriam augere cupientes....Et ideo sancti antistites archiepiscopi habeant praerogativam et omnem licentiam suam auctoritatem eis impertire et eos ordinare, et in omnibus suprascriptis provinciis primam habere dignitatem, summum sacerdotium, summum fastigium, a tua sede creentur et solum archiepiscopum habeant, nulla communione ad eum Thessalonicensi episcopo servanda...."

[48] Cf. JK, 894; *Avellana*, No. 88.

[49] Cf. Spinka, *op. cit.*, p. 13; Fliche-Martin, *Histoire*, IV, 538; Novel (131, 3): "Per tempus autem beatissimum archiepiscopum Primae Justinianae nostrae patriae habere semper sub sua jurisdictione episcopos provinciarum Daciae mediterraneae et Daciae ripensis, Privalis et Dardaniae, et Mysiae superioris atque Pannoniae, et ab eo hos ordinari, ipsum vero a proprio ordinari concilio, et in subiectis sibi provinciis locum obtineat sedis apostolicae secundum ea quae a sancto papa Vigilio constituta sunt." The expression "*iurisdictio*" was taken over by the Church from Roman law; it first appears in a letter of Gregory the Great, *Ep.* iii, 7, and is used in the same sense in *Epp.* iii, 32 and xi, 24 as in Novel (131, 3). Cf. Kerckhove, "De notione jurisdictionis in iure Romano," *Jus Pontificium*, XVI (1936), 49-65; Hilling, "Die Bedeutung der iurisdictio voluntaria im römischen Recht und im kanonischen Recht des Mittelalters und der Neuzeit," *AKK*, CV (1925), 449-473; *ibid.*, CXVIII (1938), 165-170.

"In 1272 Michael VIII Paleologus (1259-1282) by a special chrysobul transferred to the archiepiscopal see of Ohrid all the privileges which had been granted the defunct see of Prima Justiniana by Justinian; in other words, he officially identified the ancient defunct see [the Slavs destroyed the city in 602] of Prima Justiniana with Ohrid and assured Ohrid all the historic privileges possessed by both."—Spinka, *op. cit.*, p. 114. Therefore it is not true, as some authors state, that Ohrid was *originally* the name of the city which Justinian enlarged and endowed with the name of Prima Justiniana; the city so enlarged and beautified was Scupi (Skolpye). Cf. Duchesne, "L'Illyricum ecclésiastique," *Byzantinische Zeitschrift*, I (1892), 535; Caspar, *Geschichte des Papsttums*, II, 209, note 2; Mann, *Lives of the Popes in the Early Middle Ages* (18 vols. in 19, St. Louis: B. Herder, 1902-1932), I, 69, note 2.

Though Gregory's relations with the bishops of Eastern Illyricum will be considered more fully later, it may be noted here that two of his letters are addressed to the metropolitans of the Balkan Peninsula; in both, Eusebius of Thessalonica is listed first, while John of Prima Justiniana is listed sixth and fifth respectively.[50]

---

[50] *Epp.* viii, 10; ix, 156. *Ep.* ix, 196, is addressed: "Eusebio archiepiscopo Thessalonicensium;" *Ep.* xi, 55: "Eusebio episcopo Thessalonicensi."

CHAPTER II

THE ELECTION OF BISHOPS IN THE LETTERS OF GREGORY THE GREAT

That Gregory the Great took an active interest in the election and appointment of bishops throughout various parts of the world is evident from the many letters written by him on the subject. The following letters treat of elections of bishops in that part of Italy that was directly subject to the Pope as metropolitan of Rome: *Epp.* vi, 21—sees of Brindisi, Gallipoli and Lecce in Calabria; ii, 39. 40—see of Croton in Bruttium; xiii, 20. 21—sees of Taurianum, Turris and Cosenza in Bruttium; ii, 19—see of Taurianum in Bruttium; v, 9—see of Myria in Bruttium; vii, 38—see of Locri in Bruttium; ii, 5. 12. 13. 14. 18. 26; iii, 1. 2. 15. 35. 60; x, 19—see of Naples in Campania; x, 6. 7—see of Sorrento in Campania; ii, 25. 44—see of Cuma in Campania; ix, 80. 81—see of Miseno in Campania; ix, 142—see of Atella in Campania; iii, 39—sec of Nocera in Campania; i, 58—see of Perugia in Etruria; x, 13; xi, 3—see of Balnoreggio in Etruria; ii, 17—see of Velletri in Latium; vii, 16—sees of Terracina and Formia in Latium; iii, 11—see of Albano in Latium; iii, 13. 14—sees of Fondi and Terracina in Latium; i, 55. 56; ii, 28; iii, 24. 25; ix, 138. 139. 140. 210—see of Rimini in Umbria; xiv, 11—see of Ancona in Picenum; ix, 184. 185—see of Tadino in Picenum; ix, 99. 100—see of Auximo in Picenum; xii, 4. 5—see of Aprutium in Picenum; iv, 39—see of Hortona in Samnium; i, 78; ix, 166—see of Bevagna in Umbria.

Sicily and Corsica were also directly subject to the Pope as metropolitan of Rome; the following letters treat of episcopal elections in these two islands: a) in Sicily: *Epp.* i, 18; ii, 24; iv, 11—in general; ii, 19. 51—see of Lipari; v, 20; 54; vi, 18—see of Syracuse; v, 23; vi, 13—see of Lilybaeum; vi, 9—see of Carinis; xiii, 14. 16. 17. 40—see of Palermo; b) in Corsica: *Epp.* i, 76. 79—see of Saona; i, 77. 79; xi, 58—see of Aleria;

xi, 58—see of Aiaccio. One letter treats of an episcopal election for the island of Malta: *Ep.* x, 1.

Sardinia had its own metropolitan at Cagliari, and Gregory permitted him to control episcopal elections, as is evident from *Epp.* iv, 26. 29; xiv, 2.

In northern Italy there were the three metropolitan sees of Ravenna, Milan and Aquileia. There is no reference in any of Gregory's letters to an episcopal election at the latter see or in any of the sees subject to Aquileia, for all were in schism over the so-called Three Chapters.[1] The following letters were written concerning an election of a bishop at Ravenna: *Epp.* v, 21. 22. 24. 51. One letter, *Ep.* vii, 39, treats of the election at a suffragan see of Ravenna. During Gregory's pontificate, a vacancy occurred twice at Milan, in 592 and again in 600. *Epp.* iii, 26. 29. 30. 31 deal with the election in 592; *Epp.* xi, 6. 14 with the election in 600. The election at one of the suffragan sees to the bishop of Milan is treated in *Ep.* vii, 14.

None of Gregory's letters treats directly of an episcopal election in Africa, though two letters, *Epp.* i, 72. 75, are concerned with the hierarchy there. There are only two references in the extant letters of Gregory to a specific episcopal election in Gaul; they occur in *Epp.* xiii, 7. 8, while the references in

[1] Since 569 the metropolitan of Aquileia lived at Grado, whither he had fled at the coming of the Lombards, and since 557 he had been in schism. Though Gregory succeeded in winning one bishop and several ecclesiastics back into union with Rome, the schism was not healed until 698. Cf. Mann, *Lives of the Popes*, I, 28-38; 317ff.; Wisbaum, *Die wichtigsten Richtungen und Ziele der Thätigkeit des Papstes Gregors des Grossen* (Köln: Druck von M. Dumont-Schauberg, 1884), pp. 33, 45; Schroeder, *Disciplinary Decrees*, pp. 128-134; Caspar, *Geschichte des Papsttums*, II, 368-373; 423-426. The people of the "insula Capreae Histricae provinciae" ("probably to be identified with a village named Isola, situated in the neighborhood of Cittanuova"—Dudden, *Gregory the Great*, I, 450), subject to the metropolitan of Aquileia, returned to union with Rome and requested that a non-schismatic bishop be given them. Gregory requested Bishop Marinian of Ravenna to warn the schismatic bishop of Isola to submit to the Pope; if he refused to do so, Bishop Marinian was delegated to consecrate another bishop for the see and to have the see as part of his metropolitan province until the Istrian bishops returned to the Catholic faith. Cf. *Epp.* ix, 150. 152. 154. 155.

the following letters are all general: *Epp.* v, 58. 59. 60; viii, 4; ix, 213. 215. 218. 222.

In Dalmatia or Western Illyricum the metropolitan see was Salona. The election of a successor to Bishop Natalis of Salona, who died early in 593, was a very complicated affair, as is evidenced by the many letters which treat of it: *Epp.* iii, 22. 32. 46; iv, 16. 20. 38; v, 6. 29. 39; vi, 3. 25. 26. 46; vii, 17; viii, 11. 36; ix, 149. 155. 158. 176. 177. 234. 237; x, 15.

The bishops of Thessalonica and Prima Justiniana were papal vicars in Eastern Illyricum. There was no election at Thessalonica during Gregory's reign, but in 594 Bishop John of Prima Justiniana died and was succeeded by another of the same name—*Epp.* v, 10. 16 are concerned with his election. Vacancies also occurred in the metropolitan sees of Corinth and Nicopolis; the election of a successor to Bishop Anastasius of Corinth, who was deposed and degraded in 595, is spoken of in *Epp.* v, 62. 63; the election at Nicopolis is mentioned in *Ep.* vi, 7.

During Gregory's pontificate, vacancies occurred in three of the four Eastern patriarchal sees.[2] However, Gregory only refers to the election of the patriarch at Constantinople; a brief reference is found in *Ep.* vii, 6. In *Epp.* ix, 135; xi, 28; xiii, 44 Gregory refers in general terms to episcopal consecrations in the other patriarchates. In a letter, *Ep.* viii, 29, to the patriarch of Alexandria, Gregoy tells in glowing terms of Augustine's success in Britain. In this account there is a casual reference to Augustine's consecration by the bishops of Gaul.

---

[2] John of Constantinople died in Sept., 595, and was succeeded by Cyriacus; cf. *Epp.* vi, 15. 62. John of Jerusalem died in 593 and was succeeded by Amos; the latter died in 601 and was succeeded by Isacius; cf. *Ep.* vii, 29, note 4; *Epp.* viii, 6; xi, 28. Gregory of Antioch died in 593, and was succeeded by Anastasius, who had been deposed from Antioch in 570; the latter died in 599, and was succeeded by another of the same name, Anastasius; cf. *Ep.* ix, 135; Hartmann's notes *ibid.*, and ad *Ep.* v, 41.

SECTION I. ELECTIONS IN SEES DIRECTLY SUBJECT TO ROME

1. FORM LETTERS

Before considering the above-mentioned letters individually, it must be noted that some of them are identical since they are written according to two formulas, one containing the appointment of an episcopal visitor with special instructions for the holding of an election, and the other an announcement to the clergy and people of the widowed diocese of the appointment of the visitor and an exhortation to proceed to the election without delay. The following letters belong to the first group: *Epp.* ii, 25. 39; v, 21; vi, 21; vii, 16; ix, 80. 99. 184; xiii, 16. 21;[3] the following belong to the second: *Epp.* ii, 40; iv, 39; v, 22; ix, 81. 100. 185; xiii, 17. 20.

The first point to be noted is that all but two of the above-mentioned form letters refer to an election in cities of Italy and Sicily that were directly subject to the Pope as metropolitan of Rome; the two exceptions, *Epp.* v, 21. 22, refer to the election of a metropolitan at Ravenna. But more of that later.

In Sickel's edition of the *Liber Diurnus* there are no formulas which correspond to the letters of the two groups mentioned above. In an appendix Rozière gives formula 109, "Praeceptum de visitanda ecclesia destituta episcopo," and formula 110, "Item clero, ordini et plebi."[4] Concerning for-

---

[3] *Ep.* ix, 166 refers to a formula in the words: "more scrinii;" *Epp.* iii, 11 and ix, 210 are written according to a different formula; ix, 139. 140 contain only part of the formula.

[4] *Liber Diurnus ou Receuil des Formules usitées par la Chancellerie Pontificale du Ve au Xie siècle* (Paris, 1869), pp. 251-253; cf. *ibid.*, p. CCII. The critical edition of the *Liber Diurnus* is that of Sickel, *Liber Diurnus Romanorum Pontificum* (Vindobonnae: Apud G. Geroldi Filium Bibliopolam, 1889). Sickel's studies on the formation of the *Liber Diurnus* are: "Prolegomena zum Liber Diurnus I," No. VII in *Sitzungsberichte der philosophisch-historischen Classe der kaiserlichen Akademie der Wissenschaften*, CXVII (1889); "Prolegomena zum Liber Diurnus II," No. XIII, *ibid.*; cited hereafter as *Prolegomena* I and II.

Concerning formulas 109 and 110 Sickel states that they were taken from the letters of Gregory the Great and added to the *Liber Diurnus* by Holste; Sickel adds that they were never part of the original collection of

mula 109 the editor states: "Hanc formulam vulgavit Holstenius, n. xxvii, ex Regestro, ut videtur, S. Gregorii, lib. xiii, 13 [which is *Ep.* xiii, 16 in Ewald's and Hartmann's edi-

---

the *Liber Diurnus* and should not be classed as such. Cf. *Prolegomena,* I, 72f.

Scholars today are not in agreement as to the date of the formation and use of the *Liber Diurnus*; cf. Caspar, *Geschichte des Papsttums,* II, 782; Peitz, *Das vorephesinische Symbol der Papstkanzlei* (Vol. I, *Miscellanea Historiae Pontificiae,* Romae: Typis Pontificiae Universitatis Gregorianae, 1939), p. 3; Hartmann, "Die Entstehungszeit des 'Liber Diurnus,' " *Mittheilungen des Instituts für Oesterr. Geschichtsf.,* XIII (1892), 239-254—cited by Caspar, *op. cit.,* II, 784; Steinacker, "Zum Liber Diurnus und zur Frage nach dem Ursprung der Frühminuskel," *Studi e Testi* XL (Miscellanea Francesco Ehrle, IV, Roma: Biblioteca Apostolica Vaticana, 1924), pp. 105-176.

Peitz has proposed the theory that the major portion of the *Liber Diurnus* was in existence and in use in pre-Gregorian times; cf. "Liber Diurnus—Beiträge zur Kenntnis der ältesten päpstlichen Kanzlei vor Gregor dem Grossen," *Sitzungsberichte, Akademie der Wissenschaften in Wien, Philosophisch-historische Klasse* CLXXXV (1918), 1-144. His theory has been subjected to much criticism, and in 1939 he admitted that it was not accepted by most; yet he still continues to defend it; cf. *Das vorephesinische Symbol der Papstkanzlei,* pp. 1-3, 99. Sickel, whose edition of the *Liber Diurnus* is used by most authors, divided it as follows: formulas 1 to 63 make up *Collectio I,* formed between the years 625 and 680, though individual formulas may have been in use before 625; formulas 64 to 81 make up *Appendix I,* formed between the years 683 and shortly after 700; formulas 82 to 99 make up *Collectio II,* formed between the years 772 and 795. Cf. *Prolegomena* I, pp. 1-76; *Prolegomena* II, pp. 1-94. In general the system of Sickel has been accepted, though there has been much argument about the dating of individual formulas; cf. Gramatica-Galbiati, *Il Codice Ambrosiano del Liber Diurnus Romanorum Pontificum* (Analecta Ambrosiana VII, Milano-Roma: Editori Alfieri & Lacroix [1921]), p. 19f; Bresslau, *Handbuch der Urkundenlehre für Deutschland und Italien* (2 vols., vol. 2, 2. ed. by Hans-Walter Klewitz, Berlin-Leipzig: Verlag Walter de Gruyter & Co., 1931), p. 243; Boüard, *Manuel de diplomatique française et pontificale* (Paris: Éditions Auguste Picard, 1929), pp. 138-142. While the majority of scholars accept the theory that the *Liber Diurnus* was actually a book for use in the papal chancery, the theory that it was only a canonical collection has a few adherents. A brief review of the various opinions on the *Liber Diurnus* is given by Santifaller, who concludes: "Der sog. Liber Diurnus ist eine kanonistische Sammlung, die neben zahlreichen anderen Texten auch einige Formulare von Papsturkunden enthält; die Entstehung dieser Sammlung reicht in das 6. Jahrhundert zurück, und ihre uns heute überlieferten, dem 9. Jahrhundert angehörenden Hand-

tion]."[5] Certainly the editor is wrong in stating that the formula was taken from *Ep.* xiii, 16, for the formula adds at the end the words: "Monasteria autem, si qua sunt in ipsius constituta parochia, sub tua cura dispositioneque, quousque illic proprius fuerit ordinatus episcopus, esse concedimus."[6] That sentence is lacking in *all* of these form letters, except in *Ep.* vi, 21; in this letter, however, a comma follows "*concedimus*" and an additional clause is added: "Ut sollicitudinis tuae vigilantia proposito suo congrua Deo adiuvante actione respondeat."

Apparently Ewald considered formula 109 of Rozière's edition of the *Liber Diurnus* as genuine.[7] Hartmann, on the contrary, states: "In Diurno formula visitationis desideratur; nam formulae 109, 110, quas Rozière exhibet, non sunt genuinae, sed adiecticiae."[8]

Is Gregory, then, the first to have used this formula for the appointment of a visitor specifically charged to conduct an election? An affirmative answer appears necessary, despite the fact that two of the letters, *Epp.* ii, 39; v, 21, are incomplete; the former ends: "*et cetera;*" the latter, "*et cetera secundum morem.*" The "*et cetera*" of *Ep.* ii, 39, written in July of 592, and the "*et cetera secundum morem*" of *Ep.* v, 21, written in February of 595, may refer to *Ep.* ii, 25, the first letter in which this form is used, written in March of 592. It is, of course, possible that *Epp.* ii, 39 and v, 21 refer to an earlier form which has not been preserved. But since the portion which we have of these two letters is identical with the beginning of those

---

schriften sind sehr wahrscheinlich im östlichen Ober-italien entstanden; der heutige Titel LD hat sich allem Anscheine nach erst sehr spät, vermutlich in der 2. Hälfte des 11. Jahrhunderts gebildet. Entgegen der bisherigen Lehre war der LD keinesfalls seit dem 9. Jahrhundert und sehr wahrscheinlich niemals das wirklich verwendete Formularbuch der päpstlichen Kanzlei und dementsprechend ebensowenig ein Schulbuch für die Heranbildung des Kanzleinachwuches und hat als Ganzes mit der päpstlichen Kanzlei nichts zu tun gehabt."—"Zur Liber Diurnus-Forschung," *Historische Zeitschrift*, CLXI (1939-1940), 538.

[5] *Liber Diurnus*, p. 251.

[6] *Ibid.*, p. 252.

[7] Cf. Notes ad *Epp.* ii, 25. 39.

[8] Note ad *Ep.* v, 13.

letters that give the formula in full, it is more probable that they refer to the formula used by Gregory and not to an earlier one.[9]

In *Ep.* ix, 99 Gregory tells Bishop Serenus of Ancona that since the church of Auximo has been recovered from the Lombards it is necessary "ut eidem ecclesiae *ex more* visitator accedat;" the letter then proceeds to clarify the "ex more" and does so by giving the formula in full. *Ep.* ix, 166 refers to a former appointment of a bishop as visitor in these words: "In quo dum *more scrinii nostri* etc.;" the remainder of the letter leads one to the conclusion that the letter of appointment, which is no longer extant, was written according to the formula under consideration here.[10]

It must be admitted that a formula for the appointment of bishops existed before Gregory's time.[11] However, the formula under consideration here, that of the appointment of an episcopal visitor for the express purpose of conducting an election, was first used by Gregory the Great.[12]

---

[9] There are slight variations in the opening phrases of some of these letters, but these opening phrases are not an essential part of the formula, and hence it is permissible to consider the formulas identical in spite of these differences.

[10] Gregory's use of "scrinii *nostri*" may indicate that he is referring to the practice of *his* own notaries, and not merely to the notaries of the Roman Church. (The word *scrinium* refers both to the archives, established in a special building by Pope Damasus [366-384] or to the office of the papal notaries. Cf. Poole, *Lectures on the History of the Papal Chancery*, [Cambridge: At the University Press, 1915] pp. 14-17.). But the argument is not conclusive, for Gregory is not consistent in his reference to the *scrinium*, i.e., in *Ep.* ix, 206 "in scrinio nostro" refers to one of Gregory's own documents in the archives; the same phrase in *Ep.* iii, 54 refers to a document of one of Gregory's predecessor's. Cf. also *Epp.* ix, 220; xi, 40; xiv, 14; viii, 24; iii, 49. 66; iv, 17a; vii, 38.

[11] I.e., formula 6 of the *Liber Diurnus*; cf. *infra*, note 34.

[12] Visitors were appointed by previous Popes, e.g., by Gelasius I (JK, 725; Thiel, *Epistolae*, p. 450); by John II (JK, 886 to 890; Mansi, viii, 807-809; 856). None of these letters is similar in form to that used by Gregory. Between 558 and 560 Pope Pelagius I appointed Bishop Eucarpus of Messina as visitor of Catania and authorized him to urge an episcopal election in the latter city. Cf. JK, 977. The letter itself is very different in form from that used by Gregory. Cf. Mansi, ix, 907; also JK, 677-8; Mansi, viii, 85.

The formula, as found in *Ep.* ii, 25, reads:

> Quoniam Cumanae ecclesiae Liberius quondam antistes de hac luce migrasse cognoscitur, propterea visitationis destitutae ecclesiae fraternitati tuae operam sollemniter delegamus. Quam ita te convenit exhibere, ut nihil de provectionibus clericorum, reditu, ornatu, ministerioque, vel quicquid illud est, a quoquam praesumatur ecclesiae. Et ideo caritas tua ad praedictam ecclesiam ire properabit, et adsiduis adhortationibus clerum plebemque eiusdem ecclesiae admonere te volumus, ut remoto studio, uno eodemque consensu talem sibi praeficiendum expetant sacerdotem, qui et tanto ministerio dignus valeat repperiri, et a venerandis canonibus nullatenus respuatur. Qui dum fuerit postulatus, cum sollemnitate decreti omnium subscriptionibus roborati, et dilectionis tuae testimonio litterarum ad nos sacrandus occurrat. Commonentes etiam fraternitatem tuam, ut nullum de altera eligi permittas ecclesia, nisi forte inter clericos ipsius civitatis, in qua visitationis impendis officium, nullus ad episcopatum dignus, quod evenire non credimus, potuerit inveniri. Provisurus ante omnia, ne ad cuiuslibet conversationis meritum laicae personae adspirare praesumant, et tu periculum ordinis tui quod absit incurras.[13]

Regarding the election of a new bishop in those territories directly subject to the Pope as metropolitan of Rome,[14]

---

[13] *Epp.* ii, 39; v, 21; vi, 21; vii, 16; ix, 80. 99. xiii, 16. 21 are identical in form (prescinding from the non-essential variations of the opening phrase), but the following differences should be noted: a) all use the plural *ministeriisque* instead of *ministerioque*; b) as stated above, *Epp.* ii, 39; v, 21 are incomplete; c) all of the letters except *Ep.* ii, 39 add after "quicquid illud est" the words: "in patrimonio eiusdem a quoquam praesumatur ecclesiae;" d) *Ep.* vi, 21 adds at the end of the formula the following: "Monasteria autem si qua sunt in earum parochia constituta, sub tua cura dispositioneque, quousque illic proprius fuerit episcopus ordinatus, esse concedimus, ut sollicitudinis tuae vigilantia proposito suo congrua Deo adiuvante actione respondeat;" e) *Epp.* vi, 21 and xiii, 21 refer to three and two dioceses respectively, and therefore plural forms are used where necessary.

[14] The election and consecration of a metropolitan at Ravenna was governed by the very same rules—*Ep.* v, 21 is one of the form letters.

these form letters make clear the following rules: 1) Upon the death of a bishop, the Pope appointed a neighboring bishop as visitor;[15] his duty was to urge a speedy and orderly election of a worthy candidate, to preside at the election, and to send to Rome a letter attesting to the legality of the election and the worthiness of the candidate. 2) The clergy and people of the widowed church were the electors. 3) Only the clerics of the widowed church were eligible, except in such cases where no one of these was a suitable candidate. 4) The candidate must be free from all canonical disabilities. 5) No layman could be elected; the visitor who permitted the election of a layman was liable to the penalty of deposition. 6) The person elected was to be consecrated in Rome, whither he brought the formal document of his election, confirmed by the signatures of all the electors.

As a general rule, whenever Gregory sent a form letter appointing a visitor for an election he also sent a form letter to the clergy and people of the widowed church, telling them that a certain bishop had been appointed visitor and urging an orderly election. These form letters are the following—the corresponding form letter to the bishop-visitor is noted in parentheses: *Epp.* ii, 40 (ii, 39); v, 22 (v, 21); ix, 81 (ix, 80); ix, 100 (ix, 99); ix, 185 (ix, 184); xiii, 17 (xiii, 16); xiii, 20 (xiii, 21).[16] Three of the form letters to the bishop-visitor have no corresponding letter to the clergy and people: *Epp.* ii, 25; vi, 21; and vii, 16. There is no reason for presuming that no corresponding letters were written; on the contrary, it seems only reasonable to presume that such letters were written but have not been preserved. This presumption, based on the fact that the two formulas are complementary, is

[15] That is the general rule, also in those cases in which a form letter is not used. There is one exception: *Ep.* i, 78 urges the clergy and people of Bevagna to hold an election; until the one elected is consecrated, the priest Honoratus was given full charge of the diocese.

[16] *Ep.* iv, 39, written to the clergy and people of Hortona, is the same as the form letters just mentioned, except that in the middle a statement is added that the visitor has received special permission to ordain priests and deacons before the election is held. The corresponding letter to the bishop-visitor is no longer extant. Cf. Ewald's notes ad *Ep.* iv, 39.

strengthened by the fact that *Ep.* ii, 40 is incomplete and ends: "et cetera." Since no earlier formula is known to which this "et cetera" might refer, it must be supposed that it referred to the letter complementary to *Ep.* ii, 25.[17]

A formula addressed to the clergy and people of a widowed church is given in Rozière's edition of the *Liber Diurnus*, number 110, "Item clero, ordini et plebi."[18] The editor states: "Hanc formulam vulgavit Holstenius ex Regestro, ut videtur, S. Gregorii, lib. iv, ep. 41 [which is *Ep.* iv, 39 according to Ewald-Hartmann's enumeration]; maximam autem cum ep. 14, lib. xiii [which is *Ep.* xiii, 17], ac pluribus aliis similitudinem exhibet."[19] In reality, the formula is identical with *Ep.* xiii, 17, and could hardly have been taken from *Ep.* iv, 39, since that letter, differing in this respect from the other form letters of the group, inserts a special permission granting the visitor the right to ordain priests and deacons.[20] The writer is of the opinion that Gregory the Great first made use of this formula.[21]

As found in *Ep.* xiii, 17, the formula reads:

> Vestri antistitis obitum cognoscentes, curae nobis fuit destitutae ecclesiae visitationem fratri et coepiscopo nostro Barbaro sollemniter delegare. Cui dedimus in mandatis, ut nihil de provectionibus clericorum, reditu, ornatu ministeriisque a quoquam usurpari patiatur. Cuius vos adsiduis adhortationibus convenit oboedire; et remoto strepitu uno eodemque consensu talem vobis praeficiendum expetite sacerdotem, qui et a venerandis canonibus nulla discrepet ratione et tanto ministerio dignus valeat repperiri; qui, dum fuerit postulatus, cum sollemnitate decreti omnium subscriptionibus roborati et visitatoris pagina prosequente ad nos veniat ordinan-

---

[17] Cf. *supra*, p. 24.

[18] Pp. 252-253.

[19] *Liber Diurnus*, ed. Rozière, p. 252.

[20] Cf. *supra*, note 16.

[21] There is a letter extant of Pope Pelagius I (555-560) to the clergy of Catania concerning the election of a bishop; cf. *supra*, note 12. It is very different from the form employed in such cases by Gregory. Cf. JK, 982; *Mansi*, ix, 907.

dus; provisuri ante omnia, ne cuiuslibet vitae vel meriti laicam personam praesumatis eligere. Et non solum ille ad episcopatus apicem nulla ratione provehatur, verum etiam vos nullis intercessionibus veniam promereri posse cognoscite, sed omnes quos ex vobis de laica persona adspirasse constiterit, ab officio et a communione alienos faciendos procul dubio noveritis.[22]

As these form letters are complementary to those sent to the bishop visitor who was to preside at the election, the same six rules are found in both,[23] except that in the letters to the clergy and people[24] it is stated that if a laymen should seek to be elected he will be removed from his office and excommunicated.

2. ELECTIONS IN ITALY

Form letters were sent only to those sees which were directly subject to the metropolitan of Rome, but to these sees other letters, not written according to any formula, were also sent. These letters will help in clarifying the above-listed rules, for they often add more details concerning a particular situation; it is necessary, therefore, to consider some of the more important letters in some detail, beginning with those written to dioceses in Italy itself.

---

[22] The following letters are written according to the same formula: *Epp.* ii, 40; v, 22—these two are incomplete; the former ends, "et cetera;" the latter, "et cetera secundum morem;" iv, 39; xiii, 20. These four letters begin as does *Ep.* xiii, 17, quoted above: "Vestri antistitis obitum cognoscentes..." *Epp.* ix, 81. 100. 185 are written according to the same formula, but refer to dioceses that have been vacant for some time, either because the bishop was deposed (*Ep.* ix, 81) or because it had been recovered from the Lombards (*Epp.* ix, 100. 185); these three letters, therefore, begin thus: "Cognoscentes ecclesiam vestram sacerdotis regimine destitutam...;" the remainder is the same as that of *Ep.* xiii, 17, except that *Ep.* ix, 100 has its own proper ending: "Provisuri ante omnia, ne cuiuslibet vitae meriti laicam personam praesumatis eligere et non solum ille ad episcopatus apicem nulla ratione *perveniat, verum etiam et vos culpae reatus excipiat.*"

[23] Cf. *supra*, p. 26f.

[24] All of these form letters are addressed: "Clero, ordini et plebi consistenti..." Other inscriptions are used in letters treating of the election of bishops but which correspond to no formula, e.g., *Ep.* ii, 5: "Clero, nobilibus, ordini et plebi." The point is discussed more fully in Chapter IV.

The election of a bishop at Rimini, a city situated on the Adriatic sea close to the boundaries of the metropolitan province of Ravenna, was the first and also one of the more interesting cases with which Gregory had to deal. Upon the death of the former bishop, Bishop Severus of Cervia, situated between Ravenna and Rimini, was appointed visitor, and presumably received instructions to conduct an election—the letter of appointment is no longer extant. The election resulted in the choice of a Roman cleric, a certain Ocleantinus, whom Gregory refused to cede:

> Fraternitatis tuae edocti sumus epistola, in persona Ocleantini de electione episcopatus aliquos consensisse. Quem quoniam non cedimus, in eius non debeant immorari persona. Sed habitatoribus eiusdem civitatis edicito, ut si in eadem ecclesia dignum ad hoc opus invenerint, in ipsius cuncti electione declinent. Alioquin praesentium portitor personam, de qua ei diximus, indicabit, in cuius debeat fieri electione decretum....[25]

The clergy and people of Rimini then elected Castorius, a Roman subdeacon,[26] whom Gregory, though unwilling, consecrated, as Gregory stated in a letter to Bishop John of Ravenna (whom he thanked for having visited Castorius after he became sick and for having brought him to Ravenna for care): "Quem quidem ipse pro simplicitate sua illic ordinare omnimodo renuebam. Sed petentium importunitas fecit, ut contradicere nullatenus potuissem. Si autem fieri potest, multum mihi et ipsi consuletis, si eum ad me vel per Siciliam transmittatis, si tamen ei non grave iter esse perpenditis."[27]

---

[25] *Ep.* i, 55, addressed to the bishop visitor, Bishop Severus. The same refusal to cede Ocleantinus is made known to the clergy and people of Rimini in *Ep.* i, 56. No reason for the refusal is given, but it appears that Gregory considered Ocleantinus unworthy of the episcopate. A cleric could not leave his diocese without the permission of his bishop; cf. *infra*, note 58; Chapter III, note 17.

[26] Cf. John the Deacon, *Sancti Gregorii Papae Vita*, lib. iii, c. 7.

[27] *Ep.* ii, 28. Basing his statement on this letter Dudden says: "Gregory was not pleased with the choice, but he found himself unable to resist the importunities of the electors, *backed by a strongly worded recommendation from the archbishop.*"—*Gregory the Great*, I, 380; italics inserted by the writer. The statement is wholly unfounded; the bishop of Ravenna would

Bishop Castorius went to Rome to recuperate; in the meanwhile Gregory appointed Bishop Leontius of Urbino as visitor of Rimini, granting him full rights there, except the right of ordination: "...praeter ordinationes clericorum omnia in praedicta ecclesia tamquam cardinalem et proprium te volumus agere sacerdotem."[28] After four years in Rome, Castorius did not feel well enough to return to his diocese, despite the pleadings of the Pope and the clergy and people of Rimini. Finally, as Gregory said in a letter to Bishop Marinian of Ravenna, Bishop Castorius resigned in writing: "...data scriptis supplicatione nos petiit, ut, quia ad eiusdem ecclesiae regimen vel susceptum officium pro eadem qua detinetur molestia adsurgere nullatenus posset, ecclesiae ipsi ordinare episcopum deberemus."[29] Gregory unwillingly accepted the resignation, and in May, 599, ordered that a new election should be held.[30] The holding of the election is ordered in terms similar to those of the form letters considered above,

hardly have intervened in an election outside the limits of his jurisdiction; if he had, Gregory would have specifically mentioned the fact. At this time, in 592, the relations between Rome and Ravenna were excellent, for the last paragraph of the letter quoted above, *Ep.* ii, 28, grants to the bishop of Ravenna certain rights over some of the bishops subject to the Pope as metropolitan: "De episcopis vero ad nos pertinentibus, qui tamen huc pro interpositione hostium venire non possunt, curam vestra fraternitas gerat. Ita tamen ut pro causis ad Ravennatem urbem nullatenus revocentur, ne eos hoc tempore vexare aut fatigare in aliquo videamur. Sed si qua sunt, quae in eis videantur iuste reprehendi, debent semper per fraternitatis vestrae epistolas ammoneri. Sin vero aliqua, quod absit, graviora contigerint, haec ad nos subtiliter referre vos volumus, ut inquisitionis vestrae testimonio roborati, quae legibus canonibusque conveniunt, salubri iuvante Domino consilio disponamus."

[28] *Ep.* iii, 24. *Ep.* iii, 25 informs the inhabitants of Rimini that Bishop Leontius of Urbino has been appointed visitor until Castorius should be well enough to return; moreover he bade them pray for forgiveness for their former hostility to Castorius: "Si culpam vestram, fratres dilectissimi, intentius velitis adtendere, adsidua vos apud Deum debeatis oratione purgare, quod episcopum vestrum non devota mente nec ut filii suscepistis."

[29] *Ep.* ix, 138. The same account of Castorius' illness and resignation is found in the opening lines of *Epp.* 139. 140.

[30] Cf. *Ep.* ix, 139 to the clergy and people of Rimini; *Ep.* ix, 140 to Bishop Sebastian who succeeded Bishop Leontius at Urbino and as visitor of Rimini.

but before the person elected is to be sent to Rome for consecration, he is to be examined by Bishop Marinian of Ravenna; if the latter judges that the person elected is worthy, he is to send him to Rome along with a written testimonial.[31] This is the only time that the bishop of Ravenna was authorized to examine a candidate for one of the suffragan sees of Rome. There is nothing strange in the procedure, for Gregory often authorized neighboring persons to investigate the character and attainments of those elected to an episcopal see.[32] The visitor of Rimini was also to send his testimony, as well as the decree of election signed by the clergy and people of Rimini, to Rome.[33]

Apparently the electors agreed without hesitation upon a candidate, whom the Pope found suitable, for in July of the same year, Gregory wrote to the clergy and people of Rimini: "Probabilibus desideriis nihil attulimus tarditatis; fratrem iam et coepiscopum nostrum Johannen vobis ordinavimus sacerdotem. Et cetera secundum morem."[34]

If at all possible the person elected to the episcopacy was to be a member of the widowed diocese. This regulation is brought out clearly in the election at Bevagna, a city in Umbria. In August of 591 Gregory wrote to the inhabitants of

---

[31] Cf. *Epp.* ix, 138. 139.

[32] Cf. *Epp.* ii, 24; vii, 38; xiii, 14; xiv, 11.

[33] Cf. *Ep.* ix, 140.

[34] *Ep.* ix, 210. There is no doubt that the *"et cetera"* of this letter refers to formula 6 of the *Liber Diurnus*, which originated with Pope Gelasius I (492-496.) Cf. Ewald, "Zwei unedierte Briefe Gregors I.," *Neues Archiv*, VII (1881), 587-589; Thiel, *Epistolae*, pp. 379-380, and notes *ibid.* pp. 32-33; JK, 675. The formula specifically forbids the bishop to perform illicit ordinations or to advance those who were illicitly ordained: "Ne bigamum, aut qui virginem non est sortitus uxorem, neque inliteratum, vel in qualibet corporis parte vitiatum, aut expoenitentem, vel curiae aut cuilibet conditioni obnoxium notatumque, ad sacros ordines permittat accedere; sed si quos huiusmodi forte repererit, non audeat promovere." Baptism and ordinations are limited to certain days, and the bishop is to protect and increase the goods of his church and to divide the revenues thereof into the four prescribed portions. Cf. *Liber Diurnus*, Sickel, p. 5; ed. Rozière, pp. 22-29. *Ep.* iii, 11, written to the clergy and people of Albano, is the same as *Ep.* ix, 210, except that the "et cetera" is lacking. Undoubtedly a portion of *Ep.* ii, 37 is written according to formula 6; cf. *infra*, Chapter IV.

that city to inform them that the priest Honoratus had been authorized to care for and guard the rights of their church until the person they should elect would be consecrated.[35] No fit person could be found in Bevagna, and Honoratus continued to care for the church for six years; then Bishop Chrysantus of Spoleto was appointed visitor, but he was specifically ordered not to ordain any clerics. Two years later, because of the complaints of the people of Bevagna over the lack of priests, Gregory authorized Bishop Chrysantus to hold an election; if a fit person could be found there, he was to be sent in the usual way to Rome for consecration. Gregory continues: "Sin vero hoc inveniri non potest, cum omni studio ac vivacitate personas exquirite, qui illic in presbyterii ordine valeant consecrari. Quorum vitam actusque ita suptili primitus inquisitione discutite, ut in nullo eis vel sacri canones vel ecclesiasticae regulae valeant obviare, ut hac prosivione populus illic degens communionem, qua se privatos ob sacerdotum necessitatem flebiliter conqueruntur, recepisse se gaudeant et in ecclesiis illis sacra missarum solemnia deesse non debeant. Sed et pro consignandis infantibus fraternitas tua illic curet accedere, ut nihil sit, quod pastoralis sollicitudinis neglecta vos cura remordeat."[36]

The account of the election of a bishop at Naples not only provides an interesting commentary on episcopal elections in general at the end of the sixth century, but also serves to illustrate the entire procedure of such an election. A year after he became Pope, Gregory wrote to the clergy and people of Naples, informing them that Bishop Demetrius had been degraded because of his scandalous life and urging them to hold a new election.[37] Bishop Paul of Nepi was appointed visitor,

---

[35] Cf. *Ep.* i, 78; *supra*, p. 27, note 15.

[36] *Ep.* ix, 166. Only a bishop could administer the sacrament of confirmation. Cf. *Epp.* xi, 3; xiii, 22, and the decree of Pope Innocent to Bishop Decentius of Gubbio in the *Collectio Dionysiana*: "De consignandis vero infantibus manifestum est non ab alio quam ab episcopo fieri licere."—PL, LXVII, 239; JK, 311.

[37] "Demetrius siquidem, qui nec ante episcopus dici meruerat, tantis ac talibus negotiis inventus est involutus, ut si secundum suorum qualitatem facinorum iudicium sine misericordia suscepisset, divinis mundanisque legibus durissima proculdubio fuerat morte plectendus. Sed quia

and presided at the ensuing election. Contrary to custom, the Neapolitans desired to have Bishop Paul transferred to the see of Naples, and sent their request to the Pope. Gregory refused "quia summis in rebus citum non oportet esse consilium, et nos quid fiendum sit matura subinde Christo aiduvante deliberatione disponimus..."[38] To Bishop Paul Gregory granted permission to ordain clerics in Naples until he should have decided on a new bishop; meanwhile Bishop Paul was not to change anything regarding the customary stipends paid to the Neapolitan clergy.[39]

While Bishop Paul was engaged at Naples, the care of his city of Nepi and of the material goods of his church was entrusted by the Pope to a certain Leontius, a layman, in January of 592.[40] A month later Gregory again wrote to Bishop Paul at Naples, urging him to be patient and faithful in his present task despite his great desire to return to his own diocese at Nepi.[41] In order that the paschal solemnities might be properly celebrated at Nepi during Bishop Paul's absence, Gregory, in March, appointed a certain Bishop John as visitor of Nepi; it is not known to what see Bishop John belonged.[42]

During the summer months of 592, Bishop Paul continued his ministrations at Naples, despite the opposition of a certain part of the inhabitants. The opposition grew steadily

---

misericordiae reservatus sacerdotii honore privatus est, ecclesiam Dei sine doctore diu vacare non patimur. . . ." *Ep.* ii, 5.

[38] *Ep.* ii, 12.

[39] Cf. *Ep.* ii, 13.

[40] "Leontio viro clarissimo, praesentium portitori, curam sollicitudinemque civitatis iniunximus, ut in cunctis invigilans, quae ad utilitatem vestram, vel rei publicae pertinere cognoscit, ipse disponat. . . ." —*Ep.* ii, 14. Dudden states that, because of the imminent danger from the Lombards, Gregory "actually presumed, on his own initiative, to appoint a military governor at Nepi." —*Gregory the Great,* II, 10; cf. also Ewald's notes ad *Ep.* ii, 14; *Ep.* ii, 34 and Caspar, *Geschichte des Papsttums,* II, 472.

[41] Cf. *Ep.* ii, 18.

[42] "Quoniam Paulo fratri et coepiscopo nostro Neapolitanae ecclesiae operam visitationis iniunximus, idcirco fraternitas tua ecclesiae Nepesinae visitationem non desistat adsumere, quatenus exigente paschali festivitate, quicquid sacrorum sollemnitas poscit, te operante, modis omnibus impleatur. . . ." —*Ep.* ii, 26.

more bold and near the end of the summer Bishop Paul was waylaid and subjected to personal indignities by a gang of ruffians, including some of the slaves of Clementina, one of the artistocratic ladies of Naples. Gregory was highly indignant when he heard of the outrage, and sent his regrets to Bishop Paul, assuring him that two persons were being sent from Rome to investigate the incident and to take proper measures against any repetition of the affair.[43] At the same time he instructed Peter, rector of the patrimony in Campania, to assist at the investigation of the crime and to proceed against those who were found guilty.[44]

The incident seems to have cleared the air at Naples, for somewhat later the clergy and people elected Florentius, subdeacon of the Roman church. Though he was not of the Neapolitan clergy, Gregory gladly approved the election in order that the long vacancy at Naples might be ended. His joy was shortlived, for Florentius, hearing of his election and the papal approval, fled and remained in hiding. Recalling perhaps his own efforts to escape the papal dignity, Gregory did not insist on Florentius' consecration but ordered a new election by the nobles and people of the city. If these could not agree on one person, they were to choose three men, whom they were to endow with a general mandate, and send to Rome to choose a fit candidate.[45] Yet Gregory did not intend to deprive the clergy of Naples of their right to participate in the election, despite their failure to come to an agreement. In May of 593 he ordered Peter, rector of the patrimony, to call the clergy together:

> quatenus duos vel tres de suis eligere ut huc ad eligendum episcopum transmittere non omittant. Sed et sua nobis relatione insinuant, quoniam hi quos transmiserint omnium in hac electione vice fungantur.... Electos sicut diximus de clero transmitte ut quia diversi huc nobiles civitatis Neapolitanae praesentes sunt [cf. *Ep.* iii, 15],

---

[43] Cf. *Ep.* iii, 2—Sept. 592.

[44] Cf. *Ep.* iii, 1.

[45] Cf. *Ep.* iii, 15—Dec. 592. The election of "electors" appears to be a new element, introduced by Gregory in this instance to hasten the ending of the long vacancy at Naples.

> una cum eis de episcopali ordinatione et tractare et deliberare possimus.[46]

If any of the clergy proved refractory, Peter was to proceed against them with canonical penalties.

The delegates of the clergy and people assembled in Rome shortly thereafter, and they chose as bishop a certain Fortunatus, whom Gregory consecrated during the summer of 593, almost two years after Bishop Demetrius had been deposed. Bishop Fortunatus was well received in Naples[47] and continued to rule his see peaceably for five years, but in 598 he began to meddle in civic affairs, for which he was reprimanded by Gregory.[48] The affair was apparently satisfactorily adjusted, for the Pope makes no further reference to it in the last letter written to Bishop Fortunatus in April of 600.[49]

Not long after this letter was written, Bishop Fortunatus died, and another election had to be held at Naples, concerning which Gregory wrote in July of 600. The letter brings out clearly three qualities which were required in an episcopal candidate: continency, adequate knowledge, and freedom from usury.

> Nec novum nec reprehensibile est in eligendo episcopo populi se vota in duas partes dividere...Prius enim quam scripta ad nos vestra discurrerent, Iohannem diaconem, qui ab altera parte electus est, parvulam habere filiam quorundam relatione cognovimus. Unde si rationem voluissent attendere, nec alii eum eligere nec ipse debuerat consentire. Nam qua praesumptione ad episcopatum audet accedere, qui adhuc longam corporis sui continentiam filiola teste convincitur non habere? Petrus autem item diaconus, quem a vobis electum asseritis omnino, quantum dicitur, simplex est. Et nostis,

---

[46] *Ep.* iii, 35. The letter gives no clue as to why there was an interval of five months between it and *Ep.* iii, 15. Peter is also told to assure Bishop Paul that he may return to his own church at Nepi; he is to be given a hundred solidi and a slave boy from the Neapolitan church for his work as visitor.

[47] Cf. *Ep.* iii, 60.

[48] Cf. *Ep.* ix, 47. 76.

[49] Cf. *Ep.* x, 9.

quia talis hoc tempore in regiminis debet arce constitui, qui non solum de salute animarum, verum etiam de extrinseca subiectorum utilitate et cautela sciat esse sollicitus. Nam de eo insuper ad nos pervenisse cognoscite, quia solidos dederit ad usuras; quod vos oportet cum omni suptilitate requirere; et si ita constiterit, alium eligite et ab huius vos persona sine mora suspendite. Nam nos amatoribus usurarum nulla ratione manus imponimus. Si vero suptili habita inquisitione hoc falsum esse patuerit, quia persona nobis eius ignota est et, utrum ita sit de simplicitate eius quod ad nos perlatum est, ignoramus, cum decreto a vobis facto ad nos eum venire necesse est...Studii praeterea vestri sit etiam alium qui aptus sit, providere, ut ne forte, si huic ordini hic non videatur idoneus, sit in quo se vestra declinare possit electio. Nam grave cleri illius erit opprobrium, ut, si hic fortasse adprobatus non fuerit, alium se dicant, qui eligi debeat, non habere.[50]

Neither of the two candidates mentioned in the preceding letter was consecrated by Gregory. Sometime before January of 601, Pascasius was consecrated and installed as bishop of Naples; it is not known just how he was chosen or whence he had come, though it is probable that he was a Neapolitan.[51] Even after Pascasius' installation Gregory kept a watchful eye on the church of Naples through the rector of the Church's patrimony in Campania.[52] These affairs do not concern us here, as they have no relation to episcopal elections.

In the later years of his pontificate Pope Gregory never hesitated to reject a candidate whom he considered unfit,[53] even though such an exalted person as the exarch of Ravenna desired that a certain candidate be consecrated. Thus, in the election at Ravenna, Gregory refused to accept the archdeacon Donatus, favored by the exarch, as he was unworthy. He also

---

[50] *Ep.* x, 19. The sources which Gregory may have used are indicated *infra*, Chapter IV.

[51] Cf. *Ep.* xi, 19.

[52] Cf. *Epp.* xi, 22. 53; xiii, 15.

[53] In 592 he had allowed his objections to be overruled by the importunities of the electors. Cf. *supra*, p. 30.

refused to accept the priest John, who did not know the psalms.[54] Apparently for the same reason and also because he was not zealous for the Divine Office,[55] Gregory rejected the deacon John who had been elected bishop for the camp of Balnoreggio near Chiusi.[56]

In an election held at Ancona toward the end of 603, three candidates were chosen, and Gregory ordered that they should be examined there by the bishop visitor and a neighboring bishop before being sent to Rome.[57] The first candidate, Florentinus, archdeacon of Ancona, was considered unsuitable because of his advanced age and his parsimony; the second, Rusticus, a deacon of Ancona, did not know the psalter; the third, Florentinus, appreed to be suitable, but he was not of the church of Ancona, being a deacon of Ravenna. Regarding that fact Gregory wrote: "Florentino autem diacono Ravennati, si nullum sicut diximus, crimen est quod obsistat, apud episcopum eius agi necesse est, ut ei debeat cessionem concedere, non tamen ex nostro mandato vel dicto, ne contra suam eum voluntatem cedere videatur. Sed hoc ut norunt hi qui eum eligunt, ex se agant. . . ."[58] It is not known whether Florentinus of Ravenna became bishop of

---

[54] "Sed nec Johannem presbyterum psalmorum nescium praevidimus ordinare." —*Ep.* v, 51. The election at Ravenna then resulted in the choice of the priest Marinian, a former associate of Gregory in his Roman monastery, whom Gregory gladly consecrated. Cf. *Epp.* v, 21. 22. 24. 51. The same rules applied to an election at Ravenna as applied to the suffragan sees of Rome. The letter referring to the election of a suffragan to Ravenna is considered *infra*, p. 47.

[55] Gregory ordered Bishop Ecclesius of Chiusi to investigate the candidate, "si in opere Dei studium habuit." —*Ep.* x, 13. St. Benedict called the Divine Office the *Opus Dei*: "Operi Dei nihil praeponatur." —*Regula*, c. 43.

[56] Cf. *Epp.* x, 13; xi, 3. The reasons for the rejection of a candidate at Sorrento and Locri are not given in *Epp.* x, 7; vii, 38.

[57] At Nocera in Campania the rector of the patrimony, the subdeacon Peter, was authorized to investigate a candidate; if he was found suitable, he was to be sent to Rome for consecration. Cf. *Ep.* iii, 39.

[58] *Ep.* xiv, 11. It was necessary for a cleric to obtain his bishop's permission before he could leave his diocese; cf. *supra*, p. 30, *infra*, Chapter III, note 17. Cf. also *Epp.* i, 81; v, 20; vi, 20.

Ancona or not, as Gregory wrote no more letters to Ancona before his death.

The see of Teramo (Aprutium)[58a] had long been vacant,[59] for no suitable candidate who was a cleric or a monk could be found. Gregory had heard good reports of Oportunus, a layman. He therefore wrote to Bishop Passivus of Fermo to investigate further. If Oportunus seemed to be suitable, "tonsurandus est, ut vel monachus vel a vobis subdiaconus fiat et post aliquantum temporis, si Deo tum placuerit, ipse ad pastoralem curam debeat promoveri...."[60] Nothing further is known concerning the proposed plan; it serves to illustrate the point, however, that only monks or clerics were eligible for the episcopacy.[61]

[58a] Though Gregory nowhere specifically calls Teramo a diocese, the wording of *Ep.* xii, 4 seems to imply that he is speaking of the consecration of a bishop: "Aprutium *pastoralis curae* sollicitudine destitutum;" "ad *pastoralem curam* promovere." For Gregory never uses the word *pastoralis* to refer to an office below that of a bishop, but only to refer to his own work as Pope or to that of bishops. The following phrases refer to himself as Pope: "pastoralis cura" —*Epp.* i, 76; ii, 37; "pastorali regimine" —*Ep.* i, 26; "pastoralis regiminis necessitate" —*Ep.* i, 62; "pastoralis officii continentia" —*Ep.* i, 5; while the following refer to bishops: "pastorali sollicitudine (vigilantia, regimine)" —*Epp.* ii, 37; xi, 13, vii, 6; "pastoralis officii (curae, regiminis)" —*Epp.* xi, 42; iv, 9; iii, 29; iv, 5; "pastoralem sollicitudinem (curam)" —*Epp.* viii, 11; xiii, 14; "pastorali regimine (sollicitudine)" —*Epp.* ix, 138. 139. 140; i, 18; ix, 100; "pastoraliter" —*Ep.* v, 3. Only in one instance in his letters does Gregory use the word "pastor" to refer, not to a bishop, but to an actual shepherd. Cf. *Ep.* ii, 38. It may be noted also that in the *Dialogues* the word *pastoralis* "is used with *cura*, and in each instance refers to the duties of a bishop." —Kinnirey, *The Late Latin Vocabulary of the Dialogues of St. Gregory the Great* (The Catholic University of America Studies in Medieval and Renaissance Latin, Vol. IV, Washington, D.C.: The Catholic University of America, 1935), p. 77.

[59] This was an unusual situation, for it was one of Gregory's chief concerns that there should be no delay in the holding of an episcopal election. Cf. *Epp.* i, 58; ix, 142; vii, 14. 39—the latter two letters state that a diocese should not be vacant longer than three months. The same rule was given in canon 25 of the Council of Chalcedon; cf. Bruns, *Canones*, I, 32. Justinian set a limit of six months; cf. N. (123. 1).

[60] *Ep.* xii, 4. Cf. also *Ep.* xii, 5. The latter is addressed: "Gregorius Oportuno de Aprutio;" it contains no mention of the plan proposed in *Ep.* xii, 4.

[61] Cf. also *Ep.* i, 18: "de clero ecclesiarum ipsarum, vel ex monasteriis."

Normally a vacant diocese was ruled by a bishop visitor, who also presided at the election. In one instance, at Myria in southern Italy, no visitor appears to have been appointed, probably because at the coming of the Lombards the bishop and his clergy fled to Squillace. At the latter city the bishop of Myria died, and when Myria had been freed from the barbarians, Gregory ordered the archdeacon Leo to return to Myria with his clergy to hold an election. It appears that the archdeacon in this instance governed the church during the vacancy.[62]

3. EPISCOPAL ELECTIONS IN SICILY

The very first letter which Gregory wrote after his consecration was directed to the bishops of Sicily. It announced to them that Peter the subdeacon had been appointed as his representative or vicar, with whom the bishops were to meet once a year in synod.[63] A few months later, January of 591, Gregory bade his vicar to strive earnestly to overcome the old custom of leaving a diocese vacant when the bishop thereof had been deposed, lest those who had been removed strive to regain their former sees. At the same time Peter was told to seek worthy candidates from the vacant dioceses and send them to Rome for further investigation and possible consecration. If it was impossible to find worthy candidates in the vacant dioceses, Peter was to inform the Pope, who would provide a bishop. In this latter instance there is no mention of an election by the clergy and people.[64]

Peter remained papal vicar but little more than a year; in October, 591, Gregory appointed Bishop Maximian of Syracuse to the position, specifying that it was a personal privilege which did not accrue to the see of Syracuse.[65] Having heard that a certain priest of Sicily was a fit candidate for the epis-

---

[62] Cf. *Ep.* v, 9.

[63] Cf. *Ep.* i, 1—Sept. 590.

[64] Cf. *Ep.* i, 18.

[65] Cf. *Epp.* ii, 8; iv, 11. In the latter letter Gregory lists some of the evils of the Sicilian church, which he asks Maximian to correct. Of interest here is the regulation that a detailed inventory was to be made after a bishop's death or removal, and the regulation that episcopal visitors were to receive compensation from the church which they temporarily served.

copacy, Gregory asked Bishop Maximian to investigate. He continued: "Quem si ad hunc gradum dignum esse perspexerit, ad nos studeat destinare, ut eum Domino disponente loco cui praeviderimus possimus ordinare pastorem."[66] Again there is no mention of an election by clergy and people.[67]

Bishop Maximian of Syracuse died in November of 594. Thereafter the rector of the ecclesiastical patrimony around Syracuse acted more or less as the papal vicar, though that title was only once bestowed upon one rector, i.e., upon Peter the subdeacon, who had been recalled to Rome in 592. The rector at this time, in 594, was the deacon Cyprian, who had been appointed in July, 593.[68] To him Gregory wrote concerning the election of a successor to Bishop Maximian. The Pope was not pleased with the first choice of the clergy and people, and ordered that a more suitable candidate should be chosen. Meanwhile, he told Cyprian that he believed no one to be more fitted than John, archdeacon of Catania. He added that if John was elected, "etiam frater et coepiscopus noster Leo [i.e., of Catania] ei cessionem debet dare, ut liber ad ordinandum possit inveniri."[69] Cyprian apparently succeeded in convincing the nobles of John's worthiness, but the clergy and people chose a certain Agatho, and Gregory ordered both candidates to come to Rome so that he might himself decide.[70] John the archdeacon was chosen and consecrated; shortly thereafter Gregory sent him the pallium, but he did not create him papal vicar.[71]

Bishop Theodore of Lilybaeum died early in 595. No bishop was appointed as visitor, but the deacon Cyprian, rector of the patrimony, was commissioned to see that an election was held without delay.[72] The inhabitants chose Decius, a priest

[66] *Ep.* ii, 24.

[67] Cf. *infra*, Chapter IV, section III.

[68] Cf. *Ep.* iii, 55.

[69] *Ep.* v, 20. Cf. also *Ep.* vi, 20.

[70] Cf. *Ep.* v, 54.

[71] Cf. *Ep.* vi, 18.

[72] Cf. *Ep.* v, 23.

of another diocese, whom Gregory consecrated in September, 595.[73]

The island of Malta also came under the care of the rector of the ecclesiastical patrimony at Syracuse. In October, 599, Gregory wrote to Roman, who had succeeded Cyprian as rector in 598,[74] concerning the request of Bishop Trajan of Malta, who desired that four or five of his former monks might be permitted to come to live with him—Bishop Trajan had been Abbot of a monastery at Syracuse before his election as successor to Bishop Lucillus of Malta, deposed because of his crimes. While Gregory favored the request, he did not wish to infringe upon the rights of Bishop John of Syracuse, and therefore left the final decision to him.[75] The fact which is of interest here is that an abbot became a bishop, for a few years later, in 602, Gregory refused to disturb the quiet of Abbot Urbicus of the monastery of St. Hermas at Palermo. Upon the death of Bishop Victor of Palermo, the patrician Venantius wrote to Gregory, asking that Abbot Urbicus or the deacon Crescentius, director of the *xenodochium*,[76] be appointed as bishop of Palermo. Concerning Abbot Urbicus Gregory wrote: "Sed quia ceteris sic est aliquis praeponendus, ut, dum ipse exterius proficit, interius non decrescat, quietem ipsius turbare non possumus, ne, cum eum ad altiora producimus, minorem illum se ipso fieri in fluctibus compellamus."[77]

In the same letter Gregory told Venantius to investigate the character and achievements of Crescentius more closely; if he then considered him worthy, he should strive to have him elected by all; if not, all should agree in electing a candidate, a suitable cleric of Palermo if at all possible. The tone

[73] Cf. *Ep.* vi, 13.

[74] Cf. *Epp.* ix, 28 to 32; Ewald's notes ad *Ep.* ii, 38.

[75] Cf. *Ep.* x, 1.

[76] "Place to lodge strangers." —O'Donnell, *The Vocabulary of the Letters of Saint Gregory the Great* (The Catholic University of America Studies in Mediaevel and Renaissance Latin, II, Washington, D.C.: Catholic University of America, 1934), p. 77; cited hereafter as *Vocabulary*. Cf. also the legislation of Justinian: C (I, 2) 19; (I, 3) 34, and Schönfeld, "Die Xenodochien in Italien und Frankreich im frühen Mittelalter," *ZSS*, Kan. Abt., XII (1922), 1-54.

[77] *Ep.* xiii, 14.

of Gregory's letter seems to imply that he was not pleased with the interference of Venantius; he stresses the point that a candidate is to be elected by all. At the same time he appointed Bishop Barbarus of Carina as visitor with instructions to preside at the election. The two letters are written according to the regular formula.[78] There is no further mention of this election in Gregory's letters, but in July, 603, the Pope sent the pallium to Bishop John of Palermo;[79] it may, therefore, be presumed that everything proceeded regularly after the appointment of the bishop visitor. Had it not, there would have been a longer vacancy.

In the early years of his reign Gregory interfered more in episcopal elections in Sicily than elsewhere, for he himself seems to have provided bishops for certain sees without any election by the inhabitants of the see, and in one instance the candidate he favored in preference to the choice of the clergy and people was consecrated. However, these unusual measures were most probably necessitated by the conditions in Sicily in the early years of Gregory's pontificate, for after 595 the elections in Sicily proceeded regularly.[80]

4. EPISCOPAL ELECTIONS IN CORSICA

Only two episcopal elections in Corsica are mentioned in the extant letters of Gregory the Great, and both of these are mentioned in a letter to the *defensor* Boniface in Corsica,[81] whom Gregory chides for being remiss in urging the clergy and people of Aleria and Aiaccio to elect a bishop:

> Quae quoniam sine proprio amplius non debent esse rectore, praesenti auctoritate suscepta, clerum et populum singularum civitatum hortari festina, ut inter se dissentire non debeant, sed uno sibi consensu unaquaeque civitas consecrandum eligant, et facto decreto ad nos is qui fuerit electus adveniat. Si autem in uno consentire

[78] Cf. *Epp.* xiii, 16. 17; *supra*, p. 22 ff.

[79] Cf. *Ep.* xiii, 40.

[80] Cf. *Epp.* i, 18. 39. 39a. 42. 68. 70; iv, 11.

[81] Cf. *Ep.* xi, 58: "Bonifatio Defensori Corsica." The institute of the ecclesiastical *defensor* is ably treated by Fischer, "Die Entwicklung des Instituts der Defensoren in der römischen Kirche," *Ephemerides Liturgicae* XLVIII (1934), 443-454.

noluerint, sed in duorum se electione diviserint, similiter decretis ad nos ex more factis adveniant, ut requirentes de vita, actu ac moribus eorum is qui visus fuerit ordinetur.[82]

Section II. Episcopal Elections in Territories Outside of the Roman Metropolitan Province

1. IN SARDINIA

The bishop of Cagliari was metropolitan of the island of Sardinia. During Gregory's pontificate, the bishop of Cagliari was Januarius, whom Dudden has well characterized as a "petulant, unprincipled, grey-headed child, overcome with infirmities of mind and body."[83] Gregory often had to write to him and to others in Sardinia in reference to ecclesiastical discipline in the island.[84] Regarding ordinations in general, Gregory wrote as follows to Bishop Januarius in May, 594:

> Pervenit etiam ad nos, quosdam de sacris ordinibus lapsos, vel post poenitentiam, vel ante poenitentiam ad ministerii sui officium revocari, quod omnino prohibemus, et in hac re sacratissimi quoque canones contradicunt. Qui igitur post acceptum ordinem lapsus in peccato carnis fuerit, sacro ordine ita careat, ut ad altaris ministerium ulterius non accedat. Sed ne umquam hi qui ordinati sunt pereant, provideri debet quales ordinentur, ut prius aspiciatur si vita eorum continens in annis plurimis fuit, si studium lectionis, si elemosynae amorem habuerunt. Quaerendum quoque est, ne fortasse fuerit bigamus. Videndum etiam, ne sine litteris aut ne obnoxius curiae compellatur post sacrum ordinem ad exactionem publicam redire....Ea autem quae fraternitati vestrae scripsimus, cunctis sub vobis episcopis innotescite, quia ego illis scribere nolui, ne honorem vestrum viderer imminuere.[85]

---

[82] *Ep.* xi, 58.

[83] *Gregory the Great*, I, 370.

[84] Cf. *Epp.* ii, 47; iv, 9. 23-27. 29; ix, 11. 202-204; xiv, 2. Six bishops of Sardinia, besides Januarius, are listed in *Ep.* ix, 202.

[85] *Ep.* iv, 26. The sources which Gregory may have had in mind are indicated *infra*, Chapter III.

A month later Gregory requested Bishop Januarius to reestablish a diocese that had long been without a bishop:

> Pervenit ad nos, in loco qui intra provinciam dicitur Fausiana consuetudinem fuisse episcopum ordinari, sed hanc pro rerum necessitate longis aboluisse temporibus. Quia autem nunc sacerdotum indigentia quosdam illic paganos remanere cognovimus, et ferino degentes modo Dei cultum penitus ignorare, hortamur fraternitatem tuam, ut illic secundum pristinum modum ordinare festinet antistitem...[86]

Gregory did not interfere directly in episcopal elections in Sardinia, though he urged Januarius to consecrate only those who were worthy. In a letter to his *defensor* in Sardinia, Gregory also stated that he had written to Januarius not to fill all episcopal sees from the clergy of his own church. Gregory's letter to Januarius is no longer extant, but his reason apparently was to uphold the rule that bishops should be chosen from the diocese which they were to govern.[87] More exact information about episcopal elections in Sardinia is lacking.

2. AT MILAN

The metropolitan see of Milan became vacant at the death of Bishop Lawrence in August, 592.[88] During the vacancy, the Pope lifted the ban of excommunication which Bishop Lawrence had placed upon Magnus, a priest of Milan, for some un-named crime; Gregory, moreover, declared Magnus not to have been guilty of any crime and restored him to his former office.[89] At the same time he urged Magnus to exhort the clergy and people to delay no longer in electing a worthy bishop. A month later, April of 593, Gregory wrote

---

[86] *Ep.* iv, 29.

[87] "De ecclesiis autem quas vacare sacerdotibus indicasti praedicto reverentissimo Januario fratri et coepiscopo nostro scripsimus, ut eas debeat ordinare, sic tamen, ut non omnes ad episcopatum de ecclesia ipsius eligantur...."—*Ep.* xiv, 2.

[88] Cf. Ewald's notes ad *Ep.* i, 80.

[89] Cf. *Ep.* iii, 26—Mar. 593.

three letters[90] concerning the election at Milan. The first was addressed: "Presbiteris, diaconibus et clero Mediolanensis ecclesiae" in reply to an unsigned document from them indicating their unanimous choice of Constantius, a deacon of Milan. Although Gregory had known the latter while both were in Constantinople, during which time the Pope had found nothing reprehensible in Constantius' conduct, he refused to give his approval until he was assured that the Milanese clergy living at Genoa[91] consented to the election of Constantius. He therefore delegated the subdeacon John, rector of the patrimony in Liguria, to go to Genoa "quia multi illic Mediolanensium coacti barbarica feritate consistunt, eorum te voluntates oportet convocatis eis in communi perscrutari. Et si nulla eos diversitas ab electionis unitate disterminat, siquidem in praedicto filio nostro Constantio omnium voluntates atque consensum perdurare cognoscis, tunc eum a propriis episcopis, sicut antiquitatis mos exigit[92] cum nostrae auctoritatis adsensu, solatiante Domino, facias consecrari, quatenus huiusmodi servata consuetudine et apostolica sedes proprium vigorem retineat et a se concessa aliis sua iura non minuat."[93] The third letter is written to the exarch at Ravenna; it repeats the preceding account, and requests the exarch to assist Constantius whether he be elected or not.[94] The Milanese clergy at Genoa agreed in the election of Constantius, and he ruled at Milan until his death in September of the year 600.[95]

---

[90] *Epp.* iii, 29. 30. 31. Concerning the relation of these letters, cf. Ewald's notes ad *Ep.* iii, 29.

[91] Since the Lombard invasion in 569 the bishop and many of the clergy of Milan lived at Genoa. Cf. Ewald's notes ad *Ep.* iii, 29; Dudden, *Gregory the Great*, I, 429.

[92] Pelagius I (556-561) had decreed that the bishop of Milan was to consecrate the bishop of Aquileia, and vice versa, since their sees were so far removed from Rome. Cf. JK, 983. Bishop Lawrence, however, had been consecrated at Milan by his suffragans, probably because the bishop of Aquileia was then in schism. Cf. Ewald's notes ad *Ep.* iii, 29.

[93] *Ep.* iii, 30.

[94] Cf. *Ep.* iii, 31.

[95] Cf. Hartmann's notes ad *Ep.* xi, 6.

The election of a successor to Constantius followed exactly the same pattern as the election of Constantius, except that the Lombard King Agilulf (591-615) attempted to put forth a candidate of his choice. Gregory wrote to the clergy at Milan that no attention whatsoever was to be given to the King's actions, especially since he was not a Catholic but an Arian.[96] No further trouble ensued and Deusdedit, in whose election all had consented, was consecrated by his suffragans with the consent of the Pope.[97]

To each of the metropolitans of Milan and Ravenna Gregory wrote one letter about the election of a bishop in one of their suffragan sees. The two cases are exactly parallel, both of Gregory's letters being an answer to a request for advice from each of the metropolitans on the procedure to be followed when a bishop had been deposed for crimes. The following three points were mentioned in each letter: a) the deposed bishop can never regain his see; b) the canons (and pontifical decrees) do not permit an episcopal see to be vacant beyond three months; c) the metropolitans shall, therefore, consecrate a bishop for the vacant see without delay.[98] Since Gregory wrote no other letters about the elections of suffragans at either Milan or Ravenna, it must be presumed that he did not concern himself with these except when his advice was asked.

3. IN DALMATIA OR WESTERN ILLYRICUM

The metropolitan see of Dalmatia was the city of Salona. During the early years of Gregory's pontificate, Bishop Natalis governed the see of Salona in a haphazard manner. Frequently Gregory called him to a sense of his duties as bishop, with but little effect except in the case of the archdeacon whom Natalis had removed from his office and, in order to disqualify him for that office, had forcibly advanced to the priesthood. Gregory indignantly commanded Natalis to restore Honoratus to his office, threatening the bishop with the loss

---

[96] Cf. *Ep.* xi, 6.

[97] Cf. *Epp.* xi, 6. 14; xii, 14.

[98] Cf. *Ep.* vii, 14 for Milan; *Ep.* vii, 39 for Ravenna. The pontifical decrees are mentioned only in *Ep.* vii, 39.

of the pallium, with excommunication, and even with deposition.[99] The threats were effective, and Honoratus was restored to his position of archdeacon; the disputes between the bishop and his archdeacon were to be settled by Gregory in Rome, whither the bishop was to send a proxy to represent him.[100] Before the affair was entirely settled Bishop Natalis died, sometime between October 592 and March 593.

At once Gregory wrote to the subdeacon Antoninus, rector of the patrimony in Dalmatia:

> ...experientia tua omni instantia omnique sollicitudine clerum et populum eiusdem civitatis ammonere festinet quatenus uno consensu ordinandum sibi debeant eligere sacerdotem; factoque in persona quae fuerit electa decreto, ad nos transmittere studebis, ut cum nostro consensu, sicut priscis fuerit temporibus, ordinatur.... De rebus vero vel ornamento eiusdem ecclesiae fideliter rerum inventarium facito praesente te conscribi. Et ne rebus ipsis possit aliquid deperire Respectum diaconum et Stephanum primicerium notariorum, ut ipsarum rerum omnino gerant custodiam, ammonito, interminans eis de propria eos satisfacturos esse substantia, si quicquam exinde eorum negligentia fuerit imminutum.... Expensa vero quae necessaria fuerit per oeconomum, qui tempore mortis praedicti episcopi inventus est erogetur, quatenus rationes suas futuro episcopo ipse ut novit exponat....[101]

---

[99] Cf. *Epp.* i, 10. 19; ii, 20. 21. 22. 23; iii, 32. Cf. also JK, 1060, 487, 488. The latter two letters of Pope Leo I (440-461) refer to the removal of the archdeacon Aetius by the patriarch of Constantinople. Silva-Tarouca lists these two letters as spurious; cf. *supra*, p. 15, note 42. Cf. JK, 509.

[100] Cf. *Ep.* ii, 50.

[101] *Ep.* iii, 22. The Council of Chalcedon had ordered an *oeconomus* to be appointed in every diocese—Can. 26; cf. Bruns, *Canones*, I, 32; Schroeder, *Disciplinary Decrees*, p. 123. This official is mentioned but twice in Gregory's letters: in the letter just quoted, and in *Ep.* xiv, 2. In the latter Gregory deputed the *oeconomus* and the archpriest of Cagliari to look after the *xenodochia* there. For Justinian's legislation on the *oeconomus*, cf. C. (I, 2) 1, 3, 4, 5, 8, 9; C. (I, 3) 25; N. (3, 2); N. (59, 1) 2; N. (65); N. (67, 3); N. (123, 9); N. (131, 7). Cf. also, Grashof, "Die Gesetze der römischen Kaiser über die Verwaltung und Veräuserung des kirchlichen Vermögens," *AKK*, XXXVI (1876), 193-214; Knecht, *System des Justinianischen Kirchenvermögensrechtes*, Kirchenrechtliche Abhandlungen hrsg. v. Ulrich

The clergy of Salona wrote to Gregory that they had elected the archdeacon Honoratus. To this Gregory replied that he commended them for their choice, and that he had written to the rector of the patrimony urging him to try to get all to agree to the election of Honoratus. But the opposition to Honoratus was not to be won over, and Gregory did not order his consecration, since he would only give his consent if the person chosen were elected by all and found worthy. He positively excluded from consideration a certain Maximus, of whom he had heard much evil.[102] Reports of an impending consecration contrary to the canons had reached Gregory; he therefore addressed himself to all the bishops of Dalmatia: "...praecipimus ut nulli penitus extra consensum permissionemque nostram, quantum ad episcopatus ordinationem pertinet, in Salonitana civitate manus praesumatis imponere, nec quemquam in civitate ipsa aliter quam diximus ordinare. Quod si contra haec quippiam vel sponte vestra, vel a quolibet coacti praesumpseritis vel temptaveritis agere, decernimus vos Dominici corporis et sanguinis participationem privatos...nec quem ordinaveritis habeatur episcopus....[103]

Gregory's fears were not unfounded. The letter just quoted was written in November of 593; in April of the following year Gregory addressed a letter to:

> Maximo praesumptori in Salona:...Cognovimus itaque quod vel subrepta vel simulata piissimorum principum iussione dum vita dignus non fueris, te ad sacerdotii ordinem cunctis venerabilem prorupisse. Quod nos ideo sine ulla haesitatione credidimus, quia vitam aetatemque tuam non habemus incognitam ac deinde, quia serenissimi domini imperatoris animum non ignoramus, quod se in causis sacerdotalibus miscere non soleat, ne

Stutz, XXII (Stuttgart: Verlag von Ferdinand Enke, 1905), 108-116; Comyns, *Papal and Episcopal Administration of Church Property* (Catholic University of America Canon Law Studies No. 147, Washington, D. C.: The Catholic University of America Press, 1942), p. 14.

[102] Cf. *Epp.* iii, 46; iv, 16.

[103] *Ep.* iv, 16. The metropolitan of Salona, like the metropolitan of Milan, was to be consecrated by his own suffragans with the consent of the Pope.

nostris in aliquo peccatis gravetur. Additur inauditum nefas, quod post interdictionem quoque nostram, quae sub excommunicatione tua ordinantiumque te facta est, caesis presbyteris, diaconibus, ceteroque clero, manu militari diceris ad medium deductus. Quam rem nos consecrationem dicere nullo modo possumus, quia ab excommunicatis est hominibus celebrata....[104]

Various officials of Dalmatia interceded for Maximus, to whom Gregory replied that justice would be done if Maximus would come to Rome.[105] Even the Emperor intervened, bidding Gregory to overlook the irregularity of Maximus' consecration and to receive him with honor as the metropolitan of Salona.[106] Gregory obeyed the Emperor insofar as he forgave Maximus for his presumption in permitting himself to be consecrated without the Pope's permission, but he would not overlook the other transgressions:

> ...Alia vero perversa illius, scilicet mala corporalia, quae cognovi, vel quia cum pecuniis est electus vel quod excommunicatus missas facere praesumpserit, propter Deum inrequisita praeterire non possum. Sed opto et Dominum deprecor, quatenus nihil in eo de his quae dicta sunt valeat inveniri et sine periculo animae meae causa ipsius terminetur....Hoc tamen breviter suggero, quia aliquantulum expecto et, si ad me venire diu distulerit, exercere in eo districtionem canonicam nullo modo cessabo....[107]

Gregory waited for four months: the above letter was written in June, 595, and in September Gregory wrote to Maximus himself: "...Hortamur, ut ad nos venire omni postposita excusatione festines, quatenus servata iustitia haec

---

[104] *Ep.* iv, 20. Regarding the emperor's orders, cf. *Ep.* v, 6: "De causa Maximi praevaricatoris quid actum sit, cognovisti. Sed postquam serenissimus domnus imperator iussione transmisit, ut ordinari minime debuisset, tunc ad altiorem superbiam erupit. Nam homines gloriosi viri Romani patricii, qui ab eo praemia acceperunt, eumque ita ordinari fecerunt, Antonium, subdiaconum et rectorem patrimonii, nisi fugisset, occiderent...."

[105] Cf. *Epp.* iv, 38; v, 29. 39.

[106] Cf. *Ep.* v, 39.

[107] *Ep.* v, 39.

et cognoscere et finire secundum canonica instituta Christo revelante possimus. . . ."[108] Gregory again summoned Maximus to Rome in January, 596, despite the fact that the latter had requested the Pope to send a representative to Salona to try the case, as he claimed the Emperor had ordered. Gregory replied that he had received no such order from the Emperor, and that he would send a representative to Salona "si umquam ratio ei qui accusatur necessitatem probationis imponeret. At postquam non tibi sed accusantibus hoc onus incumbit[109] ad nos, sicut praefati sumus, dilatione cessante, venire non desinas. . . ."[110] At the same time the clergy and people of Salona were warned against communicating with the excommunicated bishop; a similar warning was sent to the clergy and people of Jadera in Dalmatia.[111]

More than a year went by before the Pope's insistence had any effect. In April of 597 Bishop Sabinian of Jadera submitted to the Pope, by whom he was summoned to Rome to obtain absolution for having taken part in the consecration of Maximus and for having communicated with him.[112] Bishop Sabinian answered the summons without delay. Having been found guilty, he promised to avoid all communication with Maximus for the future and imposed upon himself the penalty of doing penance in a monastery, after which Gregory joyfully received him back into communion with the Holy See.[113]

Bishop Maximus was obstinate in his refusal to come to Rome. Gregory had summoned him the second time in January, 596. In May, 599, Gregory yielded to Maximus' request, backed by the entreaties of the exarch, to have the trial elsewhere, and delegated Bishop Marinian of Ravenna, to whom

---

108 *Ep.* vi, 3.

109 "Marcianus in D. xxii, 3. 21: 'semper necessitas probandi incumbit illi qui agit.'"—Hartmann, note 1 ad *Ep.* vi, 25.

110 *Ep.* vi, 25.

111 Cf. *Epp.* vi, 26. 46.

112 Cf. *Ep.* vii, 17.

113 Cf. *Ep.* viii, 11. In this same letter Gregory asked Bishop Sabinian to investigate the request of the inhabitants of Epidaurum in Dalmatia that their bishop, wrongfully deposed by Natalis, be restored. Cf. *Epp.* iii, 8. 9.

he wrote: "....quod non amplius facere debuissem, nisi ut eiusdem Maximi causam tuae fraternitati committerem. Si igitur ad fraternitatem vestram venerit isdem Maximus, deducatur et Honoratus ecclesiae eius archidiaconus, et cognoscat sanctitas tua, si recte ordinatus est, si in simonica heresi lapsus non est, si ei de criminibus coporalibus nihil obviat, si se non cognovit excommunicatum, quando missas facere praesumpsit et quicquid sub timore Dei tibi visum fuerit, decerne, ut nos dispositioni tuae consensum Deo auctore praebeamus. Si autem tuam fraternitatem suspectam praedictus filius noster habuerit, etiam reverentissimus vir frater noster Constantius Mediolanensis episcopus Ravenna veniat, tecum resideat, et de eadem causa pariter decernite et, quod utriusque vobis placuerit, mihi placiturum esse certum tenete...."[114]

Instead of holding a regular trial, Bishop Marinian asked the Pope whether an oath of purgation would suffice. Gregory replied in the affirmative: "....si isdem Maximus coram vobis et praedicto cartulario nostro de simoniaca heresi praestito se sacramento purgaverit, atque de illis ante corpus sancti Apollinaris, sicut scripsimus, tantum modo requisitus liberum se esse responderit, causam ipsius fraternitatis vestrae de eo quod excommunicatus missarum sollemnia agere praesumpsit, iudicio committimus, qua debeat paenitentia talis culpa purgari...."[115] Finally, after six years, Bishop Maximus was

[114] *Ep.* ix, 155. *Ep.* ix, 149 informs Constantius of Milan that Bishop Marinian of Ravenna has been delegated to try Bishop Maximus; it then continues: "Si autem persona sius suspecta forsitan habetur, volumus, ut vestra quoque fraternitas, si ei laboriosum non est, ad eandem civitatem fatigare se debeat et cum praedicto fratre in eodem iudicio pariter sedere..."

[115] *Ep.* ix, 177. *Ep.* ix, 176 was addressed to Bishop Maximus and was to be handed to him by Castorius, papal notary at Ravenna, after his penance had been performed. Cf. *Ep.* ix, 178. Oaths of purgation are also mentioned in *Epp.* ii, 30; vii, 18; xiii, 7. Pope Pelagius I (556-561) by means of an oath cleared himself of the suspicion that he has been accessory to the death of his predecessor. Cf. *Liber Pontificalis*, I, 303. The oath of purgation seems to have been common among the Germanic peoples; cf. Schröder-Künssberg, *Lehrbuch der deutschen Rechtsgeschichte* (7. ed., Berlin und Leipzig: Verlag Walter de Gruyter & Co., 1932), pp. 378, 394, 410, 414. The laws of the Visigoths contain numerous references to it; cf. *MGH* Legum Sectio i, *Leges Nationum Germanicarum*, Tomus i, *Leges Visigotho-*

recognized as the lawful metropolitan of Salona, for in August. 599, Gregory wrote to him that Bishop Marinian of Ravenna had given sufficient assurance of the penance he had performed. At the same time the pallium was sent to Bishop Maximus, and he and the Pope remained on good terms.[116]

4. IN EASTERN ILLYRICUM

When Justinian created the see of Prima Justiniana and raised it to the dignity of a metropolitan see, he had decreed that the bishop thereof was to be chosen and consecrated by his suffragan bishops.[117] Although Gregory did not hesitate to revoke a decision of the bishop of Prima Justiniana[118] he did not attempt to change the arrangement made by Pope Vigilius and Justinian. In 594 Bishop John of Prima Justiniana was succeeded by another of the same name.[119] Only after this second Bishop John's election and consecration was Gregory informed of the fact by the suffragan bishops of Prima Justiniana, and the Pope then ratified and confirmed the consecration.[120] To Bishop John, Gregory wrote:

> Manifestum bonitatis esse liquet indicium in unius electione cunctorum convenire consensum. Quia igitur suscepta fratrum et coepiscoporum nostrorum relatio ad locum vos sacerdotii totius concilii unito consensu et serenissimi principis voluntate declarat accersiri, gratias Creatori nostro magna cum exultatione retulimus.... Quibus nos quoque in persona fraternitatis tuae per omnia consentimus....Pallium vero ex more transmisimus

rum edidit Karolus Zeumer (Hannoverae et Lipsiae: Impensis Bibliopolii Hahniani, 1902), Lexica et grammatica, s.v. *sacramentum*. Oaths of purgation are mentioned in canon 3 of the I Council of Orleans of 511, in canon 39 of the Council of Epâon of 517, and in canon 9 of the III Council of Orleans of 538. Cf. *MGH*, Legum Sectio iii, *Concilia Aevi Merowingici*, Tomus i, pp. 3, 28, 76. Gregory of Tours speaks of such oaths in *Liber in gloria martyrum*, I, 38, and in *Liber in gloria confessorum*, n. 92—*MGH, SS. Merov.*, pp. 512, 807. Cf. also Exod. 22:11; Num. 5:19ff.

116 Cf. *Epp.* ix, 234; viii, 36, and Hartmann's notes *ibid.*

117 Cf. N. (11); (131, 3); *supra*, p. 16f.

118 Cf. *Ep.* iii, 6.

119 Cf. Hartmann's notes ad *Ep.* v, 10.

120 Cf. *Ep.* v, 10.

> et vices vos apostolicae sedis agere iterata innovatione decernimus. . . .[121]

The remainder of the letter urges the bishop to uproot the vice of simony, particularly at the time of ordinations.

The bishop of Corinth was the metropolitan of the province of Achaia. Like the metropolitan of Prima Justiniana, Bishop John of Corinth was elected and consecrated by his own suffragans; the Pope was informed only after the event had taken place, although he had taken an active part in the trial and deposition of Bishop John's predecessor at Corinth, Bishop Anastasius.[122]

In the province of Epirus Vetus, the bishop of Nicopolis exercised metropolitan rights.[123] Again, as in the two cases just mentioned, the Pope was informed of the election and consecration of a new metropolitan at Nicopolis after the event had taken place—Gregory wrote to thank the suffragans of Nicopolis for this information, advising them that he had sent the pallium to the new metropolitan, Bishop Andrew, and exhorting them to remove all traces of simony from their province.[124]

The writer cannot agree with Wisbaum's statement that the bishop of Prima Justiniana was primate of all Illyricum and had, as such, at the time of Gregory the Great, the right of consecrating the metropolitans of Illyricum and of confirming the election of their suffragans.[125] The author's conclusion is based on a faulty interpretation of the inscription of *Ep.* v, 10: "Universis episcopis per Illyricum" and on *Ep.* xii, 10. The inscription of *Ep.* v, 10 can only refer to those

---

[121] *Ep.* v, 16.

[122] Cf. *Epp.* v, 57. 62. 63. Gregory also sent the pallium to the bishop of Corinth, exhorting him to root out the vice of simony; cf. *infra*, Appendix.

[123] Epirus was divided into two provinces: Vetus and Nova; the metropolitan of the latter was the bishop of Durazzo. Cf. Hartmann's notes ad *Ep.* vi, 7.

[124] Cf. *Ep.* vi, 7. Cf. also *Avellana*, No. 119, a letter of the suffragans of Nicopolis to Pope Hormisdas in 516 to inform him of the election of their metropolitan. The concession of the pallium is considered *infra*, Appendix.

[125] Cf. *Die wichtigsten Richtungen und Ziele der Thätigkeit des Papstes Gregors des Grossen*, pp. 30 ff.

provinces listed by Justinian in Novel (131, 3)[126] and not to *all* the Illyrian provinces; it certainly did not include Thessaly [127] (metropolitan see at Larissa), nor Epirus Vetus (metropolitan see at Nicopolis), Epirus Nova (metropolitan at Dyrrhachium), nor Achaia (metropolitan at Corinth).[128] Wisbaum's reference to *Ep.* xii, 10 does not justify his conclusion. On the contrary: *Ep.* xii, 10, which deals with the restoration of a bishop in Doclea, a city in Privalis (one of the provinces placed under the bishop of Prima Justiniana by Justinian) is addressed to Bishop John of Prima Justiniana. But, and this is the important point which Wisbaum fails to mention, *Ep.* xii, 10 was *not* sent to the bishop of Prima Justiniana, but to Bishop Constantine of Scodra, metropolitan of Privalis, along with *Ep.* xii, 11. In the latter, Gregory asks Bishop Constantine to restore the bishop of Doclea and continues: "Si vero hoc tibi quibusdam forte adversantibus obstaculis vides esse difficile, studendum est ut *eadem scripta* [*Ep.* xii, 10] *nostra ad antedictum fratrem nostrum* [John of Prima Justiniana] *sine excusatione perveniant.* Cui etiam et te convenit inminere, ut ea quae ei a nobis mandata sunt districtius exequi et nulla debeant occasione lentari..."[129] This seems to indicate clearly that the bishop of Prima Justiniana did not have any rights over the suffragans of *all* Illyricum, since even in those provinces which were listed as coming under his care by Justinian the Pope commands him at times to act.

It is true that Gregory does not explicitly state that the metropolitans of Corinth and Nicopolis were consecrated by their own suffragans. Yet that seems to be implied in *Ep.* vi, 7 to the bishops of Epirus Vetus, suffragans of Nicopolis: "Scriptorum vestrorum insinuatio, fratres carissimi, patefecit An-

[126] Cf. *supra*, p. 17, note 49.

[127] Wisbaum, referring to *Epp.* iii, 6. 7, includes Thessaly. Cf. *op. cit.*, p. 30, note 5.

[128] Cf. Maps I, 14 of *Cambridge Medieval History* (8 vols., New York: Macmillan Company, 1911-1936), I, following page 754; map 15, *ibid.*, II, following page 889.

[129] *Ep.* xii, 11. Italics inserted by the writer. Cf. Caspar, *Geschichte des Papsttums*, II, 441, note 4.

dream fratrem nostrum Nicopolitaniae civitatis episcopum Deo propitio sollemniter ordinatum. Cuius quoniam consecrationem cleri et provincialium provenisse signatis assensu, gaudemus...." The writer is, therefore, of the opinion that in those provinces of Eastern Illyricum not strictly under the bishop of Prima Justiniana the metropolitans were consecrated by their own suffragans, and that these same metropolitans ratified the election and performed the consecration of their own suffragans.

5. IN GAUL

In only one of his letters does Gregory explicitly treat of an episcopal election in Gaul, though he frequently refers to them in general terms. Following the practice of his predecessors,[130] Gregory appointed as his vicar the bishop of Arles, to whom he sent the pallium. But under the papal vicar the metropolitans were to keep their ancient rights: "Itaque fraternitati tuae vices nostras in ecclesiis, quae sub regno sunt praecellentissimi filii nostri Childeberti iuxta antiquum morem Deo auctore committimus, singulis siquidem metropolitis secundum priscam consuetudinem proprio honore servato."[131] However, Gregory did order that if a bishop wished to make a journey, he could do so only with permission of the vicar, who could also clarify simple questions of faith and settle minor disputes between bishops; more serious questions were to be settled by the vicar and twelve bishops, and, if necessary, were to be sent to Rome for final decision.[132] Nowhere is it stated that the vicar has the right of approving episcopal elections or of performing episcopal consecrations, although he is told to warn the king that the evil of tonsuring laymen and of consecrating them bishops immediately thereafter must be removed from the realm; the evil of simony must also be uprooted.[133]

---

[130] Cf. *supra*, p. 12.
[131] *Ep*. v, 58.
[132] Cf. *Epp*. v, 58. 59.
[133] Cf. *Ep*. v, 58.

Gregory frequently repeats these two points: to all the bishops in King Childebert's realm;[134] to King Childebert (575-595);[135] to Queen Brunichild (†613);[136] to Kings Theoderic (595-613) and Theodebert (595-612), sons of King Childebert who succeeded him in 595;[137] to the bishops of Autun, Lyons, Arles and Vienne;[138] and again to the bishop of Autun, to whom Gregory granted the pallium after the bishop had promised to strive that a synod, frequently called for by the Pope, would pronounce against the above-mentioned evils.[139]

A certain bishop, whose name and see are both unknown, had lost his mind, though he occasionally had lucid intervals. It seems that Queen Brunichild and others wished to depose him. To the Queen and to Bishop Aetherius of Lyons Gregory wrote that he would not permit the sick bishop to be deposed, since a bishop could only be deposed because of his crimes, and not for any lack of health.[140] If the bishop, in one of his lucid intervals, resigned, another might be elected in his place, as Gregory wrote: "Quo facto [resignation] omnium solemniter electione alter qui dignus fuerit episcopus consecretur, sic tamen, ut quousque eundem episcopum in hoc saeculo vita tenuerit, sumptus ei debiti de eadem ecclesia ministrentur."[141] If the bishop did not resign, a suitable person was to be chosen to maintain ecclesiastical discipline and to care for the goods of the church. Since this person was not

---

[134] Cf. *Ep*. v, 59.

[135] Cf. *Ep*. v, 60.

[136] Cf. *Ep*. viii, 4; ix, 213; xiii, 7. The last-mentioned letter excludes from the episcopacy one guilty of bigamy.

[137] Cf. *Ep*. ix, 215.

[138] Cf. *Ep*. ix, 218.

[139] Cf. *Ep*. ix, 222. In this letter Gregory also granted to the church of Autun the privilege of ranking second after Lyons; this privilege, however, was not to work to the detriment of the metropolitans: "metropolis suo per omnia loco et honore servato." The other bishops were to take their rank according to the time of their consecration.

[140] Cf. *Epp*. xiii, 7. 8. The same principle is invoked in *Epp*. iii, 24; ix, 138; xi, 29.

[141] *Ep*. xiii, 8.

a bishop, though he had the right of succession,[142] the ordination of priests and deacons and others was reserved to Bishop Aetherius of Lyons.[143] It is not known whether the Queen obeyed the Pope's injunction.

Gregory's efforts in Gaul were not altogether unsuccessful. Neither simony nor lay ordinations could be eradicated as long as the rulers of Gaul had such an important influence on episcopal elections as that conceded them by the I Council of Orleans in 511.[144] Canon 8 of the III Council of Paris of 559

---

[142] "Qui etiam, si episcopo, qui nunc aegrotat, superstes extiterit, loco eius debeat consecrari." —*Ep.* xiii, 8. This letter is important for the history of the law on coadjutor bishops.

[143] Cf. *Epp.* xiii, 7, 8. It is noteworthy that in neither of these letters does the word "*chorepiscopus*" occur. It appears, therefore, that Gregory was either unaware of the institute of rural bishops or unwilling to use this institute as a means to provide for coadjutors.

In the East the institute of rural bishops (*χωρεπίσκοποι; ἐπίσκοποι τῶν ἀγρῶν*) arose spontaneously during the second half of the third century, and spread rapidly during the first half of the fourth. Gillmann maintains that they were true bishops, at least until the Council of Chalcedon in 451; they are last mentioned at the II Council of Nicaea in 787. Cf. Gillmann, *Das Institut der Chorbischöfe im Orient, Historisch-kanonistische Studie* (München: Verlag der J. J. Lentner'schen Buchhandlung, 1903), pp. 1-108; Fliche-Martin, *Histoire*, II, 396f; IV, 540; Leclercq, "Chorévêques," *DACL*, III, 1424f.

In the West the first mention of rural bishops occurred at the Council of Riez in 439; cf. Mansi, V, 1192. There is but one other mention of a rural bishop in the West in the first half of the fifth century, that of a certain Eugraphus in Dalmatia, whose tombstone was found in 1874 with the inscription: "Depositio Eugrafi Choreepiscopi." Cf. Zeiller, "Le chorévêque Eugraphus—Note sur le chorépiscopat en occident au Ve siècle," *RHE*, VII (1906), 27-32. Although rural bishops appear as a regular institute in the West only in the eighth century, they are mentioned several times as existing in Gaul in the last half of the sixth century. The instances in which they are mentioned are very similar to that with which Gregory dealt in *Epp.* xiii, 7, 8. Cf. Gottlob, *Der abendländische Chorepiskopat* (Kanonistische Studien und Texte, Band I, Bonn: Kurt Schroeder Verlag, 1928), pp. 1-19. Gregory, however, does not mention the institute in these or any of his letters.

[144] Canon 4—"De ordinationibus clericorum id observandum esse censuimus, ut nullus saecularium ad clericatus officium praesumatur nisi aut cum regis jussione aut cum iudicis voluntate." —Bruns, *Canones*, II, 161; *MGH*, *Legum Sectio* iii, *Concilia Aevi Merowingici*, p. 4. This canon and its effects are discussed at length by Boucharlat, *Les élections épisco-*

rejected royal influence in episcopal elections, but the canon was not observed.[145]

The Council of Paris of 613 passed over the rights of the king without any mention of them; it mentioned only the rights of the clergy and people to elect, and that of the metropolitan to consecrate, with the bishops of his province, the one elected.[146] Clotaire II (King of Neustria 584-613; King of all France 613-629) published the canons of the Council of Paris and made them obligatory for his realm. But in so doing he changed the wording of canon 1 by adding the words: "et si persona condigna fuerit, per ordinationem principis ordinetur..."[147] Vaes contends that the law of the Council of Paris of 613 can be looked upon as the culmination of Pope Gregory's strenuous efforts to better the condition of the Church in Gaul.[148]

6. IN BRITAIN

With the Celtic church Gregory was strangely out of touch. "There is no more remarkable proof of the isolation of

---

pales, pp. 48-85; Vacandard, "Les élections épiscopales sous les Mérovingiens," *Études de critique et d'histoire religieuse*, I (1913), 129-164; cf. also De Clercq, *La législation religieuse franque de Clovis à Charlemagne* (Louvain: Bureaux de Recueil Bibliothèque de l'Université, 1936), pp. 8-13.

[145] "....Nullus civibus invitis ordinetur episcopus nisi quem populi et clericorum electio plenissima quaesierit voluntate: non principis imperio neque per quamlibet conditionem contra metropolis voluntatem vel episcoporum comprovincialium ingeratur..." —Bruns, *Canones*, II, 221; *MGH*, *Concilia* I, p. 144. The date of this council is not certain; cf. De Clercq, *op. cit.*, p. 44f.

[146] Cf. canon 1 —Bruns, *Canones*, II, 256; *MGH*, *Concilia* i, 186; Boucharlat, *op. cit.*, p. 87f; Vacandard, *op. cit.*, pp. 164-167.

[147] Cf. *Edictum Clotarii*, *MGH*, Legum Sectio ii (*Capitularia Regum Francorum*, Tomus I, denuo edidit Alfredus Boretius, Hannoverae, 1883), 21; Vacandard, *op. cit.*, pp. 167-170; Boucharlat, *op. cit.*, pp. 88-93; De Clercq, *op. cit.*, 57-59.

[148] Cf. "La papauté et l'église franque à l'époque de Grégoire le Grand," *RHE*, XI (1905), 755-782. A contrary opinion is given by Caspar, who states that the Council of Paris had no connection at all with the plan of Gregory the Great for a reform-synod. He adds: "Die Pariser Synode Chlotars II. von 614 bezeichnete vielmehr den Markstein in der Entwickelung der fränkischen Landeskirche, jenseits dessen auf ein Jahrhundert fast jeder Zusammenhang zwischen Papsttum und fränkischer Landeskirche aufhörte." —*Geschichte des Papsttums*, II, 501.

the contemporary Irish Church from the rest of Christendom, than the absence of any reference or allusion to it in Gregory's correspondence. With all the other branches of the Catholic Church in the West Gregory was brought into contact in the course of his pontificate; with the Church in Ireland and Britain alone he held no communication."[149] Perhaps there is one allusion: in his letter to King Theoderic and Theodebert commending to their protection Augustine and his companions on their journey to Britain, Gregory explains why he is sending missionaries: ". . . .Atque ideo pervenit ad nos Anglorum gentem ad fidem christianam Deo miserante desideranter velle converti, sed *sacerdotes e vicino* neglegere et desideria eorum cessare sua adhortatione succendere. . . ."[150] The italicized words are explained by Hartmann: "Scil. sacerdotes in Hibernia insula habitantes."[151] Even if Hartmann's explanation is correct, the fact remains that Gregory did not concern himself with the Celtic Church, except to supply for its neglect of converting the Angles by sending Augustine, prior of Gregory's own monastery in Rome, with a band of forty monks to Britain.

The story of Augustine's mission and its success is too well known to require repetition.[152] Gregory's regulations regarding episcopal elections in the territory won from paganism are of interest here. When with his monks Augustine (†604) left Rome, late in 595, he was their prior. Before the band had proceeded far in Gaul, they delegated Augustine to return to Rome to obtain permission to give up the project. Gregory would hear nothing of this, and sent Augustine back as Abbot with a letter of encouragement.[153]

In Britain the Abbot and his monks settled at Canterbury, the capital of King Ethelbert of Kent (560-616), who received

---

[149] Dudden, *Gregory the Great*, II, 118f.

[150] *Ep.* vi, 49. Italics not in the original.

[151] Note 2 ad *Ep.* vi, 49. Caspar refers these words to the clergy of Gaul; cf. *Geschichte des Papsttums*, II, 506.

[152] Cf. e.g., Batiffol, *St. Gregory the Great*, pp. 212-226; Dudden, *Gregory the Great*, II, 99-147.

[153] "Remeanti autem Augustino praeposito vestro, quem et abbatem vobis constituimus. . . ." —*Ep.* vi, 50a.

them kindly, influenced assuredly by his Catholic wife Bertha. Gregory soon heard of the success of the missionaries and related it joyfully to Eulogius of Alexandria in a letter of July, 598: "...nuntio...ut ad eam [gentem Anglorum] monasterii mei monachum in praedicatione transmittere Deo auctore debuissem. Qui data a me licentia a Germaniarum episcopis[154] episcopus factus [est]....In sollemnitate autem Dominicae nativitatis, quae hac prima indictione [i.e., 597] transacta est, plus quam decem milia Angli ab eodem nuntiati sunt fratre et coepiscopo nostro baptizati...."[155] The letter in which Gregory granted Augustine permission to be consecrated has not been preserved.

In 601 a second group of missionaries was sent to Britain in answer to Augustine's request for more helpers. These carried with them, besides presents for the King and articles necessary for church services, letters to King Ethelbert and his Queen,[156] and three letters to Augustine.[157] The first warned the bishop against the danger of pride because of his success and the miracles he had performed; the second granted Augustine the use of the pallium and proposed a plan for the hierarchy of Britain; the third was the *Responsa*, a series of replies to questions submitted to the Pope by Augustine.[158]

---

[154] Bede states that Augustine was consecrated by Aetherius of Arles. Cf. *Historia Ecclesiastica*, Lib. i, c. 27—Plummer, *Venerabilis Bedae Opera Historica*, I, 48. Vergil, however, was at that time bishop of Arles. Cf. Hartmann's note 4 ad *Ep*. viii, 29.

[155] *Ep*. viii, 29.

[156] *Epp*. xi, 37. 35.

[157] *Epp*. xi, 36. 39. 56a.

[158] The authenticity of these *Responsa* has been called into question, but Hartmann considered them to be genuine, with a few interpolations. Cf. his notes ad *Ep*. xi, 56a. In 1932 Müller again studied the question and concluded: "Der Inhalt der besprochenen Responsa lässt die Abfassung durch Gregor den Grossen für höchst unglaublich, die Datierung aber in die Zeit nach Theodors Wirken, genauer in das letzte Jahrzehnt vor 731 als sehr wahrscheinlich erscheinen." —"Zur Frage nach der Echtheit und Abfassungszeit des Responsum b. Gregorii ad Augustinum Episcopum," *Theologische Quartalschrift*, CXIII (1932), 94-118. Against this thesis, a further study in 1938 again concluded that the *Responsa* are genuine. Cf. Wasner, "De Authenticitate 'Libelli Responsionum' B. Gregorii M. Papae

Concerning the establishment of the hierarchy in the newly-converted territory, Gregory had thought out a well-conceived plan. He wrote on this subject to Augustine as follows:

> ....per loca singula duodecim episcopos ordines, qui tuae subiacent dicioni, quatenus Lundoniensis civitatis episcopus semper in posterum a synodo propria debeat consecrari atque honoris pallium ab hac sancta et apostolica, cui Deo auctore deservio, sede percipiat.[159] Ad Eburachum vero civitatem te volumus episcopum mittere, quem ipse iudicaveris ordinandum, ita ut, si eadem civitas cum finitimis locis verbum Dei receperit, ipse quoque duodecim episcopos ordinet et metropolitani honore perfruatur...quem tamen tuae fraternitatis volumus dispositioni subiacere; post obitum vero tuum ita episcopis quos ordinaverit praesit, ut Lundoniensis episcopi nullo modo dicioni subiaceat. Sit vero inter Lundoniae et Eburachae civitatis episcopos in posterum honoris ista distinctio, ut ipse prior habeatur, qui prius fuerit ordinatus...Tua vero fraternitas non solum eos episcopos quos ordinaverit neque hos tantum modo qui per Eburachae episcopum fuerint ordinati, sed etiam omnes Brittaniae sacerdotes habeat...subiectos...[160]

The sixth question submitted by Augustine to Gregory's judgment was: "Si longinquitas itineris magna interiacet, ut episcopi non facile valeant convenire, an debeat sine aliorum episcoporum praesentia episcopus ordinari?" To which Gregory replied: "Et quidem in Anglorum ecclesia, in qua adhuc solus tu episcopus inveniris, ordinare episcopum non aliter nisi sine episcopis potes. Nam quando de Gallis episcopi veniunt, qui in ordinatione episcopi testes assistant? Sed fraternitatem tuam ita volumus episcopos ordinare, ut ipsi sibi

---

ad S. Augustinum Angliae Apostolum Animadversiones," *Jus Pontificium*, XVIII (1938-1939), 171-185; 293-299.

[159] The archiepiscopal see, however, remained at Canterbury and not at London. Cf. Dudden, *Gregory the Great*, II, 129, note 2. In 604 Augustine consecrated Mellitus bishop of London. Cf. Bede, *Historia Ecclesiastica*, Lib. ii, c. 3. —Plummer, *op. cit.*, I, 85.

[160] *Ep.* xi, 39.

episcopi longo intervallo minime disiungantur, quatenus nulla sit necessitas, ut in ordinatione episcopi pastores quoque alii, quorum praesentia valde est utilis, facillime debeant convenire. Cum igitur auctore Deo ita fuerint episcopi in propinquis sibi locis ordinati, per omnia episcoporum ordinatio sine adgregatis tribus vel quattuor episcopis fieri non debet...."[161]

7. IN AFRICA

Gregory's letters contain no information about episcopal elections in Africa,[162] but two of them refer to the hierarchy. Gregory wanted to change the African tradition whereby in *each province* the bishop who had been first consecrated held the office of primate, an office similar to that of metropolitan in other provinces of the Church—not to be confused with the primatial dignity of a *country* granted to certain sees.[163] Under that system, the primacy moved from city to city (or from village to village, since in Africa villages often had bishops) as the primate died and the next in line took over his duties. Gregory wanted the bishops of each province to select a definite city, the bishop of which would always be primate: "Ipse vero primas non passim sicut moris est per villas, sed in una iuxta eorum electionem civitate reside-

[161] *Ep.* xi, 56a.

[162] Except that the evil of simony was present in Africa. Cf. e.g., the letters cited *infra*, note 166.

[163] Cf. *Ep.* i, 72. Ewald contends (note 3 ad *Ep.* i, 72) that the Maurists wrongly interpreted this letter to refer to the time of consecration as the determining factor in obtaining the office of primate. Wisbaum maintains that in Africa at the time of Gregory the Great the time of consecration had nothing to do with the position of primate. Cf. *Die wichtigsten Richtungen und Ziele der Thätigkeit des Papstes Gregors des Grossen*, p. 23, note 2. Before Gregory's reign the time of consecration was the determining factor; cf. *supra*, p. 9f. Though Gregory's words are not very clear, the writer agrees with the interpretation of the Maurists, for both Ewald and Wisbaum seem to have overlooked *Ep.* iii, 48, addressed to the primate of Numidia who had excused himself from coming to Rome *because of his age*; to him Gregory writes: "...ad hunc ordinem [i.e., primatis] *pervenisse*...." Nowhere is there any indication that the primates were *chosen*, as Wisbaum would have it. Fliche-Martin agree with the interpretation of the Maurists; cf. *Histoire*, V, 215.

at. . . ."[164] But despite his disapproval, Gregory did not change the African custom. In a letter written to the bishops of the province of Numidia Gregory states that he has granted their request that their customs be preserved, but that he forbids those bishops who had once been Donatists to become primates: "Consuetudinem. . .immotam permanere concedimus, sive de primatibus constituendis, ceterisque capitulis; exceptis his, qui ex Donatistis ad episcopatum perveniunt, quos provehi ad primatus dignitatem, etiam cum ordo eos ad locum eundem deferat, modis omnibus prohibemus. . . ."[165] Gregory also assured the bishop of Carthage that he would defend the privileges of the Carthaginian Church.[166]

8. IN THE ORIENT

In the Orient there were the four patriarchs of Constantinople, Alexandria, Antioch and Jerusalem. The union of faith between the West and the East was guaranteed by means of the synodical letters sent by the Pope to each of the patriarchs and by these to the Pope and to one another.[167]

---

[164] *Ep.* i, 72. Concerning this sentence, Ewald (note 4) says: "Hic et aliis locis docemur, Gregorii tempore episcopos quosdam non certam sedem retinuisse. Cf. *Ep.* vi, 23, qua papa interdicit Amalfitano episcopo foris per diversa loca vagari." The words of Gregory quoted above do *not* imply that the bishop who was primate was not attached to a fixed see; his words mean, as stated already, that the *primacy* was not attached to one see, since it always moved on at the death of the primate to the see of the bishop next in line, and so on. Ewald's reference to *Ep.* vi, 23 proves nothing more than that Bishop Pimenius of Amalfi in Campania did not obey the law of residence, as Gregory states clearly: "Pervenit ad nos Pimenium Amalfitanae civitatis episcopum in ecclesia *sua* residere non esse contentum. . . ."

[165] *Ep.* i, 75.

[166] Cf. *Ep.* ii, 52. Bishop Columbus, whose see is unknown, frequently acted as Gregory's unofficial representative in Africa—"Vicaire de fait, mais sans titre." —Duchesne, *L'Église,* p. 650, note 3. Cf. also *Epp.* ii, 46; iii, 47; iv, 34; xii, 8. Yet Gregory never overlooked the privileges and rights of the primates; cf. *Epp.* ii, 52 to the bishop of Carthage; iii, 48; xii, 9 to the primate of Numidia; iv, 13 to the primate of Byzacene. In *Epp.* iii, 47, 48 Gregory warns that youths are not to be ordained "ad sacros ordines;" all simony and lay interference are also to be eschewed.

[167] "On appelle synodique la lettre officielle que les papes et autres patriarches s'expédiaient les uns aux autres peu après leur installation pour

Gregory the Great intervened in the internal affairs of the East only when such intervention was required to maintain justice and the observance of the canons, and in such cases his intervention was in response to an appeal to the authority of the Roman pontiff.[168] Nevertheless he did not hesitate at other times to address to the patriarchs a fraternal admonition when disorders were prevalent and little effort was made to correct them. One of the prevailing evils was, as in the West also, the practice of simony. To each of the three patriarchs of Alexandria, Antioch and Jerusalem Gregory addressed an urgent appeal that they remove all traces of simony from their churches:

> Quia vero pervenit ad nos in orientis ecclesiis nullum ad sacrum ordinem nisi ex praemiorum datione pervenire, si ita esse vestra fraternitas agnoscit, hanc primam oblationem omnipotenti Domino offerat, ut a subiectis sibi ecclesiis errorem simoniacae hereseos compescat. Nam, ut alia taceam, quales esse in sacris ordinibus poterunt, qui ad hoc non merito, sed praemiis evehuntur?[169]

There is no mention of simony in Gregory's letters to John of Constantinople, or to his successor, Cyriacus.[170]

---

se la notifier et aussi pour témoigner de leur enseignement doctrinal." —Duchesne, *Liber Diurnus et les élections pontificales au VIIe siècle,* (Paris, 1891), p. 26, note 1; cited hereafter *Les élections pontificales.* Cf. also Du Cange, *Glossarium Mediae et Infimae Latinitatis* conditum a Carolo du Fresne Domino du Cange auctum a Monachis Ordinis S. Benedicti, editio nova a Leopold Favre (10 vols., Paris, Librairie des sciences et des arts, 1937-1938), s.v., "synodica;" *Ep.* ix, 147. Very few synodical letters of the Popes have been preserved; those preserved are the following: JK, 746 —Anastasius II (496-498); JK, 938—Pelagius I (556-561); JK, 931—Vigilius (537-555); JK, 1054—Pelagius II (579-590); *Ep.* i, 24—Gregory the Great. But cf. also JK, 452, 460, letters of Pope Leo I (440-461) in which reference is made to the custom of sending synodical letters. Other non-papal synodical letters may be found in *Avellana,* Nos. 89, 90, 146, 169, 195—these all date from the early sixth century.

[168] Cf. e.g., *Epp.* iii, 52. 63; v, 44; vi, 14-17. 62.

[169] *Epp.* ix, 135 to Anastasius of Antioch; xi, 28 to Isacius of Jerusalem; the appeal to Eulogius of Alexandria in *Ep.* xiii, 44 is couched in different words.

[170] Cf. *Epp.* i, 4. 24; iii, 52; v, 44; vi, 15; vii, 4. 5. 28; xiii, 43.

Beyond these general appeals against simony Gregory made no further references to episcopal elections in the four eastern patriarchates, except in one letter to Emperor Maurice, whom he congratulated for having chosen Cyriacus to succeed John at Constantinople in 596:

> ....Non enim parvae potuit esse mercedis, quod Johanne sanctae memoriae de hac luce subtracto ad ordinandum sacerdotem pietas vestra diu haesitavit, tempus paulo longius distulit, cum metu omnipotentis Domini consilium quaesivit, ut videlicet causa Dei cum magno timore debuisset disponi. Unde et aptum valde existere in pastorali regimine fratrem atque consacerdotem meum Cyriacum existimo, quem ad eundem ordinem pietatis vestrae consilia longa genuerunt; qui in amministrandis dudum rebus ecclesiasticis quam sollicitus et quomodo fuerit expertus cuncti novimus...."[171]

Nothing is said against the emperor's interference in an ecclesiastical election, and Gregory's words do not indicate whether the emperor merely approved a previous selection of the inhabitants of Constantinople, or whether his choice took precedence, though the latter seems more probable. From a letter of Epiphanius of Constantinople (520-535) to Pope Hormisdas (514-523) in 520 it is evident that the emperor's choice preceded: "...sedem sacerdotalem sanctae ecclesiae catholicae regiae urbis conferre dignatus est sententia et electione christianissimi et justissimi principis Justini et piissimae reginae...His...simul et sacerdotum et monachorum et fidelissimae plebis consensus accessit...."[172]

---

[171] *Ep.* vii, 6. Gregory had known Cyriacus during the time he was *apocrisiarius* at Constantinople before his election as Pope. Cf. *Epp.* vii, 4. 5. 7.

[172] *Avellana*, No. 195; Thiel, *Epistolae*, p. 923. Cf. also *Avellana*, Nos. 234 ("Epistola synodi Constantinopolitanae de ordinatione Epiphanii"), 239, 240, replies of Pope Hormisdas to Nos. 234 and 195 respectively; the letters are also in Thiel, *Epistolae*, pp. 950, 965, 966.

SUMMARY

The preceding treatment of the letters of Gregory the Great dealing with episcopal elections has pesented a general picture of the election of a bishop in the various parts of the Church at the end of the sixth century with but few references to preceding legislation. In brief, the following points have been noted: 1) Gregory, as metropolitan, took an active share in episcopal elections within the Roman province, exercising the right of a metropolitan in confirming or rejecting a candidate elected by the inhabitants of the widowed diocese, and in consecrating at Rome the person elected and confirmed. 2) For regulating an election within the limits of the Roman metropolitan province Gregory originated two form letters, one to the bishop visitor delegated to conduct the election, the other to the electors. In these form letters the following rules were stated: a) the inhabitants of the widowed diocese were the electors, and all were normally to agree on one candidate; b) only clerics of the widowed church were eligible, except in cases wherein no suitable clerics were to be found; c) the person elected was to be free from all canonical impediments; d) canonical penalties were decreed against those who permitted or consented to the election of a layman; e) the person elected was to be consecrated at Rome by the Pope in his capacity as metropolitan. These rules were further clarified in those letters which were not written according to any form, wherein one finds various disabilities which Gregory considered as sufficient to debar a person from the episcopal office. 3) The election of the metropolitan of Ravenna was regulated by the same rules as were the elections of suffragan bishops of Rome, but in the province itself, as in all other metropolitan provinces, the metropolitan approved the election of his suffragans and performed the consecration of those suffragans. 4) The metropolitans were consecrated by their own suffragans; at Milan and at Salona the consent of the Pope had to be obtained *before* the consecration took place, while the election and consecration of the metropolitans of Prima Justiniana, Corinth and Nicopolis were ratified and confirmed by the Pope *after* these events had taken place. 5) The Pope did not interfere in the election of the four eastern patriarchs, nor in elections within the patriarchates—he interfered in the internal affairs of the eastern church only when it was necessary to uphold the canonical discipline of the Church. 6) Normally a bishop was to be consecrated by several bishops, but in cases of necessity the consecration by but one bishop was permitted.

In the chapters that follow the more important topics related to episcopal elections and Gregory's letters will be considered more in detail. The first section treats of the sources probably used by Gregory in the letters dealing with episcopal elections; it will become evident that Gregory followed closely the discipline established both by his predecessors and by preceding Councils. Thereafter, select points of law (the electors, the age of candidates for the episcopacy, absolute ordinations, transfer of bishops, oaths of bishops) will be considered in their relation to the letters of Gregory the Great.

CHAPTER III

THE SOURCES USED BY GREGORY THE GREAT

What sources does Gregory the Great use for listing the qualities of those eligible to the episcopal office? It is certain that he was well acquainted with Justinian's law,[1] and that he did not hesitate to invoke both the sacred canons and Roman law in ecclesiastical matters, particularly in the question of the trial and deposition of bishops.[2] Yet in all of the letters referring to episcopal elections and the qualities required of those who are to be ordained, Gregory emphasizes the prescriptions of the sacred canons—not once in the portions of these letters that treat specifically of episcopal elections and the qualities required does he use the word *"lex."*

By the year 590, the year of Gregory's election, there were various canonical collections in existence in the West. "In the fifth century two Latin versions of canons of Oriental Councils, the *Hispana* or *Isidoriana* and the *Prisca* or *Itala* were made in Italy, perhaps in Rome itself, and pontifical writings were preserved in the papal archives. . . .At the end of the fifth century both the collections themselves and the

---

[1] Cf. e.g., *Ep.* xiii, 50. As Max Conrat has pointed out: "Ja das Kommonitorium an den Defensor Johannes [*Ep.* xiii, 50] ist im Grunde nichts weiter als ein Gewebe von Texten der Justinianischen Kodifikation... Es sind Texte aus den Pandekten, dem Kodex, und den Novellen, und zwar originalgriechischen Novellen in lateinischer Version, von denen die eine (Nov. 123, 8. 19. 21. 22) mit der Fassung des Authenticum (134) übereinstimmt, die andere (Nov. 90, 9) eine hiervon abweichende Uebersetzung darstellt."—Conrat-Kantorowicz, "Römisches Recht im frühesten Mittelalter," *ZSS*, Rom. Abt., XXXIV (1913), 33; cf. *ibid.*, pp. 36-44; Conrat, *Geschichte der Quellen und Literatur des römischen Rechts im früheren Mittelalter* (Leipzig: J. C. Hinrichs'sche Buchhandlung, 1891), pp. 8-13. "Die Sprache Gregor's ist von Reminiscenzen wie aus der Bibel, so aus dem Justinianischen Rechtsbuche mannigfach durchsetzt."—Seckel, [in book review], *Historische Zeitschrift*, LXXIX (1897), 92.

[2] Cf., e.g., *Ep.* ii, 28: "quae legibus canonibusque conveniunt;" *Ep.* ix, 194: "et sacris canonibus et legibus esse noscitur definitum;" *Ep.* iii, 8: "quae sunt legibus canonibus placita;" *Ep.* viii, 32: "nec mundanarum legum nec sacrorum canonum statuta."

canons in each collection were multiplied....During the space of thirty years (492-523) many collections, including those of Dionysius Exiguus and that known as the *Collectio Quesnelliana*...were made."[3]

It must be noted in the first place that Gregory does not seem to quote directly or verbatim from the canonical collections which were in use at the time of his pontificate. The writer has found but one quotation made verbatim:[4] in forbidding bishops and priests to put away their wives Gregory says, in *Ep.* ix, 110: "ut hi, sicut canonica decrevit auctoritas, uxores, *quas caste debent regere non relinquant*." The rubric of canon 6 of the *Canones Apostolorum* of the *Dionysiana* is identical: "Ut episcopus aut presbiter *uxorem suam quam debet caste regere non relinquat*."[5] In the same letter Gregory forbids bishops to live with women, "exceptis eis [mulieribus] quas sacrorum canonum censura permittit, id est, *matre, amita, germana*, et aliis huiuscemodi de quibus non possit esse su-

[3] Le Bras, "Quantam partem habuerint Romani in Libris Canonum ante Decretum Gratiani confectis," *Jus Pontificium*, XIII (1933), 237. "Apud Romanam vero ecclesiam collectionem Dionysianam iamdudum vigere testatur circa 550 Cassiodorus (Div. Litt. xxii 'Dionysius...ex Graecis exemplaribus canones ecclesiasticos...composuit quos hodie usu celeberrimo ecclesia Romana complectitur'), ipsos canones apostolicos adhibet Joannis II papae (532-535) epistula ad Caesarium Arelatensem data; vide cann. xxv, xxviiii." —Turner, I, ii, 33. John II's letter quoting the *Dionysiana* (JK, 885) may be found in Schwartz, *Acta Conciliorum Oecumenicorum* (4 vols. in 12 parts, Berolini et Lipsiae: Walter de Gruyter & Co., 1914-1936), IV, ii, 206-210. Cf. also Caspar, *Geschichte des Papsttums*, II, 307-311; Sägmüller, *Lehrbuch*, pp. 211-213. The most recent critical study of the *Dionysiana* and other canonical collections is by Wurm: *Studien und Texte zur Dekretalensammlung des Dionysius Exiguus*, Kanonistische Studien und Texte hrsg. von A. M. Koeniger, Band XVI (Bonn: Ludwig Röhrscheid Verlag, 1939); cf. especially pp. 10-80. Wurm has also given a critical edition of two texts of the *Dionysiana*; cf. "Decretales selectae ex antiquissimis Romanorum Pontificum epistulis decretalibus," *Apollinaris*, XII (1939), 40-93. Cited hereafter as *Decretales selectae*.

[4] The writer's search was confined mainly to a comparison of the *Dionysiana* and the *Avellana* with the letters of Gregory; a thorough check of all of Gregory's statements with all of the possible canonical collections which he might have used would perhaps bring to light other similar quotations verbatim reproduced.

[5] Turner, I, i, 2.

spicio." Hartmann refers this quotation to the Theodosian Code (16, 2) 44.[6] Seckel (1864-1924), who maintains that the Theodosian Code was no longer cited by the Roman pontiffs after the promulgation of Justinian's laws in Italy, states that Justinian's Code should have been cited: (1, 3) 19.[7]

Both authors are wrong, for Justinian's Code, repeating the Theodosian, has: "...ut *matres filias atque germanas* intra domorum suarum saepta contineant." Novel (123, 29) forbids a bishop to have any woman whatsoever in his house: "Episcopum vero nullam penitus mulierem habere aut cum ea habitare permittimus." This was again changed by Novel (137, 1) which quoted canon 3 of the Council of Nicaea in Greek, and permitted a bishop or cleric to live with his *mother* or his *aunt* or with such women who were beyond all suspicion. It omits specific mention of the bishop's or cleric's *sister*. It seems clear to the writer, therefore, that Gregory was quoting some canonical collection and not Roman law. The Dionysian version of canon 3 of the Council of Nicaea must have been the source which Gregory had before him, for it states: "...nec alicui omnino qui in clero est licere subintroductam habere mulierem, nisi forte *matrem aut sororem aut amitam* vel eas tantum personas quae suspicionem effugiunt."[8] The *Dionysiana* also contains a decree of Pope Siricius (384-399) which may have led Pope Gregory to cite canon 3 of the Council of Nicaea: "Feminas vero non alias esse patimur in domibus clericorum, nisi eas tantum quas propter solas necessitudinum causas habitare cum eisdem synodus Nicaeni permisit."[9]

Neither of the above-mentioned cases of similarity between the wording of Gregory and that of the *Dionysiana* occurs in letters treating of episcopal elections or of the qualities required of a candidate. In those letters a further similarity of wording is found in the regulations that only the clerics of the widowed church were eligible. A letter of Pope

---

[6] Cf. Note 1 ad *Ep.* ix, 110.

[7] Cf. [Book Review], *Historische Zeitschrift*, LXXVI (1896), 111.

[8] Turner, I, ii, 257. The *versio Prisca* omits the word *matrem*. Cf. Turner, I, ii, 117.

[9] *PL*, LXVII, 236; JK, 255.

Celestine (423-432) states: "Tunc alter de altera eligatur ecclesia, si de civitatis ipsius clericis, cui est episcopus ordinandus, nullus dignus (quod evenire non credimus) potuerit inveniri."[10] Gregory's words are very similar: "...ut nullum de altera eligi permittas ecclesia, nisi forte inter clericos ipsius civitatis...nullus ad episcopatum dignus, quod evenire non credimus, potuerit invenire."[11]

These instances seem to indicate that Pope Gregory made use of the Dionysian collection. This statement is strengthened by the fact that all of the canonical prescriptions mentioned by Gregory are found also in the collection of Dionysius Exiguus. In the form letters mentioned above[12] Gregory listed five rules (omitting the first which dealt only with the appointment of the bishop visitor), and these same rules applied in all cases, even though not methodically listed in the majority of his letters. Hence it will be sufficient to show that these rules were to be found scattered throughout the *Dionysiana*. Two points must first be noted: the fifth rule of the form letters, which were written only to Ravenna and the suffragan sees of Rome, must be understood in the sense that all metropolitans had the right to consecrate their suffragans; the third rule, which is in the form letters merely a succinct statement, is clarified in Gregory's other letters.

The first rule that the clergy, nobles and people were to elect their bishop is found in the following places of the *Dionysiana*: a) a letter of Pope Celestine to the bishops of Gaul: "Nullus invitis detur episcopus; cleri, plebis et ordinis consensus et desiderium requiratur;"[13] b) in a letter of Pope Leo to the bishop of Aquileia: "Quod non habeantur episcopi quos nec clerus eligit, nec populus exquisivit...."[14] c) in a letter of the same Pope to the bishop of Thessalonica: "Ille omnibus praeponitur, quem cleri, plebisque consensus concorditer postularint...ut nullus invitis et non petentibus ordinetur."[15]

---

[10] *PL*, LXVII, 276; JK, 369.

[11] Cf. *supra*, p. 26.

[12] Cf. *supra*, p. 22.

[13] *PL*, LXVII, 276; JK, 369.

[14] *PL*, LXVII, 288; JK, 398.

[15] *PL*, LXVII, 293; JK, 404.

The second rule, that only the clergy of the widowed church were eligible, is found: a) in a letter of Pope Celestine: "Tunc alter de altera eligatur ecclesia, si de civitatis ipsius clericis, cui est episcopus ordinandus, nullus dignus (quod evenire non credimus) potuerit inveniri;"[16] b) in a letter of Pope Innocent to Victricius of Rouen: "Ut de aliena ecclesia clericum ordinare nullus usurpet, nisi eius episcopus precibus exoratus concedere voluerit."[17]

The fourth rule (the third will be considered after the fifth), that laymen were not eligible, is found: a) in a letter of Pope Zosimus (417-418) to Bishop Hesychius of Salona: "Quod monachi vel laici, nisi per gradus ecclesiae non debeant ad summum sacerdotium pervenire."[18] b) in a letter of Pope Celestine to the bishops of Gaul: "Quod per gradus ecclesiasticos ad episcopatus debeat officium pervenire."[19] c) in

[16] *PL*, LXVII, 276; JK, 369; cf. *supra*, p. 72.

[17] *PL*, LXVII, 243; JK, 286. Cf. *supra*, p. 38, note 58. Cf. also letter of Pope Leo to the bishop of Thessalonica: "Alienum clericum, invito episcopo ipsius, nemo suscipiat, nemo sollicitet...." —*PL*, LXVII, 291; JK, 404. Pope Pelagius I (556-561) specifically mentions the requirement that when a cleric of another church is elected he must first obtain his own bishop's permission. To a bishop whose deacon had been elected to another diocese he wrote: "...si eum eligunt et vis eum concedere..." —JK, 1015; *Decretum Gratiani*, c. 14, D. LXIII. Regarding the same deacon, Pelagius wrote to the bishop who was apparently visitor of the widowed diocese: "...et jussimus, ut veniat, credentes eos de persona eius ab episcopo suo dimissoriam accepisse." —JK, 1017; *Decretum Gratiani*, c. 12, D. LXXVI. Cf. also canon 12 of the Council of Sardica (343); Turner, I, ii, iii, 482-484. This canon was quoted in the fifth canon of the Council of Carthage in 348. Cf. Turner, I, ii, iii, XVII.

[18] *PL*, LXVII, 262; JK, 339. This letter also gives examples similar to those used by Gregory in *Epp*. v, 58. 60; ix, 218, but Gregory does not quote this letter of Pope Zosimus to Hesychius of Salona. In reference to the evil of laymen being made bishops in Gaul, Caspar states: "Vgl. JE, 1374 [*Ep*. v, 58] in Anlehnung an die Formulierung bei Zosimus, JK, 328 c. 3 (ein Beweis, dass das ältere päpstliche Material über Arles bei dieser Aktion Gregors d. Gr. benutzt worden ist)..." —*Geschichte des Papsttums*, II, 495, note 1.

[19] *PL*, LXVII, 275; JK, 369. A similar regulation is contained in a letter of the same Pope to the bishops of Apulia and Calabria; cf. PL, LXVII, 277; JK, 371. The examples quoted in these two letters are strikingly similar to those used by Gregory in various letters, but especially in *Epp*. v, 58. 60; ix, 238. While it is evident that Gregory certainly had these

a second letter of Pope Celestine to the bishops of Gaul: "Abstineatur etiam ab illicitis ordinationibus: nullus ex laicis. . . ."[20] d) in a letter of Pope Leo to the bishop of Thessalonica: "Quod non laici. . .ordinentur episcopi."[21] e) in canon 8 of the Council of Sardica (343): ". . .si forte aut dives, aut scolasticus de foro, aut ex administratore, episcopus postulatus fuerit, non prius ordinetur, nisi ante et lectoris munere et officio diaconii et ministerio praesbyterii fuerit perfunctus; ut per singulos gradus (si dignus fuerit) ascendat ad culmen episcopatus. . . ."[22] f) in canons 3 and 12 of the Council of Laodicea (350-381?): "Quod non oportet eos qui recens sunt baptizati in ordinem sacerdotalem promoveri." "Quod oportet episcopus judicio metropolitanorum et finitimorum episcoporum ad ecclesiasticum magistratum constitui plurimo tempore probatos. . . ."[23]

Except in the cases of necessity, the prohibition against choosing laymen extended also to monks, as is clearly stated in a decree of Pope Gelasius (492-496) to the bishops of Italy and Sicily. If no suitable monks were available, laymen could be chosen; in such cases, their past life was to be very carefully scrutinized.[24]

The fifth rule of Gregory's form letters was that the person elected was to be consecrated at Rome. That, of course, held good only for those dioceses which were subject to the Pope as metropolitan of Rome, since these form letters were addressed only to such dioceses and to Ravenna. No such specific rule for the Roman province is found in the *Dionysiana,* though it will be shown immediately that it contains several canons and decretals which proclaim that the metro-

---

examples in mind, a comparison of the texts shows that he did not quote the two letters verbatim. Cf. preceding note.

[20] *PL,* LXVII, 277; JK, 381.

[21] *PL,* LXVII, 293; JK, 404.

[22] Turner, I, ii, iii, 472-474.

[23] *PL,* LXVII, 70; Bruns, *Canones,* I, 73, 74.

[24] *PL,* LXVII, 302f.; JK, 636. Cf. *Ep.* xii, 4; *supra,* p. 82. Pope Siricius (384-399) had decreed that monks could be ordained if they had reached the age of thirty years, but they were not to be made bishops immediately: "nec statim saltu ad episcopatus culmen ascendant." —*PL,* LXVII, 237; JK, 255.

politan is normally to consecrate his suffragans. Here it may be noted first that Gregory made no innovation when he ordered the person elected to one of his suffragan sees to come to Rome to be consecrated. This had been done by his predecessors, as is evident from a letter of Pope Gelasius and two letters of Pope Pelagius I.[25]

That the metropolitan was normally to consecrate his suffragans is found in the following laws as contained in the *Dionysiana*: a) in a letter of Pope Innocent to Victricius of Rouen: "Primum ut extra conscientiam metropolitani episcopi nullus audeat ordinare..."[26] b) in a letter of Pope Leo to the bishop of Thessalonica;[27] c) in canon 19 of the Council of Antioch (341): "Episcopus praeter synodum et praesentiam metropolitani nullatenus ordinetur...."[28] d) in canon 4 of the Council of Nicaea: "Episcopum convenit maxime quidem ab omnibus qui sunt in provincia episcopi ordinari.... Firmitas autem eorum quae geruntur per unamquamque provinciam metropolitano tribuatur episcopo."[29] e) in canon 12 of the Council of Laodicea: "Quod oportet episcopos judicio metropolitanorum et finitimorum episcoporum magistratum constitui..."[30] f) in canon 13 of the *Statuta Concilii Africae* (419): "...inconsulto primate cuiuslibet provinciae, tam facile non praesumant multi congregati episcopi episcopum ordinare; nisi necessitas fuerit, tres episcopi, in quocumque loco sint, eius praecepto ordinare debebunt episcopum."[31] g) in canon 25 of the Council of Chalcedon (451): "Quoniam qui-

[25] Cf. JK, 675; Thiel, *Epistolae*, p. 380, note 2; JK, 1015, 1017.

[26] *PL*, LXVII, 242; JK, 286.

[27] Cf. No. xxxv, *PL*, LXVII, 293; No. xxxiii, *ibid.*; JK, 404.

[28] Turner, II, ii, 287-289. Cf. also canon 23: "Episcopo non licere pro se alterum successorem sibi constituere, licet ad exitum vitae perveniat, quod si tale aliquid factum fuerit, irritum esse huiuscemodi constitutum. Servetur autem ius ecclesiasticum, id continens oportere non aliter fieri nisi cum synodo et iudicio episcoporum, qui post obitum quiescentis potestatem habent eum qui dignus extiterit promovere." —Turner, II, ii, 299-301.

[29] Turner, I, ii, 258. Cf. canon 4 of the Council of Sardica; Turner, I, ii, iii, 458.

[30] *PL*, LXVII, 70; Bruns, *Canones*, I, 74.

[31] *PL*, LXVII, 188; Bruns, *Canones*, I, 162.

dam metropolitani, sicut ad nos pervenit, greges sibi commissos negligunt, et episcoporum ordinationes differunt..."[32]

The third rule of Gregory's form letters was the general statement that the candidate must be worthy and not barred from the episcopacy by the sacred canons. In none of his letters did Gregory state which canons he had in mind. Perhaps he referred to the *Collectio Dionysiana*, wherein may be found mentioned practically all[33] of the qualities which Gregory required of a candidate for the episcopal office over and above the ordinary qualifications for the clerical office. The following disqualified a person for the clerical office: immorality, bigamy (i.e., a second marriage even after the first wife had died), marriage with a widow or a woman not a virgin, ignorance of letters, liability to civil or military service, physical defects (including self-mutilation), performance of public penance.[34]

Each of these disqualifications is also mentioned in the *Collectio Dionysiana*: An incontinent cleric could not be advanced to the episcopacy, for he was even deprived of the office which he held. This is stated in a letter of Pope Innocent.[35] One who was guilty of bigamy (i.e., one who had married again after the death of his first wife) or of marrying a widow or a woman who had been rejected by her husband

---

[32] *PL*, LXVII, 92; Bruns, *Canones*, I, 32.

[33] Gregory rejected one candidate for lack of zeal for the Divine Office, and another because of his advanced age and parsimony; cf. *supra*, p. 38. These qualities are not mentioned in the *Dionysiana*. It must be emphasized, moreover, that the qualities required of a candidate for the episcopal office were almost all developed on the pattern of I Tim. iii, 1-7 and Tit. i, 5-9. Besides the early Councils and papal letters, the commentaries of the Fathers on these passages of Sacred Scripture also contributed to shape the canonical doctrine in this respect. Pertinent passages of the Fathers may be found in Cornelius a Lapide (1567-1637), *Commentaria in omnes Sancti Pauli Epistolas* recognovit subjectisque notis illustravit, emendavit et ad praesentem sacrae scientiae statum adduxit Antonius Padovani (editio secunda stereotypa, III vols., Taurini: Ex officina Marii E. Marietti, 1934), III, 47-58; 203-206.

[34] Cf. *Epp*. ii, 37; iv, 26; *supra*, p. 44.

[35] Cf. No. xxi, *PL*, LXVII, 245; No. xxxiii, *ibid.*, 250; JK, 286.

was debarred from the episcopacy.[36] One who was uneducated could not be advanced to the episcopal office. This was stated by Pope Siricius and also by Pope Gelasius.[37] One who was liable to the civil curia could not become a bishop.[38] None of

[36] Cf. Nos. vii, xi, xv of Pope Siricius — *PL*, LXVII, 235ff.; No. xix of Pope Celestine—*ibid.*, 277; Nos. ii, xxxiii of Pope Leo—*ibid.*, 279, 293; Nos. ii and xxii of Pope Gelasius—*ibid.*, 302; 308; canons 17-19 of the *Canones Apostolorum*—Turner, I, i, 15f.; canon 8 of the Council of Neocaesarea—Turner, II, i, 129; Nos. xi to xiii, xxix, li and lii of Pope Innocent—*PL*, LXVII, 242f., 249, 258.

[37] Cf. No. xv of Pope Siricius—*PL*, LXVII, 237; No. ii of Pope Gelasius—*ibid.*, 302; No. xvi of the latter Pope—*ibid.*, 307.

[38] In 313 Constantine exempted the Catholic clergy from the burdens (the greatest of which was the collection of taxes) of the *decurionate*. Because of the unseemly rush for the reception of Holy Orders and the consequent depletion of the *decurionate*, Constantine in 320 forbade the ordination of anyone qualified, by reason of the amount of land possessed, for the *curia*, the governing body of his city. Those liable to the *curia* were known as *curiales*, out of which the actual members of the city senate, *decuriones*, were selected. The *curiales* formed a separate class, membership in which was hereditary, and both "the Theodosian and Justinian Codes are full of enactments forbidding *curiales* to leave the place of their birth, and condemning them to a hereditary subjection to municipal charges." Certain crimes were even punished by subjection to the *curia*. Cf. *Cambridge Medieval History*, I, 10, 555-557; 591; Lot, *The End of the Ancient World and the Beginnings of the Middle Ages* (New York, Alfred A. Knopf, 1931), pp. 114-127; Abbot-Johnson, *Municipal Administration in the Roman Empire* (Princeton: Princeton University Press, 1926), pp. 65f.; 113-116, 194, 206f., 229f.; Pauly-Wissowa-Kroll, *Realencyclopädie der klassischen Altertumswissenschaft* (26 vols. in 51 and 6 supplements, Stuttgart: J. B. Metzlersche Verlagsbuchhandlung, 1893–), IV, 1815f., 2319-2354; hereafter cited Pauly-Wissowa, *Realencyclopädie*. An excellent review of the "technical terms of administration" in the *Variae* of Cassiodorus (†ca. 570) is given by Zimmermann, *The Late Latin Vocabulary of the Variae of Cassiodorus* (Catholic University of America Studies in Medieval and Renaissance Latin Language and Literature, XV, Washington, D.C.: Catholic University of America Pess, 1944), pp. 193-256. It may be noted that under the Emperor Anastasius (491-518) the burden of collecting taxes was removed from the *curiales*, but the other burdens remained, and under Justinian the position of the *curiales* has been described as wretched. Cf. Boak, *A History of Rome* to 565 *A.D.* (3. ed., New York: Macmillan Company, 1943), pp. 363-370; 471; Dudden, *Gregory the Great*, I, 20ff.; Bury, *History of the Later Roman Empire* (revised edition, 2 vols., London: Macmillan and Company, Ltd., 1923), I, 59ff., 441ff.; II, 351f. Cf. also, Stein, *Geschichte des spätrömischen Reiches* (Wien:

the early councils mentions this impediment, but it is found in the decrees of Popes Innocent and Gelasius.[39] Defect of body and self-mutilation were repeatedly mentioned as impediments in the *Collectio Dionysiana*, especially by the Council of Nicaea, the *Canones Apostolorum* and Pope Gelasius.[40] Pope Siricius had decreed that no public penitent was to be ordained a cleric.[41] However, if through ignorance such a one was raised to the clerical state, he was permitted to keep his rank, but was debarred from further promotion.[42] Pope Gelasius more specifically stated that one who had performed public penance was not to be chosen for the episcopal office.[43]

Over and above these qualities Gregory required that a cleric to be eligible for the episcopate must not have been guilty of usury, or of simony, and that he know the psalms. These requirements, except perhaps the latter, were not new, for they are contained in the *Dionysiana*. Canon 17 of the Council of Nicaea decreed that any cleric who practiced usury was to be degraded,[44] and Pope Leo forbade clerics to practice usury either in their own name or in the name of an-

---

Verlag von L. W. Seidel & Sohn, 1928), pp. 27-46; 70-75; 337-343. For Justinian's legislation regarding the ordination of those liable to the curia, cf. e.g., C. (I. 3)12; (I.3)52; N. (6, 1)1; (6, 4); (123, 1); (123, 4); (123, 15). In brief, the latest Novel forbade a *decurio* or any official to be consecrated a bishop or ordained a cleric unless he had previously spent fifteen years in a monastery; if anyone allowed himself to be consecrated without observing this law, he was to be removed from the episcopacy and restored to his former position.

[39] No. xviii of Pope Innocent—*PL*, LXVII, 244; No. ii of Pope Gelasius—*ibid.*, 302.

[40] Cf. canon 1 of the Council of Nicaea—Turner, I, ii, 255; canons 21 to 23 of the *Canones Apostolorum*—Turner, I, i, 17ff.; No. xvi of Pope Gelasius—*PL*, LXVII, 307.

[41] Cf. No. xiv—*PL*, LXVII, 237. Cf. also No. xxxiv of Pope Innocent —*ibid.*, 250; canon 9 of the Council of Nicaea—Turner, I, ii, 264.

[42] Cf. No. xv of Pope Siricius—*PL*, LXVII, 237; canon 9 of the Council of Nicaea—Turner, I, ii, 264.

[43] Cf. No. ii—*PL*, LXVII, 302; cf. also canon 27 of the *Statuta Concilii Africae*—*ibid.*, 191.

[44] "...deiciatur a clero et alienus exsistat a regula."—Turner, I, ii, 270.

other.[45] Deposition was decreed for one who attained the episcopal dignity through simony and also for those who knowingly consecrated such a one or who accepted money for the act of consecration.[46]

It is not stated specifically in the *Dionysiana* that the candidate for the episcopacy must know the psalms, though both Councils and Popes insisted on the regulation that only those who were skilled in the sacred sciences and in ecclesiastical discipline could become bishops.[47] Gregory the Great, however, specifically insisted on a knowledge of the psalms.[48]

---

[45] Cf. No. iv—*PL*, LXVII, 379; JK, 402; *Decretales Selectae*, p. 91ff. A cleric who disobeyed this rule was to be removed from his office. Cf. also canon 4 of the Council of Laodicea—*PL*, LXVII, 70; Bruns, *Canones*, I, 73.

[46] Cf. canon 30 of the *Canones Apostolorum*—Turner, I, i, 20; canon 2 of the Council of Chalcedon—*PL*, LXVII, 86; Bruns, *Canones*, I, 25f.

[47] Cf. canon 2 of the Council of Nicaea—Turner, I, ii, 256; canon 8 of the Council of Sardica—Turner, I, ii, iii, 472-474; canon 12 of the Council of Neocaesarea (314-325)—Turner, II, i, 135; No. xxxii of Pope Siricius—*PL*, LXVII, 249; Nos. i and iii of Pope Zosimus—*ibid.*, 262f.

[48] Cf. *supra*, p. 38.

CHAPTER IV

SPECIAL POINTS OF LAW

SECTION I. THE ELECTORS—ADDRESSEES OF GREGORY'S LETTERS

In his form letters to the bishop visitor who was appointed for the specific purpose of presiding at the election of a bishop Gregory bade the visitor to admonish the clergy and people ("*clerum plebemque*") to agree in their choice of a suitable candidate. There is no specific mention of the nobles in these letters. Yet the corresponding form letters to the members of the widowed church are all addressed: "Clero, ordini et plebi consistenti. . . ."[1]

This same inscription is found also in the following letters: *Epp.* ix, 210—Rimini; i, 78—Bevagna; ii, 12—Naples; ii, 14—Nepi; iii, 11—Albano; i, 58—Perugia; iii, 14—Terracina. Other inscriptions are used in letters exhorting the election of a bishop: *Epp.* i, 56—"Arsicino Duci, clero, ordini et plebi consistenti Ariminensis;" iii, 25—"Universis habitatoribus Arimino;" ix, 139—"Clero et plebi consistenti Arimino;" ii, 5—"Clero, nobilibus, ordini et plebi consistenti Neapolim;" iii, 15—"Scolastico judici Campaniae;" iii, 35—"Petro subdiacono Campaniae;" x, 19—"Clero et nobilibus Neapolim;" v, 54—"Nobilibus Syracusis;" v, 23 and vi, 13—"Cypriano diacono rectori;" xiii, 14—"Venantio patricio Panormo;" iii, 26—"Magno presbytero ecclesiae Mediolanensis;" iii, 29 and xi, 6—"Presbyteris, diaconibus et clero Mediolanensis ecclesiae;" iii, 30—"Johanni subdiacono;" iii, 31—"Romano patricio et exarcho Italiae;" xi, 14—"Pantaleoni notario;" i, 79—"Clero, nobilibus Corsicae;" xi, 58—"Bonifatio defensori Corsica;" iii, 22—"Antonio subdiacono rectori in Dalmatia;" iii, 46—"Clero ecclesiae Salonitanae;" iv,

[1] Cf. *supra*, p. 27ff.

16—"Universis episcopis per Dalmatias;" vi, 26—"Dilectissimis filiis clero, nobilibus Salonis consistentibus."[2]

Wisbaum contends that the word "ordo" in these inscriptions can only mean the nobility.[3] The author explains why both the nobles and the *ordo* are mentioned in the inscription of *Ep*. ii, 5: "Clero, nobilibus, ordini et plebi consistenti Neapolim" as follows: "...diese Adresse ist für falsch überliefert zu halten. Ein Teil der Handschriften hat die Variante 'Clero, nobilibus et plebi,' der einige Monate später in gleicher Angelegenheit nach Neapel abgeschickte Brief Reg. ii, 12 trägt die sonst gewöhnliche Aufschrift 'Clero, ordini et plebi consist. Neapoli.' "[4]

In his footnotes Ewald does not mention the variant given by Wisbaum, and therefore one cannot accept the latter's statement regarding the inscription of *Ep*. ii, 5. Diehl held that the word *ordo* in the inscriptions of Gregory's letters does not suffice to prove the existence and functioning of the municipal senate, to which the word *ordo* in an earlier period was properly applied,[5] for he states that *ordo* was an official word of the Roman chancery. This last statement he bases on the fact that *ordo* was used in exactly the same way ("Clero ordini et plebi...") by Pope Gelasius (492-496) and by Pope Gregory II (715-731). He continues: "L'ordo mentionné dans la suscription disparaît absolument dans le texte. Seules, trois catégories de personnes jouent un rôle dans l'élection: le

---

[2] All these letters were written to dioceses subject to the Pope as patriarch of the West, but those directed to the dioceses of Eastern Illyricum are not included in the list even though Eastern Illyricum was also part of the western patriarchate. Cf. *infra*, p. 85.

[3] "Unter dem ordo sind also die Nobiles zu verstehen."—*Die wichtigsten Richtungen und Ziele der Thätigkeit Gregors des Grossen*, p. 40.

[4] Wisbaum, *op. cit.*, p. 50.

[5] Cf. *Études sur l'administration byzantine dans l'exarcat de Ravenne* 568-751 (Paris, 1888), pp. 81-193, esp. 94ff. He admits that other texts do prove that municipal instituions did continue to exist in Byzantine Italy. Cf. also Hartmann, *Geschichte Italiens*, I, 22, 355; II, 124-135; Hodgkin, *Italy and Her Invaders* (2. ed. 8 vols., Oxford, At the Clarendon Press, 1892-1899), II, 576-596; VI, 509-560; Pauly-Wissowa, *Realencyclopädie*, XVIII, 930-934. O'Donnell, however, translates the word *ordo* as "a municipal council or senate" and his references are to the inscriptions of Gregory's letters. Cf. *Vocabulary*, p. 100.

clergé, la noblesse et le peuple; pas un mot n'est dit du sénat municipal. . . . Le sénat municipal, s'il existe, se confond avec le *populus*. . . . Une chancellerie conservatrice peut, dans l'intitulé de ses lettres, conserver une antique formule; mais les faits montrent que cet ordo n'a plus qu'un rôle effacé et secondaire et que des distinctions sociales nouvelles commencent à se former dans la cité."[6]

Granted that the word *ordo* proves nothing as to the existence of a particular body, the municipal senate, in the cities of Italy at the time of Gregory the Great, the writer doubts Diehl's statement that it was merely an official word of the Roman chancery, taken over from the time of Pope Gelasius. For it must be remembered that the majority of inscriptions "Clero, ordini et plebi" are found in letters written according to a special formula, which formula Gregory himself first used.[7] If the formula itself is new with Gregory, the presumption seems to be that an inscription fitting the conditions for which the formula was intended would be chosen. If the municipal senate, to which the word *ordo* properly referred formerly, was submerged in the people ("se confond avec le *populus*"), the word must have received a new meaning in the inscriptions of Gregory's letters. Since three categories are frequently described as participating in an episcopal election, the clergy, aristocracy and people, it seems probable that *ordo* refers to the aristocracy.

Not only were there various classes of society in Byzantine Italy at the end of the sixth century, but there were also various gradations in the aristocracy itself.[8] Under the term "aristocracy" the writer includes both the *ordo* and the *Nobiles*, for that interpretation seems to explain most adequately all of Gregory's letters, though it does not explain the inscription of *Ep.* ii, 5 to Naples: "Clero, nobilibus, ordini et plebi." In no other inscription of Gregory's letters are the two words "*nobilibus*" and "*ordini*" joined. In *Ep.* ii, 12, written three months after *Ep.* ii, 5, and treating of approximately the same matter, the inscription is "Clero, ordini et plebi." If the in-

[6] Diehl, *op. cit.*, p. 105f.

[7] Cf. *supra*, p. 22ff.

[8] Cf. authors cited in Chapter III, note 38; *supra*, note 5.

scription of *Ep.* ii, 5 had any special significance, why was it not repeated in *Ep.* ii, 12?

Relatively considered the great majority of the letters treating of episcopal elections are addressed: "Clero, ordini et plebi."[9] In those letters wherein other inscriptions are used the three categories of electors are generally included. Thus *Epp.* iii, 15 and iii, 35 must be considered together. The former is addressed; "Scolastico judici Campaniae" and bids him call together "priores vel populum civitatis;" the latter is addressed "Petro subdiacono" and bids him to call together the "clerum ecclesiae Neapolitanae;" the delegates chosen by these groups were to meet in Rome to elect a bishop.[10] *Ep.* x, 19 is addressed "Clero et nobilibus Neapolim," but in the body of the letter Gregory mentions "populos" also.

The three elements are clearly distinguished in *Ep*, v, 54, addressed: "*Nobilibus* Syracusanis: Laudis vestrae testimonium quam direxistis gerit epistola, quod electionis vos onera sapienter declinasse significat. Et quoniam hoc nostro arbitrio commisistis....Sed et quia a *clero* et *plebe* Syracusanae ecclesiae Agatho, ab aliquibus autem alter eligitur, hunc, qui a clero et plebe electus est, ad nos interim venire necesse est, ut utrisque comminus constitutis ille qui utilior visus fuerit et Deo placuerit, ordinetur..."

Ep. xiii, 14 is addressed "Venantio patricio Panormo," in answer to a letter in which the latter had presented to the Pope his own choice for the vacant see of Palermo. Gregory refused to accept the choice of Venantius, and told the patrician that the "clerus et populus" are to be exhorted to elect a fit candidate. The phrase "clerus et populus" here seems to include also the aristocracy, for at the same time Gregory addressed a letter: "Clero, ordini et plebi consistenti Panormo."[11]

Though *Epp.* i, 79 and xi, 58 are separated by a lapse of ten years, they must be considered together, and in them the

[9] Fourteen letters are thus addressed; if *Epp.* ii, 5 and i, 56 be added, there would be a total of sixteen. No other inscription is used more than three times: "Clero et nobilibus..."—*Epp.* x, 19; i, 79; vi, 26.

[10] Cf. *supra*, p. 35.

[11] *Ep.* xiii, 16.

three elements are to be found. The former is addressed "Clero nobilibus Corsicae" and omits all reference to the people; the latter is addressed "Bonifatio defensori Corsica," whom Gregory scolds for not having urged the "clerum et populum" to proceed to an election. Only the clergy and people are mentioned in the inscription of *Ep.* ix, 139, dealing with an election at Rimini. However, the following letters also deal with the same situation and show clearly that the aristocracy shared in the election: *Epp.* i, 56, "Arsicino duci, clero, ordini et plebi civitatis Ariminensis;" iii, 25, "Universis habitatoribus Arimino;" ix, 210, "Clero, ordini et plebi Arimino."

Epp. iii, 22. 46; iv, 16, and vi, 26 deal with the election at Salona in Dalmatia. The first is addressed to the rector of the patrimony, urging him to warn the "clerum et populum" to elect a bishop; the second is addressed only to the clergy; the third to all the bishops of Dalmatia, and the fourth, while omitting mention of the people, includes the nobles: "Dilectissimis filiis clero, nobilibus Salonis consistentibus." Thus, if taken together, these four letters include mention of the three elements.

In the following letters there is no mention of the aristocracy, but they seem to be at least implicitly included. Both *Epp.* v, 23 and vi, 13 are addressed "Cypriano diacono," rector of the patrimony in Sicily, about an election at Lilybaeum. The former mentions the clergy and people; the latter only the clergy. There is no apparent reason why the aristocracy of Lilybaeum should be excluded, for in other places of Sicily they were included.[12] *Epp.* iii, 26. 29. 30. 31; xi, 6. 14 treat of an election at Milan. Neither in the inscriptions nor in the bodies of these letters is there specific mention of the aristocracy but only of the clergy and people. Yet the latter three letters use the phrases: "*omnium* consistit electio;" "*cunctorum* in eius electione concordat assensus;" "a *cunctis* electus est." In these phrases the aristocracy seems to be implicitly included. The conclusion seems justified, therefore, that in Italy, Sicily, Corsica and Dalmatia Gregory the Great recognized the right of the clergy, aristocrats and people to

[12] Cf. *Ep.* xiii, 16.

elect their bishops. From Gregory's letters no conclusion can be drawn as to the electors in Sardinia, Africa, Gaul and Spain.

Nor can a specific conclusion be drawn as to who the electors were in Eastern Illyricum or in the Eastern patriarchates. Although Eastern Illyricum was part of the Western patriarchate, it would be rash to state, on the basis of Gregory's letters, that, as in other portions of the West, the electors were the clergy, nobles and people of each widowed church. For Gregory's letters concerning elections in Eastern Illyricum are all written *after* an election has taken place, and thus give but little information about the electors.[13] Concerning the election at Prima Justiniana Gregory wrote to all of the bishops of Illyricum: "...in persona Joannis fratris et coepiscopi nostri consensum omnium vestrum et serenissimi principis convenisse cognovimus voluntatem...."[14] To John himself Gregory wrote: "Quia igitur suscepta...relatio ad locum vos sacerdotii totius concilii unito consensu et serenissimi principis voluntate declarat accersiri gratias Creatori ...retulimus."[15] There is no mention of any choice by the clergy, aristocracy or people in these two letters, and no mention of an election at all in the other three letters to episcopal sees in Eastern Illyricum.[16] Authors state that in the East after the fourth century the part of the people in episcopal elections waned, and that later in practice the will of the emperor or his representative was the decisive factor.[17] The meager information given by Gregory's letters appears to corroborate this statement.

---

[13] Cf. *supra*, p. 53ff.

[14] *Ep.* v, 10.

[15] *Ep.* v, 16. The word "concilii" here undoubtedly means province, as it does also in *Ep.* i, 72. Cf. Ewald's note 1 ad *Ep.* iii, 47.

[16] Cf. *Epp.* v, 62. 63; vi, 7; *supra*, p. 53ff.

[17] Cf. Parsons, *Canonical Elections* (Catholic University of America Canon Law Studies, No. 118, Washington, D.C.: Catholic University of America Press, 1939), pp. 22ff.; Fliche-Martin, *Histoire*, IV, 538; Fuchs, *Der Ordinationstitel von seiner Entstehung bis auf Innozenz III.*, Kanonistische Studien und Texte hrsg. v. A. M. Koeniger, Band IV (Bonn: Kurt Schroeder Verlag, 1930), p. 53f.; Pargoire, *L'Église byzantine de 527 à 847* (Paris: Librairie Victor Lecoffre, 1905), p. 57.

SECTION II. THE AGE OF ELIGIBLE CANDIDATES

It has been seen above that Gregory refused a candidate because of his advanced age and parsimony.[18] In none of his letters, however, does Gregory set a specific age before which a man could not be chosen bishop. The only indications he gives are the following: boys are not to be admitted to sacred orders;[19] only those advanced in age are to be admitted to sacred orders;[20] it was wrong to ordain a boy ("*puerum*") to the diaconate.[21]

SECTION III. ABSOLUTE ORDINATION

Absolute ordination, i.e., ordination without reference to a particular, specified office, began both in the East and in the West in the middle of the fourth century. Canon 6 of the Council of Chalcedon (451) strictly forbade such absolute ordinations.[22] Despite the prohibition of the Council of Chalcedon, the custom of absolute ordinations spread further, and was found in the East in the time of Justinian, and in the West particularly in the time of the Carolingians.[23]

Gregory the Great does not refer to absolute ordinations, and the writer knows of no instance where he permitted such

---

[18] Cf. *supra*, p. 38.

[19] "Ut pueri ad sacros ordines nullatenus ammittantur."—*Ep.* iii, 47.

[20] "Et ad sacros ordines nisi provectiores aetate et mundos opere nullatenus ammittatis."—*Ep.* iii, 48.

[21] Cf. *Ep.* xiii, 44. Cf. also Blokscha, "Die Altervorschriften für die höheren Weihen im ersten Jahrtausend," *AKK*, CXI (1931), 31-83, especially p. 61f. Justinian first set the age for bishops at thirty-five years —N. (123, 1); later he set it at thirty years—N. (137, 2). Cf. Blokscha, *op. cit.*, p. 45. In note 3 *ibid.* the author states that Novel (123, 13) set the age for priests at thirty-five years; he is, however, quoting the Latin *Authenticum*, for the original Greek sets the age for priests at thirty years. Regarding the place and time of the translation known as the *Authenticum* cf. Kübler, *Geschichte des römischen Rechts* (Leipzig: A. Deichertsche Verlagsbuchhandlung Dr. Werner Scholl, 1925), p. 417f.

[22] Bruns, *Canones*, I, 27. Canon 6 is also found in the *Collectio Dionysiana*—*PL*, LXVII, 172. Cf. Fuchs, *Ordinationstitel*, pp. 103-137; Piontek, "De Acephalis in Jure Canonico," *Jus Pontificium*, XIII (1933), 29.

[23] Cf. Fuchs, *op. cit.*, p. 138.

ordination.[24] In *Ep.* i, 18, Gregory bade Peter, papal vicar in Sicily at the time, to seek out suitable candidates who could be sent to Rome for ordination. This command was given, however, because there existed a number of vacant sees in Sicily, and these candidates were to be ordained for these sees. To the bishop of Syracuse Gregory wrote that a certain priest should be sent to Rome, for the Pope had heard that he was a suitable candidate for the episcopacy: "ut eum Domino disponente loco cui praeviderimus possimus ordinare pastorem."[25] These are the only two instances in which Gregory speaks of consecrating men for unspecified sees, but in neither instance is the person to be consecrated until a definite place has been provided for him. These two instances cannot, therefore, be considered as examples of absolute ordination.

But how are these two instances to be explained in view of the regulation that an episcopal candidate be chosen from the clergy of the widowed church itself?[26] Be it noted that the afore-mentioned letters are both concerned with conditions in Sicily, where the custom existed of leaving a diocese vacant after a bishop had been deposed. Gregory ordered that this custom be abolished, and in *Ep.* i, 18 he expressly stated that fit candidates were first to be sought from the vacant churches themselves. If no one there was found worthy, a suitable candidate was to be sought elsewhere. To provide for this latter contingency, *Ep.* ii, 24 seems to have been written.[27]

---

[24] Piontek states that at the time of Pope Gregory the sixth canon of the Council of Chalcedon was accurately observed. Cf. *op. cit.*, p. 30, note 2.

[25] *Ep.* ii, 24.

[26] Cf. *supra*, p. 27.

[27] Caspar (1879-1935) interprets the phrase "veteri quae iam inoleverat consuetudine postposita" of *Ep.* i, 18 as referring to the custom by which the clergy and people elected their bishops: " 'unter Hintansetzung der alten Gewohnheit', d. h. des Wahlrechts von Klerus und Volk."—*Geschichte des Papsttums*, II, 409. The author gives no reason for this interpretation, and the writer believes, with Dudden (Cf. *Gregory the Great*, I, 379) that the phrase refers to the custom of leaving a church vacant after a bishop had been deposed, for Gregory states that he wishes the vacant dioceses

SECTION IV. THE OATH OF BISHOPS

In 599 Gregory the Great wrote to his rector in Sicily about one of the Istrian bishops living in Sicily who wished to return to union with Rome; the Pope demanded that the bishop, if he preferred to remain in Sicily rather than to come to Rome, had to sign a "*cautela*," in which he was to state his intention of remaining loyal to the true Faith.[28] Such a "cautela," signed most probably by another Istrian bishop who was reunited with Rome, has been preserved in *Ep.* xii, 7.[29]

It has been conjectured that at the end of the sixth century the Popes demanded from all bishops whom they consecrated some assurance of the orthodoxy of their belief and of their devotion to the Holy See.[30] This conjecture has been based in part upon the use in the papal chancery[31] of formu-

---

to be filled so that the deposed bishops may no longer have any hope of being restored to their former sees.

[28] Cf. *Ep.* ix, 150.

[29] Cf. Hartmann's notes *ibid.*, and *Ep.* xii, 13.

[30] Cf. Gottlob, *Der kirchliche Amtseid der Bischöfe* (Kanonistische Studien und Texte hrsg. v. A. M. Koeniger, Band IX, Bonn: Ludwig Röhrscheid Verlag, 1936), p. 10; hereafter cited as *Amtseid.* Cf. also Schneider, "Der kanonische Gehorsam," *AKK*, LXXXII (1902), 290-324. The first to demand an oath of fidelity from his followers was the antipope Novatian in 251. At the end of the fifth century conditions in southern Italy and in Sicily were unsettled, and Pope Gelasius (492-496) gave his suffragans at the time of their consecration a detailed list of instructions, and sent a record of their consecration to the diocese. Cf. *Epp.* 15, 16—Thiel, *Epistolae*, p. 379; JK, 674, 675. *Ep.* 15 became formula 6 of the *Liber Diurnus* —ed. Sickel, p. 5; ed. Rozière, pp. 22-29. Pope Hormisdas (514-523) demanded a profession of faith from all oriental bishops returning from schism to union with Rome. Cf. *Ep.* 61—Thiel, *Epistolae*, p. 852; Appendix 4, "Incipit libellus professionis fidei quam constituit papa Hormisda sedis apostolicae dari a singulis episcopis Graeciarum."—*Avellana, CSEL*, XXXV, 800f. Pope Pelagius I (556-561) demanded a written promise from the bishop of Syracuse before the latter's consecration. Cf. JK, 984; Mansi, IX, 734. In 571 Pope John III (561-574) received a "*cautio*" from Archbishop Lawrence of Milan, to which Gregory refers in *Epp.* iv, 2. 37. Cf. Gottlob, *op. cit.*, pp. 2-9.

[31] Gottlob rejects Steinacker's theory [*Zum Liber diurnus und zur Frage nach dem Ursprung der Frühminuskel* (Miscellanea Fr. Ehrle—Studi e Testi, 40, Roma, 1928)] that the *Liber Diurnus* was not used in the chancery but was rather a school or practice book. Cf. *Amtseid*, p. 11, note 1.

las 73 to 76 of the *Liber Diurnus*. Formula 73, "Promissio fidei episcopi," is a quite detailed profession of faith in the teaching of the first six ecumenical Councils to which is added a promise to respect the rights of other bishops—it was given under oath. Formula 74, "Cautio episcopi," is essentially a promise of careful administration of the diocese. Formula 75, "Indiculum episcopi," is an oath to St. Peter and to the Pope to hold to the profession of the true Faith, to further the welfare of the Roman Church, and not to ally oneself against the Roman State. Formula 76, "Indiculum episcopi de Langobardia," is the same as the preceding, except that instead of a promise of loyalty to the Roman State it contains a promise to guarantee the peace between the Empire and the Lombards.[32]

After giving various opinions as to the date of composition of these four formulas, Gottlob seeks to prove that the first three, formulas 73 to 75, were in use during the time of Gregory the Great, and that formula 76 was composed shortly after the death of Pope Gregory.[33] The reasons adduced by the author for his conclusion are not completely convincing. He states that the agreement of the ending of formula 73 with *Ep.* xii, 7 must be noticed. There is some agreement between the two, but it is not sufficient to warrant any conclusion as to a relation of dependency of one upon the other. Secondly, he correctly states that formulas 45 and 46 of the *Liber Diurnus*, which treat of the granting of the pallium, prove that the grantee gave a written profession of faith before he received the pallium. He then states that the letters of Gregory in which he grants the pallium to Vergil of Arles, John of Corinth and others, as well as his letter to Anastasius of Antioch, are written according to the above-named formulas, which he claims belong to the end of the sixth century.[34]

---

[32] The formulas may be found in Sickel, *Liber Diurnus*, pp. 69-81; and in an appendix (taken from Sickel's edition) in Gottlob, *Amtseid*, pp. 170-175. Cf. Gottlob, *ibid.*, p. 11f.

[33] Cf. *Amtseid*, pp. 14-18.

[34] Cf. *Epp.* v, 58. 62. 63; ix, 135. Gottlob's reference in note 56 on page 14 to *Ep.* v, 68 must be a misprint for v, 62; there is no *Ep.* v, 68.

He fails to note, however, that only parts of the above-named letters correspond to formulas 45 and 46, and that *none* of Gregory's letters (not even those just cited) concerning the granting of the pallium contain any reference to a written profession of faith of the recipient. It is much more probable that formulas 45 and 46 were written after Gregory the Great.[35] Thirdly, he refers to the synodical letters sent by the Popes to the Eastern Patriarchs and received from them. There is no doubt that the custom of sending synodical letters existed long before Gregory the Great's pontificate, but the author fails to show any direct connection between them and the dating of the major portion of formula 73 as an oath taken by bishops at the time of their consecration.[36] Peitz admits that certain parts of formula 73 are additions made after the 6th General Council (II Constantinople) of 680, but he contends (against Caspar) that part of the text of formula 73 was used in the encyclical letter of Pope Vigilius (537-555) in 552 (JK, 931) and existed already before the Council of Ephesus (431).[37]

Regarding formula 74 Gottlob concludes thus: "Auf Gregor geht also die Terminänderung zurück, wie überhaupt das ganze Formular unter ihm in Brauch gewesen sein muss."[38] That statement is based on the fact that in formula 74 the bishop promises to come to Rome yearly on the feast of the princes of the Apostles (June 29), whereas formula 42 of the *Liber Diurnus* is an invitation of the suffragan bishops to

[35] This point is considered more fully in the Appendix, section II, n. 6.

[36] The salient points of the relationship between the synodical letters and formula 73 have been missed by Gottlob. Caspar has pointed these out, and he dates formula 73 in the period between the years 682 and 687. Cf. *Geschichte des Papsttums*, II, 770-774, 616f., 783. Stein accepts Caspar's dates; cf. "La période byzantine de la papauté," *CHR*, XXI (1935-1936), 154. Silva-Tarouca also states that formula 73 as it stands in the *Liber Diurnus* dates from the end of the 7th century. Cf. "Nuovi studi sulle antiche lettere dei Papi," *Gregorianum*, XII (1931), 424, note 1.

[37] Cf. *Das vorephesinische Symbol der Papstkanzlei*, pp. 51, 88f., 99, 101. Steinacker also admits that additions were made to formula 73 after 680; cf. *Zum Liber Diurnus und zur Frage nach dem Ursprung der Frühminuskel*, p. 166.

[38] *Amtseid*, p. 17.

visit the Pope on the anniversary of his consecration. In March of 591 Gregory drew up a list of precepts for the rectors in Sicily; the last one reads:

> Praeterea sicut moris fuit, ut ad natalem pontificis episcopi convenirent, ad ordinationis meae diem venire eos prohibe, quia ista me vana superfluitas non delectat. Sed si eos convenire necesse est, in beati Petri apostolorum principis natalem conveniant, ut ei, ex cuius largitate pastores sunt, gratiarum actiones solvant.[39]

The fact that the date for the visit of the bishops of Sicily was changed by Gregory the Great would seem to indicate that formula 74 was formed only after his death; at least there is no reference in Gregory's letters which must be considered as pertaining to formula 74.

Formula 75 contains, besides a profession of faith, an oath of fidelity to the Roman Empire. Gottlob notes that such a promise was contained in a letter of the schismatic Istrian bishops to the Emperor Maurice in 591,[40] and continues: "Es liegt nahe, dass die Kaiser Wert darauf legten, dass auch die päpstlichen Suffragane eine ähnliche Verpflichtung bei ihrer Konsekration eingingen, und damit dürfte auch F. 75 unter Gregor anzusetzen sein. Wenn aber letzteres zutrifft, muss auch F. 76 kurz nach Gregor abgefasst sein."[41]

The writer is of the opinion that neither Gottlob nor Peitz have adduced sufficient proof to warrant the conclusion that formulas 73 to 76 (formulas 74-76 are not considered by Peitz in the work here cited) were in use in the papal chancery at the time of Gregory the Great as oaths which the Pope demanded from his suffragans at the time of their consecration in Rome. Even if we grant with Peitz that formula 73 went through a long period of development, and that parts of it were used in various papal letters of the fifth and sixth centuries[42] it does not necessarily follow that this same formula was sworn to by the suffragan bishops of Rome at the

[39] *Ep.* i, 39a.

[40] Cf. *Ep.* i, 16a.

[41] *Amtseid,* p. 18.

[42] Cf. examples cited by Peitz, *op. cit.,* p. 101.

time of their consecration. In the absence of more positive proof and of any reference to these formulas of the *Liber Diurnus* in the letters of Gregory, the writer prefers to accept the opinion which dates these formulas *after* Gregory the Great, i.e., in the form in which they appear in the *Liber Diurnus* as episcopal oaths and promises of allegiance.[43]

Yet Gottlob's conjecture that at the end of the sixth century the Popes demanded from all bishops whom they consecrated a promise that they would fulfill their office faithfully and be loyal to the Roman pontiff is probably correct. For it has already been noted that Pope Gelasius gave his suffragans a detailed list of instructions, which list became formula 6 of the *Liber Diurnus*.[44] Pope Gregory made use of this formula in *Epp*. ii, 37; iii, 11, and ix, 210, written to Squillace, Albano and Rimini respectively. To this formula Gregory also referred when he replied to one of Augustine of England's questions: "Mos autem sedis apostolicae est, ordinatis episcopis praeceptum tradere...";[45] and to Bishop Paschasius of Naples: "Tempore quo fraternitas vestra ad episcopatus officium Deo auctore provecta est, constituisse nos recolet, ut ex pecuniis ecclesiae vestrae portio cleri vel pauperum quam minime decessor vester praebuerat...seorsum fieri debuissent, qui eiusdem cleri vel pauperum erogatione proficerent...."[46] To formula 6 the following words of decree V of the Roman synod of 595 also apply: "Antiquam patrum regulam sequens nihil umquam de ordinationibus accipiendum esse constituo neque ex datione pallii neque *ex traditione cartarum*

[43] Sickel dated formulas 73 to 76 at the end of the seventh century; cf. *Prolegomena* I, 52-72; *Prolegomena* II, 80-88. Duchesne contends that these formulas could not have been written before 682, but that they must have been written shortly thereafter. Cf. *Les élections pontificales*, pp. 3, 5. Cf. also the authors cited *supra*, p. 90, note 36.

[44] Cf. *supra*, p. 32, note 34.

[45] *Ep*. xi, 56a. This is also the opinion of Thiel; cf. *Epistolae*, p. 32.

[46] *Ep*. xi, 22. Perhaps Gregory had given Bishop Paschasius a special precept, but he may also merely have emphasized that section of formula 6 of the *Liber Diurnus* which regulates the distribution of the goods of the church. Possibly also the words of *Ep*. iii, 47, "ut eorum quae beato Petro apostolorum principi promisisti memor esse non desinas," refer to formula 6.

...Quia enim ordinando episcopo pontifex manum ponit, evangelicam vero lectionem minister legit, *confirmationis autem eius epistolam notarius scribit...*[47] There are but three letters of confirmation extant in Gregory's *Register*; they are *Epp.* ii, 37; iii, 11, and ix, 210. The latter two give but the beginning of formula 6, whereas a portion of *Ep.* ii, 37 agrees with a portion of formula 6. The words of the decree cited must therefore refer to formula 6.

Preceding the list of instructions in formula 6 is the phrase: "Cui dedimus in mandatis." While it is not stated that the bishop promised to obey these precepts, it would seem strange if such a promise had not been exacted before the bishop's consecration. It may also be conjectured that such a promise was given under oath, but this is merely a conjecture, for, if one does not accept Gottlob's dating of formulas 73 to 76, there is no proof that such an oath was given.

SECTION V. THE TRANSFER OF BISHOPS AND THE UNION AND DIVISION OF DIOCESES

It has already been noted that when the people of Naples desired to elect the bishop visitor, Gregory refused their request.[48] In general the transfer of a bishop from one diocese to another was prohibited.[49] But during Gregory's reign many cities were either threatened, captured or devastated by the

---

[47] *Ep.* v, 57a. Italics inserted by the writer.

[48] Cf. *supra*, p. 34.

[49] Cf. canon 15 of the Council of Nicaea—Turner, I, ii, 268; canons 13, 16-18 of the Council of Antioch—Turner, II, ii, 273-295; canon 16 of this Council was read in the *actio undecima* of the Council of Chalcedon in 451; cf. Turner, II, ii, 320. Cf. also canons 1, 2, 3 of the Council of Sardica—Turner, I, ii, iii, 452-455; canon 14 of the *Canones Apostolorum*—Turner, I, i, 14f; canon 17 of the Council of Ancyra—Turner, II, i, 101-105; canon 7 of the Council of Chalcedon—Bruns, *Canones*, I, 27. An excellent account of the legislation against the transfer of bishops is given by Fuchs, *Ordinationstitel*, pp. 77-90. The author shows that in practice this legislation did not apply to bishops who, for one reason or another, no longer had a diocese. Cf. *ibid.* pp. 88, 90. Gregory's letters furnish additional proof of this latter point.

barbarians, the Lombards in Italy[50] and the Avars or Huns in the Balkan peninsula. In one case, the episcopal see was moved to a safer place within the same diocese:

> Temporis qualitas admonet, episcoporum sedes antiquitus certis civitatibus constitutas ad alia, quae securiora putamus, eiusdem dioeceseos loca transponere, quo et habitatores nunc dirigere et barbarici possit periculum facilius declinari. Propterea te Johannem fratrem coepiscopumque nostrum Vellitrensis civitatis sedemque tuam in locum qui appellatur Arenata ad sanctam Andream apostolum praecipimus exinde transmigrari. . . ."[51]

When Bishop Peter of Terracina died, the clergy and people asked for Bishop Agnellus of Fondi as their bishop. Gregory granted the request, as he explains to Bishop Agnellus:

> Quia igitur ob cladem hostilitatis nec in civitate tua nec in ecclesia tua est cuiquam habitandi licentia, ideoque hac te auctoritate Terracinensi ecclesiae cardinalem constituimus sacerdotem. . . .[52] Illud quoque fraternitatem tuam scire necesse est, quoniam sic te praedictae Terracinensis ecclesiae cardinalem esse constituimus sacerdotem, ut et Fundensis ecclesiae pontifex esse non desinas, nec curam gubernationemque eius praetereas. . ."[53]

The city of Risano in Illyricum, Bishop Sebastian's episcopal see, was in the hands of barbarians. Anastasius, patriarch of Antioch, offered Bishop Sebastian a diocese in his patriarchate, but the latter refused to accept, for which refusal he was commended by Gregory. But at the same time Gregory offered him the possibility of a vacant episcopal see

---

[50] Cf. Blasel, "Die kirchlichen Zustände Italiens zur Zeit Gregors des Grossen," *AKK*, LXXXIV (1904), 83-93; 225-243.

[51] *Ep.* ii, 17.

[52] The term *cardinalis* was applied only to bishops when they were transferred, either permanently or temporarily, for some special reason to another diocese. Cf. Kuttner, " 'Cardinalis': The History of a Canonical Concept," *Traditio*, III (1945), 132ff. This is contrary to the opinion of Ewald; cf. note 3 ad *Ep.* i, 77.

[53] *Ep.* iii, 13. Cf. *Ep.* iii, 14, addressed to the people of Terracina, granting their request.

in Sicily, bidding him to come to Rome if he desired an appointment. To which he added: "Sin vero non placet, feliciter state, et pro nobis infelicibus exorate."[54]

In cities that were not entirely destroyed and to which some of the inhabitants returned after the barbarians had left, Gregory often entrusted the care of souls to some neighboring bishop as visitor, if it did not seem expedient to reestablish the city immediately as an episcopal see. In the first year of his pontificate Gregory entrusted the care of Populonia to Balbinus, bishop of Grosseto, ordering him to ordain there a cardinal priest and two deacons, and three priests for the parishes attached to Populonia, in order that infants might be baptized and adults might not die without the sacrament of penance.[55] For the same reason the care of Canosa was entrusted to Bishop Felix of Sipontum.[56] Only a few people remained in Terni, and hence Gregory entrusted it to the care of Bishop Constantius of Narni, since the two cities were only six miles apart.[57] The bishop of Agropoli was appointed to care for the ruined cities of Velia, Buxentum and Blanda, situated in Lucania.[58]

If the bishop of a devastated city survived, and there was little hope of the early restoration of his see, he was given some vacant diocese in the meantime. Thus, when Alessio, situated on the Adriatic Sea in Illyricum, was captured by the barbarians, Bishop John was made bishop of Squillace in southern Italy:

> Licet a tua hoste imminente depulsus sis, aliam quae a pastore vacat debeas ecclesiam gubernare, ita tamen, ut si civitatem illam ab hostibus liberam effici, et Domino protegente ad priorem statum contigerit revocari, in eam in qua es prius ordinatus ecclesiam revertaris. Sin autem praedicta civitas continua captivitate

---

[54] *Ep.* v, 40. It appears that Bishop Sebastian did not accept the offer of the vacant Sicilian see.

[55] Cf. *Ep.* i, 15.

[56] Cf. *Ep.* i, 51.

[57] Cf. *Ep.* ix, 60; Dudden, *Gregory the Great,* I, 360.

[58] Cf. *Ep.* ii, 42.

calamitate premitur, in hac in qua et a nobis incardinatus es debeas ecclesia permanere....[59]

Taurianum in southern Italy was ruined by the Lombards before February, 592, for at that time Gregory transferred Bishop Paulinus to the isle of Lipari, close to the shores of Sicily, with orders to visit his former see whenever it was opportune.[60] In October of the preceding year Bishop Maximian of Syracuse had been made papal vicar for Sicily—it was an office bestowed upon Bishop Maximian personally and not to the see of Syracuse.[61] As papal vicar Bishop Maximian was requested to install Bishop Paulinus in his new diocese at Lipari.[62]

In the above-mentioned cases, there appears to have been some hope that the cities would at some time or other be restored so that a bishop might again be installed there. In other cases, however, when there seemed to be no hope for the future restoration of a city, Gregory united the place with some neighboring bishopric. Shortly after his consecration he joined the see of Minturnae to the diocese of Formia, both of which were in Latium.[63]

In March 592, Gregory appointed Bishop Benenatus of Miseno visitor of Cuma with instructions to conduct an election.[64] Four months later, however, Gregory decreed that the two sees of Miseno and Cuma should be united, since they were close together and since there were few people left at the latter city. Bishop Benenatus was given full rights in both sees, and permission to dwell in whichever see he chose, provided that he did not neglect the one or the other.[65]

---

[59] *Ep.* ii, 37. The remainder of the letter is similar to formula 6 of the *Liber Diurnus*. Cf. *supra*, p. 32, note 34; regarding the term "incardinatus," cf. *supra*, p. 94, note 52.

[60] Cf. *Ep.* ii, 19.

[61] "Quae videlicet vices non loco sed personae tribuimus."—*Ep.* ii, 8.

[62] Cf. *Ep.* ii, 51.

[63] Cf. *Ep.* i, 8.

[64] Cf. *Ep.* ii, 25.

[65] Cf. *Ep.* ii, 44.

Also in 592 Tre-Taverne was joined to Velletri by Gregory. As this letter is the same as formula 9 of the *Liber Diurnus,*[66] it may be quoted in full:

> Postquam hostilis impietas diversarum civitatum ita peccatis facientibus desolavit ecclesias, ut reparandi eas spes nulla populo deficiente remanserit, maiori valde cura constringimur, ne defunctis earum sacerdotibus reliquiae plebis nullo pastoris moderamine gubernatae per invia fidei hostis calidi rapiantur, quod absit, insidia. Huius ergo rei sollicitudine saepe commoniti hoc nostro sedit cordi consilium, ut vicinis eas mandaremus pontificibus gubernandas. Ideoque fraternitati tuae curam gubernationemque Trium-Tavernensium ecclesiae praevidimus committendum, quam tuae ecclesiae adgregari unirique necesse est, quatenus utrarumque ecclesiarum sacerdos recte, Christo adiutore, possis existere. Quaeque tibi de eius patrimonio, vel cleri ordinatione, seu promotione, vigilanti ac canonica visa fuerint cura disponere, quippe ut pontifex proprius liberam habebis ex nostra praesenti permissione licentiam. Quapropter, frater karissime, Dominicorum reminiscens salubriter mandatorum ita in commissae plebis regimine lucrandisque animabus invigila, ut ante tribunal aeterni iudicis constitutus fructus bonae operationis, quod ad mercedem tuam pertineat, eidem redemptori nostro, in quo laetari possit, exhibeas.[67]

Early in his reign Pope Gregory found episcopal cities devastated by the barbarians in Corsica as in Italy, and in

[66] "Praeceptum de adunandis ecclesiis."—ed. Sickel, p. 8; ed. Rozière, pp. 34ff.

[67] *Ep.* ii, 48. *Epp.* iii, 20 and vi, 9 are identical in form, though the latter reveals a few minor differences. Garnier (1825-1898) notes that formula 9 is found in *Epp.* iii, 20 and vi, 9; he does not mention *Ep.* ii, 48. Cf. *Liber Diurnus*, ed. Rozière, p. 34. It is very probable that Gregory the Great was the first to use this formula as Jaffé-Kaltenbrunner list no letter of a previous Pope that might correspond to the formula. In *Ep.* iii, 20, Gregory united the church of St. Anthemius in Torre with that of Nomentum; in *Ep.* vi, 9, the church of Carina with that of Reggio. Seven years later Carina again had its own bishop. Cf. *Ep.* xiii, 16, of November, 602.

Corsica he followed the same policy of transferring the surviving bishop to some vacant diocese. After the city of Tainatis was destroyed, Bishop Martin was moved to the see of Aleria and given full rights therein in August, 591.[68] In the same month, Bishop Leo, whose see is unknown, was moved to the diocese of Saona.[69]

These instances are indicative of the Pope's supreme power in that he could a) transfer the location of an episcopal see to a new site within the diocese; b) transfer a bishop, either temporarily or in perpetuity, from one diocese to another, assigning him the care also of his former diocese; c) entrust the care of another diocese to a visitor, a bishop of a neighboring diocese; d) unite, either by a union called today *aeque principalis* or by a union *minus principalis,*[70] two dioceses in perpetuity or temporarily. In only one instance is there an indication that the wishes of the inhabitants played a part in the arrangement made by the Pope, i.e., when Bishop Agnellus of Fondi was transferred to Terracina at the request of the inhabitants of the latter see.[71]

In none of Gregory's letters is there mention either of a *divisio* or *dismembratio* of a diocese.[72] On the contrary: his

---

[68] Cf. *Epp.* i, 77. 79.

[69] Cf. *Epp.* i, 76. 79.

[70] Cf. *Epp.* ii, 44. 48; iii, 20; vi, 9—*aeque principalis*; *Ep.* i, 8—*minus principalis.* Cf. also canon 1419.

[71] Cf. *Epp.* iii, 13. 14.

[72] It has been noted above (p. 20, note 1) that the see of Isola was probably removed from the jurisdiction of the schismatic metropolitan of Aquileia and placed within the jurisdiction of the metropolitan of Ravenna until such time as the Istrian bishops returned to union with Rome. Gregory also placed some of Rome's suffragan sees (including Rimini) under the care of the metropolitan of Ravenna. Cf. *supra,* p. 30, note 27. Both of these instances reflect only temporary measures. Caspar, citing Kehr, states: "Auf Rimini wurden denn auch in der Folgezeit Ravennater Oberhoheitsanspruch geltend gemacht."—*Geschichte des Papsttums,* II, 427, note 2. But it must be noted that the attempts of the archbishops of Ravenna to subject Rimini to themselves were ineffectual for a thousand years; only in 1604 did Pope Clement VIII subject Rimini and Ferrara to Ravenna. Cf. Kehr, *Regesta Pontificum Romanorum, Italia Pontificia,* 8 vols. in 12 (Berolini: Apud Weidmannos, 1906-1935), IV, 158. Hereafter cited *Italia Pontificia.*

letters are evidence that the dioceses as constituted were not to be divided. In the first year of his reign Gregory was notified, through Jobinus, Pretorian Prefect of Illyricum, of an imperial order that the bishops who were forced to leave their dioceses because of the invasions of the Avars were to be received by those bishops whose dioceses were not threatened. The Pope confirmed the imperial order, appealing to the law of charity. But he added:

> Non quidem ut per communionem episcopalis throni dignitas dividatur, sed ut ab ecclesia iuxta possibilitatem sufficientia debeant alimenta percipere. Sic enim et proximum in Deo et Deum in proximum diligere comprobamur. Nullam quippe eis nos in vestris ecclesiis auctoritatem tribuimus, sed tamen eos vestris solatiis contineri summopere hortamur.[73]

Bishop John of Euria in Epirus Vetus came, bringing with him the body of St. Donatus, to the island of Corfù for refuge and dwelt in a place called Cassiopi Castrum. Contrary to all canonical statutes Bishop John sought to remove the place from the jurisdiction of the bishop of Corfù, thus constituting it a new diocese for himself. The case was first tried, at the emperor's orders, before Bishop Andrew of Nicopolis, metropolitan of Epirus Vetus, and his decree that Cassiopi Castrum should remain part of the diocese of Corfù was solemnly confirmed by Gregory the Great. Before the sentence was promulgated, Bishop Andrew died and Emperor Maurice was dethroned by Phocas. The latter decreed that Cassiopi Castrum should be removed from the jurisdiction of the bishop of Corfù and given as a diocese to Bishop John of Euria. As soon as he learned of this decree, Gregory ordered his *apocrisiarius* in Constantinople to make every effort to induce the emperor to change his decree, which was "omnino pravum, omnino iniustum, omnino inlicitum et sacris valde canonibus inimicum." He was also to urge the emperor to issue a new decree in conformity with the decision first

---

[73] *Ep.* i, 43.

given by the metropolitan and confirmed by the Pope, so that later no doubts could arise.[74]

It may be presumed that the emperor revoked his decree, for later Bishop John sent a representative to Rome to plead for permission to remain at Cassiopi Castrum and to place the body of St. Donatus in the church there. Gregory was not averse to the granting of such permission, but he demanded that two written guarantees be first made out: Bishop John was to sign a guarantee that he would never seek to assert for himself any jurisdiction or any privilege in Cassiopi Castrum "tamquam proprius episcopus;" the bishop of Corfù was to sign an agreement that, when the barbarian menace was removed, Bishop John could freely remove the body of St. Donatus to his former episcopal see.[75] Apparently the affair was thus settled, for nothing more is heard of it in Gregory's letters.

---

[74] Cf. *Epp.* xiv, 7. 8.

[75] Cf. *Ep.* xiv, 13; also xiv, 7: "nullam tanquam cardinalis episcopus . . .auctoritatem."

APPENDIX: THE PALLIUM

SECTION I. THE ORIGIN AND EARLY USE OF THE PALLIUM

1. ORIGIN OF THE PALLIUM

As is well known, the pallium today signifies the jurisdiction of a metropolitan; until an archbishop has received it from the Pope he is forbidden to exercise certain of his powers, and he is obliged to petition the Pope for it within three months of his consecration, or, if already consecrated, of the time of his appointment.[1] It is, therefore, one of the most important of ecclesiastical vestments, and yet the origin and early history of the pallium have been hidden in obscurity. Gregory the Great frequently granted the pallium to various bishops during the course of his pontificate, and in certain instances the granting of the pallium coincided with the papal approval of a bishop's election and consecration. Two of Gregory's letters have also been used by authors to prove that the pallium originally was an imperial grant, and that even at the end of the sixth century the Pope was dependent upon the emperor in the granting of the pallium.

Of the various theories that have been proposed, one of the more common is that which holds that the pallium originated as an imperial gift and closely resembled the *lorus* which certain Roman officials wore as a mark of honor. This theory is upheld by De Marca (1594-1662),[2] Thomassinus (1619-1695),[3] Barthel (1697-1771),[4] Thurston (1856-1939),[5]

[1] Cf. canons 275, 276.

[2] *De Concordia Sacerdotii et Imperii seu de Libertatibus Ecclesiae Gallicanae* (8 books in 4 vols., Neapoli, 1771), III, 259.

[3] *Vetus et Nova Ecclesiae Disciplina* (Magontiaci, 1787), pars I, lib. ii, c. 53.

[4] *Dissertatio Historico-Canonico-Publica de Pallio* (2 ed., Herbipoli, 1753), pp. 6, 19. (Printed in edition of Vespasiani, *De Sacri Pallii Origine* (Romae: Typis S. C. de Propaganda Fide, 1856).

[5] "The Pallium," *Month*, LXXV (1892), 305-325.

and Duchesne (1843-1922)[6]. This theory is based upon the false Donation of Constantine, in which it is stated that the emperor bestowed upon Pope Sylvester *superhumerale videlicet lorum qui imperiale circumdare assolet collum;*[7] upon the *discolora pallia* granted by the emperor as a distinctive garb to certain officials;[8] upon consular diptychs and ancient mosaics representing the use of the *lorus;*[9] upon the fact that the Pope at times apparently requested the emperor's permission before granting the pallium; and upon the fact that Archbishop Maurus of Ravenna (642-671) requested the pallium from Constans II (642-668) and obtained it.[10]

In refutation of this theory the following may be adduced: the false Donation of Constantine proves nothing, for it was composed only in the ninth century; there is nothing whatever in Christian literature to link up the *discolora pallia* of the Theodosian Code with the ecclesiastical pallium; the classical *lorus* was not worn in quite the same manner as the pallium, for it passed *under* the right arm and over the left shoulder, whereas the pallium was worn over both shoulders.[11]

To prove that the pallium must have been originally an imperial grant, authors point to four instances in which it is claimed the Pope requested the emperor's permission before granting the pallium: Pope Vigilius (537-555), before granting it to Auxanius of Arles, and to his successor, Aurelian; Pope Gregory, regarding the use of the pallium by Anastasius, the

---

[6] *Origines*, p. 405.

[7] Hinschius, *Decretales Pseudo-Isidorianae* (Lipsiae, 1863), p. 253. Cf. Duchesne, *Origines*, p. 405; Barthel, *Dissertatio Historico-Canonico-Publica de Pallio*, p. 19.

[8] C. Th., (14, 10) 1. Cf. Duchesne, *Origines*, p. 406.

[9] Cf. Thurston, "The Pallium," p. 306; Duchesne, *Origines*, p. 406.

[10] Cf. Duchesne, *op. cit.*, p. 405; *infra*, at note 72.

[11] Cf. Trombetta, *De Pallio Archiepiscopali* (Surrenti: Ex Typographia Hen. D. Onofrio, 1923), p. 37; Braun, *Die liturgische Gewandung* (Freiburg im Breisgau: Herder'sche Verlagsbuchhandlung, 1907), p. 652; Sägmüller, *Lehrbuch*, p. 601; Hinschius, *Kirchenrecht*, II, 26, n. 7; Garnier, *De Usu Pallii* (printed in Rozière's edition of the *Liber Diurnus*, pp. 341-360), p. 345; Thurston, "The Pallium," *Month*, LXXV (1892), 309. The last-mentioned author notes the difference between the wearing of the *lorus* and the pallium, and yet he prefers to believe that the *lorus* was changed into the ecclesiastical pallium.

deposed patriarch of Antioch,[12] and before granting it to Syagrius of Autun. It cannot be proved from the texts of the letters of Pope Vigilius or of Pope Gregory[13] that either Pope formally requested permission of the emperor before granting the pallium, for the texts might be interpreted as indicating merely that the Popes informed the emperor of their intention to confer the pallium in order to forestall any unpleasant reaction. It must be remembered that Pope Vigilius was under the suspicion of Theodora and Justinian, and that Pope Gregory was for a time under the suspicion of Emperor Maurice—both knew that Pope Sylverius (536-537), because he was accused of treasonable relations with the Goths, was deposed by Belisarius at the wish of the emperor.[14]

---

[12] Cf. *infra*, Section II, n. 3.

[13] Cf. JK, 912, 913, 918 *MGH*, Epistolarum Tomus III, *Epistolae Merovingici et Karolini Aevi*, Tomus I (Berolini: Apud Weidmannos 1892), pp. 59, 62, 66; JE, 1491—*Ep*. viii, 4. The pertinent passages are:

JK, 912: "....De his vero, quae caritas vestra tam de usu pallei quam de aliis sibi a nobis petiit debere concedi, libenti hoc animo etiam in praesenti facere sine dilatione potuimus, nisi cum christianissimi domni, filii nostri, imperatoris, hoc, sicut ratio postulat, voluissemus perficere, Deo auctore, notitia, ut et vobis gratia praestitorum causa reddatur, dum, quae postulastis, cum consensu christianissimi principis conferuntur, et nos honorem fidei eius servasse competenti reverentia iudicemur."

JK, 913: "....quia digna credimus ratione compleri, ut agenti vices nostras pallei non desit ornatus, usum tibi eius, sicut decessori tuo prodecessor noster sanctae recordationis Symmachus legitur contulisse, beati Petri functi auctoritate contulimus."

JK, 918: "....Sed ne in aliquo sedis nostrae vicarius minor suis decessoribus videatur, necessarium fore credidimus pallii vobis usum, quemadmodum decessori vestro hactenus dederamus, praesenti auctoritate concedere, ut et morum et omnium bonarum rerum vobis, beato Petro apostolo suffragante, non desit ornatus."

Ep. viii, 4: "....Syagrio [of Autun] pallium dirigere secundum postulationem vestram voluimus. Propter quod et serenissimi domni imperatoris quantum nobis diaconus noster, qui apud eum responsa ecclesiae faciebat innotuit, prona voluntas est et concedi hoc omnino desiderat."

[14] Cf. *Liber Pontificalis*, I, 293; Braun, *Die liturgische Gewandung*, 635-637; Vespasiani, *De Sacri Pallii Origine*, pp. 18-20; P. Syxtus, "Indumenta Sacra," *Ephemerides Liturgicae*, XXIII (1909), 642; Sägmüller, *Lehrbuch*, p. 601; Grisar, "Rom und die fränkische Kirche vornehmlich im sechsten Jahrhundert," *ZKT*, XIV (1890), 489ff.; Dudden, *Gregory the Great*, I, 436, n. 3; II, 60; Garnier, *De Usu Pallii*, p. 344.

One point stands out clearly: these instances are exceptional, even if one were to grant that they were a true request of the emperor's permission to bestow the pallium, and, as exceptions, cannot be used to prove that the pallium was originally an imperial gift. The better opinion seems to be that the Popes did not ask the emperor's consent, but only sought to find out how their act would be considered at Constantinople. Their assurance to the Frankish rulers that the emperor was perfectly agreeable would certainly tend to foster good relations between the three concerned, the Pope, the emperor and the Frankish rulers.

Several other theories on the origin of the pallium have been proposed,[15] but the writer prefers to accept that of Braun, namely, that the pallium, from its very origin, was a distinct liturgical vestment both in the East and the West, and was not the result of a gradual development from some secular garment.[16]

---

[15] 1. The pallium replaced the rational worn by the High Priest of the Old Testament—supported by Devoti, *Institutionum Canonicarum Libri IV*, Tom. I, lib. I, tit. 3, sect. 3, ¶42, note 1; Gagliardi, *Institutiones Iuris Canonici Communis et Neapolitani* (2. ed., Neapoli, 1766-1771), Lib. I, tit. 17, n. 3.

2. The pallium originated in Apostolic times from the mantle of St. Peter—supported by Vespasiani, *De Sacri Pallii Origine*, pp. 15-27; Schmalzgrueber, *Ius Ecclesiasticum Universum* (5 vols. in 12, Romae, 1843-1845), Lib. I, tit. 8, n. 1; Trombetta, *De Pallio Archiepiscopali*, pp. 38-40.

3. The pallium originated from the ordinary garment, the "mantle-pallium" which was gradually folded into a long, narrow band, and worn as a sign of honor in the Church in the fourth century—supported by Wilpert, whose works are cited by Walsh, *Mass and Vestments of the Catholic Church* (New York: Benziger Brothers, 1916), p. 433; also by Sägmüller, *Lehrbuch*, p. 602.

4. The pallium originated from the sacred "mantle-pallium," worn somewhat like the classical toga, gradually developing into the ecclesiastical pallium—supported by Garrucci, as cited by Trombetta, *op. cit.*, p. 38; Braun, *op. cit.*, p. 655.

[16] "Das Pallium tritt stets als durchaus liturgisches Gewandstück auf, und das gleichmässig in Rom wie in der Ostkirche. . . . Das Pallium ist ihr zufolge nicht das Produkt einer langsamen Entwicklung, nicht ein durch die Umstände verkümmertes Obergewand; es wurde vielmehr zu Rom von Anfang an als das eingeführt, als was es uns stets in der Geschichte begegnet, als auszeichnender Schmuck und als Abzeichen des

2. USE OF THE PALLIUM BEFORE GREGORY THE GREAT

a. Use of the Pallium in the West

Before the early years of the sixth century there is no definite reference to the use of the pallium as an ecclesiastical vestment.[17] The oldest document in the West referring to the use of the pallium is a letter of Pope Symmachus (498-514) to Bishop Caesarius of Arles; the latter was created papal vicar and was granted the use of the pallium in 513.[18] Pope Vigilius (537-555) conferred the pallium upon Bishops Auxanius and Aurelian, both of Arles; his successor, Pope Pelagius I (556-561), conferred it on Bishop Sapaudus of Arles, and forbade its use by Secundus of Taormina. Pope John III (561-574) granted the pallium to Bishop Peter of Ravenna, and Pope Pelagius II (579-590) is said to have decreed that all metropolitans must, within three months of the time of their consecration, make a profession of faith and request the use of the pallium. The document upon which this latter statement is based has been marked as spurious by Jaffé-Kaltenbrun-

obersten Hirten der Kirche und des Patriarchen des Abendlandes, des römischen Bischofs. . . ."—Braun, *Die liturgische Gewandung*, pp. 653, 662; cf. also *ibid.*, 620-676. Eisenhofer accepts the hypothesis of Braun, but adds that undoubtedly the Roman bishops followed the practice of the bishops of the Orient who wore the *ὠμοφόριον*, the oriental counterpart of the Roman pallium, from the beginning of the 5th century. Cf. *Handbuch der katholischen Liturgik* (2 vols., Freiburg im Breisgau: Herder, 1932), I, 459. Hereafter cited as *Handbuch.*

[17] Traces of the pallium have been found in the tomb of Pope Leo I (440-461); cf. Braun, *Die liturgische Gewandung*, p. 625, note 1. It is noted in the life of Pope Mark (336) that he granted the pallium to the bishop of Ostia to be used in the consecration of the Pope; cf. *Liber Pontificalis*, I, 81. No modern scholar, however, dates the composition of the first part of the *Liber Pontificalis* before the early sixth century. Bibliography for further study of the question is indicated by Braun, *op. cit.*, p. 250, note 2.

[18] Cf. JK, 766. The claim that Pope Symmachus also granted the pallium to Theodore of Lorsch, metropolitan of Pannonia and Noricum, is based on a spurious document; cf. JK, †767; Hinschius, *Kirchenrecht*, II, 25, n. 3. The pallium is mentioned also in the lives of Pope Felix IV (526-530) and Pope Silverius (536-537); cf. *Liber Pontificalis*, I, 282, 293. Eisenhofer, noting the fact that the pallium was removed from Pope Silverius before he was deposed by Belisarius, believes that the Roman pontiffs wore the pallium even when not engaged in liturgical functions. Cf. *Handbuch*, I, 462.

ner.[19] The oldest monuments which depict the pallium are the mosaics in the churches of St. Vitalis in Ravenna and of St. Apollinaris in Classe. These mosaics date from about the middle of the sixth century and point, therefore, to the use of the pallium in that city before Pope John III granted it to Bishop Peter.[20]

Though one finds only few references to the granting of the pallium before the time of Gregory the Great, authors maintain that in the West, as in the East, it was widely used before his time: in Africa,[21] in Sicily,[22] and in Gaul. To show the use of the pallium in the latter country, authors rely on the sixth canon of the I Council of Mâcon in 583: *Ut episcopus sine pallio missas dicere non praesumat.*[23] Up to modern times some authors, relying upon a false rendition of this canon, *Ut archiepiscopus sine pallio missas dicere non praesumat,*[24] supposed that there existed a special *pallium Gallicanum,* worn by all Gallican archbishops and existing side by side with the *pallium Romanum,* worn by vicars of the Pope

---

[19] Cf. JK, 912, 914—letters of Vigilius; JK, 944, 1000—letters of Pelagius I. Leclercq ("Pallium," *DACL*, XIII, 931) states that Pelagius I *granted* the pallium to Bishop Secundus; the Pope, however, undoubtedly *forbade* Bishop Secundus to use the pallium; cf. Loewenfeld, *Epistolae Pontificum Romanorum ineditae ab a.* 493 *ad a.* 1198 (Lipsiae: Veit et Comp., 1885), p. 16, n. 30. Cf. JK, 1041—letter of John III; JK, †1064—spurious letter of Pelagius II.

[20] Cf. Braun, *Die liturgische Gewandung*, p. 626.

[21] Cf. Duchesne, *Origines*, p. 408. He refers to the *Life of St. Fulgentius*, c. 18—*PL*, LXV, 136. This reference, however, is not to the liturgical pallium, but rather to an ordinary scarf worn to protect the neck and shoulders. Thus the word "pallium" is used in the *Rule of Cassian* (*PL*, XLIX, 72), and in the *Life of St. Martin* (*PL*, XX, 169). Cf. Kleinschmidt, "Das bischöfliche Rationale und der 6. Kanon der Synode von Mâcon," *Historisches Jahrbuch*, XXVII (1906), 800.

[22] Cf. Eisenhofer, *Handbuch*, I, 459. Cf. *infra*, section II, 6.

[23] *MGH*, Legum Sectio III, *Concilia* I, p. 157. Usually this Council is dated in 581; Maassen, however, believes that the date 583 is more correct, for he maintains that in Gaul at the end of the sixth century events were dated, not according to the *Indictio*, but according to the year of the king then ruling. Cf. also Hefele-Leclercq, *Histoire des Conciles*, III, 202. The date 581 is given by De Clercq, *La législation religieuse franque de Clovis à Charlemagne*, pp. 49-51; 92.

[24] Mansi, ix, 933.

only.[25] Kleinschmidt, after a study of the use of the word *pallium,* and after a comparison of the *Expositio Brevis Antiquae Liturgiae Gallicanae,* which he ascribed to St. Germain of Paris (†576)[26] with the sixth canon of Mâcon, concludes: "Das Pallium der gallikanischen Messerklärung und des Mâconer Konzils ist nichts anders als die priesterliche Stola."[27] It seems best to hold that in the West, except perhaps in Sicily, the pallium was from the beginning restricted to the Pope and to those to whom it was conceded by him.

b. *Use of the Pallium in the East*

In the East, contrary to the practice of the West, every bishop wore the Omophorion, as is shown by Isidore of Pe-

---

[25] Cf. Marriot, *Vestiarium Christianum* (London: Rivingstons, Waterloo Place, 1868), p. 209—the author relied upon the works of Hefele (1809-1893) and Ruinart (1657-1709). Hinschius also used the false rendition, but he rejected the theory of a special Gallican pallium and interpreted the canon to mean that those who had the pallium must wear it; cf. *Kirchenrecht,* II, 27, n. 5.

A modern liturgist, while accepting the correct reading *episcopus* for *archiepiscopus,* still maintains that a special pallium was meant. Cf. Eisenhofer, *Handbuch,* I 459.

[26] The *Expositio* was most probably composed by an anonymous author of the seventh or even of the beginning of the eighth century. Cf. Quasten, "Oriental Influence in the Gallican Liturgy," *Traditio,* I (1943), 55f. The text of the *Expositio* is found in *PL,* LXXII, 97; the critical edition is that of Quasten, *Expositio antiquae liturgiae Gallicanae Germano Parisiensi ascripta* (Münster, 1934).

[27] "Das bischöfliche Rationale und der 6. Kanon der Synode von Mâcon," *Historisches Jahrbuch,* XXVII (1906), 799-803. Kleinschmidt's view has been accepted by: Sägmüller, *Lehrbuch,* p. 601; Braun, *Die liturgische Gewandung,* pp. 563, 569, 674ff. Kleinschmidt's supposition that the *Expositio* was written about the time of the Council of Mâcon does not invalidate his conclusion that the former treated of garments common to both priests and bishops. If a seventh century writer used the word *pallium* to refer to vestments common to bishops and priests, a sixth century council could have used it with the same meaning.

The 28th canon of the IV Provincial Council of Toledo (633) refers, not to the episcopal pallium but to the stole. Cf. Bruns, *Canones,* I, 231f; Braun, *op. cit.,* p. 674f.; Duchesne, *Origines,* p. 412.

lusium († ca. 435)[28] and by Liberatus of Carthage (sixth century).[29]

It has been said that apparently the patriarchs of Constantinople in the sixth century wore the omophorion (or pallium) not only in liturgical functions but in others as well.[30] This statement is based on two passages of Eustratius in the *Life of St. Eutychius*, patriarch of Constantinople from 552-582[31] and on a passage in the *Ecclesiastica Historia* of Theodore (early seventh century).[32]

In the first passage of Eustratius' *Life* the bishop is represented as standing in prayer at the altar, after the people had been dismissed, and as wearing his usual vestments "*καὶ τὸ ὠμοφόριον ὅπερ καὶ μεθ' ἑαυτοῦ λαβὼν εἶχεν ἀεί;*" in the second, the bishop spent the night in the temple, and then went to the church of St. Mary, wearing the omophorion—"*καὶ φορέσας ἔωθεν τὸ ὠμοφόριον, ὅπερ καὶ μεθ' ἑαυτοῦ λαβὼν εἶχεν ἀεί.*" Why does Eustratius stress, by an identical phrase used twice, the fact that Bishop Eutychius always carried (or wore) the omophorion? If this had been customary, it would scarcely have merited mention, much less a double mention. It seems more logical to conclude that Bishop Eutychius acted contrary to custom than to conclude that all patriarchs wore the omophorion outside of liturgical functions.

The passage in the *Ecclesiastica Historia* of Theodore likewise does not give any conclusive proof. Euphemius was

---

[28] Cf. *Epistolae*, lib. 1, n. 136—Migne, *Patrologiae Cursus Completus, Series Graeca* (161 vols., Parisii, 1856-1866), LXXVIII, 272. Cited hereafter as *PG*. Isidore states that the Eastern bishops wore the pallium during Mass but put it off during the singing of the Gospel. No such custom is spoken of in the West.

[29] Cf. *Breviarium Collectum a Liberato Ecclesiae Carthaginensis*—*PL*, LXVIII, 1036. He who succeeded the patriarch at Alexandria is said to have removed from his predecessor the pallium to place it on his own shoulders; Liberatus traces this custom back to the time of St. Mark. Braun is of the opinion that a pallium in the time of St. Mark would have been an anachronism. Cf. *Die liturgische Gewandung*, p. 666.

[30] Cf. Braun, *op. cit.*, p. 668.

[31] *PG*, LXXXVI², 2317, 2360. Eustratius was a contemporary of Eutychius.

[32] *PG*, LXXXVI¹, 189.

deposed as patriarch of Constantinople at the order of Emperor Anastasius (491-518), and was succeeded by Macedonius (496-511). Theodore praises the latter because he obtained the emperor's permission to assure Euphemius that he would be safe in exile; before going to speak with Euphemius, Macedonius had his own omophorion removed by his deacon, but it is not clear whether or not he had just come from a liturgical function, since the account states that Euphemius was in the baptistry—"*ἐν τῷ βαπτιστηρίῳ τοῦ Εὐφημίου ὄντος τὸ ὠμοφόριον τὸ ἐπισκοπικὸν ἑαυτοῦ ἀφαιρεθῆναι ὑπὸ τοῦ διακόνου προσέταξε, καὶ οὗτος εἰσελθεῖν πρὸς τὸν Εὐφήμιον.*"

In speaking of the conflict over the use of the pallium between Pope Gregory and Bishop John of Ravenna, Hartmann says: "Es handelte sich um das Recht, das Pallium zu tragen, das Johannes unterstützt von den kaiserlichen Beamten, in einem Umfange beanspruchte, wie es offenbar bei den orientalischen Kirchen gebräuchlich war, während Gregor es nur für die Zeit der Messe und für jährlich vier feierliche Litanien zugestehen wollte."[33] The author does not quote any source for his statement regarding the use of the pallium by the oriental Church. It seems better to the writer, therefore, to suspend judgment regarding the use of the pallium in the East in other than liturgical functions until more conclusive proof for such use has been found.

SECTION II. THE PALLIUM IN THE LETTERS OF GREGORY THE GREAT

1. CONTROVERSY WITH THE BISHOP OF RAVENNA

During the fourteen years in which Gregory the Great ruled as supreme pontiff (590-604) he treated of the pallium and its use in thirty-six of his letters.[34] Of these letters eight

---

[33] *Geschichte Italiens*, II, 165.

[34] *Epp.* i, 7. 27. 66; ii, 20, 21. 22; iii, 54; iv, 1; v, 10. 11. 15. 16. 58. 60. 61. 62. 63; vi, 7. 8. 18. 31; vii, 37; viii, 4. 36; ix, 167. 176. 213. 219. 220. 222. 227. 228. 234; xi, 39. 56a; xiii, 40. To these must be added the decree of the Roman Synod of 595, given as *Ep.* v, 57a.

refer to the use of the pallium at Ravenna.[35] One may consider these first, since they show more clearly than do the other letters the mind of Pope Gregory regarding the pallium and its use. At the time of Gregory Ravenna was the residence of the exarch. In 404 Honorius (395-423) had moved the imperial residence from Milan to Ravenna. After the overthrow of the last Western emperor, Odoacer (476-493) made his home at Ravenna, being killed there by the treachery of Theoderic (493-526), leader of the Ostrogoths, who likewise took up his residence in the city. In 539 Ravenna was captured by Belisarius, Justinian's able general, and it became shortly thereafter the residence of the exarch, the first of whom was Narses (554-567), appointed after the recall of Belisarius. "The Exarch exercised a viceregal authority throughout Imperial Italy. As head of the civil service, he superseded the Pretorian Prefect; as chief of the Army, he held all troops in Italy at his absolute command. He appointed to all military, and possibly to all civil, offices."[36]

The episcopal see of Ravenna seems to have been founded about the beginning of the third century, or perhaps a little earlier. It was at first a suffragan see of the metropolitan see of Milan, which was the only metropolitan see in northern Italy until the formation of the metropolitan see of Aquileia early in the fifth century. A little later the province of Aemilia was detached from the jurisdiction of Milan, and thus there were furnished a number of suffragan sees to the bishop of Ravenna, who however remained a suffragan of the Roman see.[37]

Why Ravenna was raised to the dignity of a metropolitan see is not clear. Was it because since 404 it had been the imperial residence? Or was it because of Milan's preponderant influence? No definite answer can be given. It is of course well known that towards the end of the fourth century, and particularly in the beginning of the fifth, Milan was a center

---

[35] *Epp.* iii, 54; v, 11. 15. 61; vi, 31; ix, 167. *Ep.* iii, 66, is a letter of John of Ravenna to Pope Gregory; *Ep.* iii, 67, from Pope John III to Peter of Ravenna.

[36] Dudden, *Gregory the Great,* I, 180.

[37] Cf. *supra,* p. 7f.

of influence, so much so that it appears that for a time the bishops of the West recognized a double hegemony, that of the Pope and that of the bishop of Milan.[38] "Such a situation could have worked to the detriment of Rome's pre-eminence; though we do not know what part the Popes had in the formation of Aquileia as a metropolitan see, we are sure that they helped create the metropolitan see of Ravenna."[39]

Batiffol (1861-1929) is of the opinion that Ravenna became a metropolitan see by decree of the Pope and emperor:

> Ravenne devint métropole sous l'épiscopat de saint Pierre (Chrysologue). 'Decreto, dit-il, principis Christiani et decreto beati Petri' c'est-à-dire de Valentinien III et du pape Célestin. D'une lettre de Théodoret, en 431, addressée aux évêques de Rome, Milan, Aquilée, Ravenne, on peut inférer que, à cette date, Ravenne était métropole.[40]

Apparently his reference is to the 175th Sermon of St. Peter Chrysologus, which was preached on the occasion of the first consecration of a suffragan at Ravenna, Marcellinus as bishop of Vicohabentinus: "...Sancta Ecclesia Ravennas, ut primum pareret, viam fecit, angores pertulit, sensit dolores.... [Refers to the trials of Mary at the birth of Christ.] Edicto Caesaris et pagani universorum Dominus obtemperaturus occurrit, et decreto beati Petri, decreto principis christiani, servus adhuc aliquis irreverenter obsistit?"[41]

Batiffol also refers presumably to the privileges granted by Valentinian III (425-455) to Ravenna, which privileges

---

[38] Cf. Duchesne, *Origines*, pp. 30-38; Kirsch, *Kirchengeschichte* (4 vols., Freiburg im Breisgau: Herder and Company, 1930-1933), I, 742; Batiffol, *Le siège apostolique* 359-451 (2. ed., Paris: Librairie Victor Lecoffre, 1924), pp. 157, 171ff.; Zeiller, *L'Empire romain et l'église* (Paris, E. De Boccard, Éditeur, 1928), pp. 332-340; Fliche-Martin, *Histoire*, IV, 242; Palanque, *Saint Ambroise et l'empire romain* (Paris, E. De Boccard, Éditeur, 1933), pp. 387-404; Grisar, *History of Rome*, I, 347.

[39] Duchesne, *Origines*, p. 38. He refers to Sermon 175 of St. Peter Chrysologus, who became bishop of Ravenna in 433.

[40] *Le siège apostolique*, 359-451, p. 178.

[41] *PL*, LII, 656. The episcopal see was soon removed from Vicohabentinus to Ferrara. Cf. Kehr, *Italia Pontificia*, V, 16.

are thus cited by Agnellus, the author of the *Liber Pontificalis Ecclesiae Ravennatis*:[42]

> Non post multos dies idem augustus [Valentinian III] sub consecratione beati antistitis Joannis 14 civitates cum suis ecclesiis largitus est archigeratica potestate, et usque in praesentem diem 14 civitates cum episcopis sub Ravennense ecclesia redactae sunt. . . . Iste primus ab ipso augusto pallio ex candida lana accepit, ut mos est Romanum pontifici super diploidem induere, quo usus est ipse et successores sui usque in praesentem diem.[43]

Regarding this statement of Agnellus, Holder-Egger remarks:

> Fortasse Agnellus iam diploma supposititium Valentiniani III prae oculis habuit (Marini, *Papiri diplomatici*, p. 94), quo episcopo Ravennati 14 episcopatus subiciuntur et 'honor pallii' confertur; nota verba chartae: *Ravennatem eccl. . . . archieratica dignitate erectam.* Attamen, quamvis privilegium falsum sit, haud plane reiicienda esse judico, quae hoc loco de honoribus ecclesiae Ravennati collatis traduntur. Constant quidem ex Petri

[42] Very little is known of the life of Agnellus, except that which he himself tells. He was born of a rich and noble family at Ravenna about the year 805, and early in life became a cleric at the cathedral. As he was outstanding among the priests of the cathedral both in knowledge and in eloquence, he states that he was practically forced to compose a history of the archbishops of Ravenna. The book was written in sections, and Agnellus was wont to read each section to his brethren of the clergy; he tells that they could hardly wait for him to finish a section. Throughout the work he constantly sought to uphold the liberty of the church of Ravenna over against the authority of the Holy See. The work was finished probably about the year 847. Cf. preface of O. Holder-Egger, *MGH*, *Scriptores Rerum Langobardicarum et Italicarum Saec. VI-IX* (Hannoverae: Impensis Bibliopolii Hahniani, 1878), pp. 267-272. Abbreviated hereafter *SS. Lang.* Cf. also, Bishop, *Liturgica Historica* (Oxford: At the Clarendon Press, 1918), pp. 370-383.

[43] *Liber Pontificalis Ecclesiae Ravennatis*, n. 40, in *Vita Johannis.*—*MGH*, *SS. Lang.* The editor (Holder-Egger) notes: "In hac Vita Agnellus duos episcopos eiusdem nominis confundit, quorum alterum Joannes II, 477-494, et alterum Joannes I tempore Valentiniani III, circa 418 et ante 440."—p. 298.

> Chrysologi sermone 175 Vicohaventinam (i.e., Ferrariensem) ecclesiam, cuius in charta mentio fit, Valentiniani III tempore sub potestatem metropolitanam Ravennatis episcopi reductam esse *decreto beati Petri* et *decreto principis christiani*, i.e., Valentiniani. . . . Ante tempora vero Valentiniani III de metropolitana potestate huius ecclesiae nihil constat.[44]

Kehr simply states that the concession is spurious, and that it belongs without doubt to the eighth century.[45]

Definite evidence that Ravenna enjoyed the status of a metropolitan see for the province of Aemilia toward the end of the fifth century, and that the Pope fearlessly called the metropolitan of Ravenna to task without any reference to the emperor or to imperial privileges, is found in a letter of Pope Simplicius, written in 482 to John II of Ravenna (477-494). After severely reprimanding John for ordaining a certain Gregory to the priesthood and for consecrating him a bishop against his (i.e., Gregory's) will, the Pope concludes: "Denuntiamus autem quod si posthac quidquam tale praesumpseris, et aliquem seu episcopum seu presbyterum seu diaconum invitum facere forte credideris, ordinationes tibi Ravennatis ecclesiae vel Aemiliensis noveris auferendas."[46]

After this letter of the Pope, there is no indication in the sources that the relations between Ravenna and Rome were not normal uutil the year 545. But then one finds in the *Liber Pontificalis Ecclesiae Ravennatis* the following account, which is used by some authors to prove the independent spirit of Ravenna and the emperor's right to grant the pallium:

---

[44] *MGH*, *SS. Lang.*, p. 304, note 12.

[45] Cf. *Italia Pontificia*, V, 15. Hinschius was of the opinion that this concession of Valentinian III was very doubtful; cf. *Kirchenrecht*, II, 4, n. 4; 25, n. 3. Schmidt likewise doubted the authenticity; cf. "Die Kirche von Ravenna im Frühmittelalter, 540-967," *Historisches Jahrbuch*, XXXIV (1913), 729. Vespasiani concluded that the concession was false; cf. *De Origine Pallii*, p. 20. A like conclusion was reached by Marriot, *Vestiarium Christianum*, p. 210ff.; Walter, "Ueber den Ursprung des erzbischöflichen Palliums," *AKK*, VI (1861), 215; Brandi, "Ravenna und Rom. Neue Beiträge zur Kenntnis der römisch-byzantinischen Urkunde," *Archiv für Urkundenforschung*, IX (1926), 15-21.

[46] Thiel, *Epistolae*, p. 201. Cf. JK, 583.

> Contigit eo tempore [545] ut moriretur Victor episcopus, huius civitatis Ravennae, et euntes cives Ravennatis sacerdotes cum universa plebe ad imperatorem, palleum postulantes ad electio. Post praecepit augustus petitoribus moras habere. Qui, excogitato consilio, iussit consecrari beatum Maximianum Polensem diaconum episcopum a Vigilio papa in civitate Patras apud Achaiam pridie Idus Octubris, ind. 10., quinquies p. c. Basilii iunioris, anno nativitatis suae 48, et dato pallio Ravennam misit.[47]

But it must be remembered that Pope Vigilius was removed from Rome in November of 545, at the order of Empress Theodora, and exiled in Sicily for over a year; he was subsequently taken to Constantinople, where he arrived in January of 547.[48] On his journey thither, Vigilius consecrated Maximian at Patras in October, 546.[49] While the Pope was thus absent from Rome, in exile because of the empress and also because of his refusal to sign Justinian's edict of 543, it is not surprising that the clergy of Ravenna should go to the emperor for permission to elect a new bishop. It is in the light of these facts that the above-quoted account of Agnellus must be considered: if the Pope had been exercising his functions in the normal way at Rome, it is unlikely that an appeal would have been made to the emperor at this time, though such an appeal was made about a century later. This consclusion is borne out by the fact that Pope John III (561-574) granted the pallium "as his predecessors had done" to Bishop Peter of Ravenna (569-578).[50]

---

[47] Agnellus in "Vita de Sancto Maximiano"—*MGH, SS. Lang.*, n. 70, p. 326.

[48] Full details are given in Dudden, *Gregory the Great*, I, 63-65; 200-205; cf. also Batiffol, *Cathedra Petri, Études d'histoire ancienne de l'église* (Paris: Les éditions du Cerf, 1938), p. 293.

[49] Cf. Hartmann, *Geschichte Italiens*, I, 390. Of Agnellus' work the author states that he composed in the ninth century "aus Wahrheit, Dichtung und Missverständnis die Biographien der Bischöfe seiner Vaterstadt." —I, 391.

[50] The letter granting the pallium is quoted fully *infra*, p. 116. Cf. Ewald, "Studien zur Ausgabe des Registers Gregors I.," *Neues Archiv*, III (1878), 601ff.

About twenty years later there took place the controversy between Pope Gregory and John of Ravenna regarding the use of the pallium. At the time of Gregory's election to the papacy, John had ruled the see of Ravenna for over a decade, having succeeded Bishop Peter in 578. The two men were close friends, as is evident fron the fact that Gregory sent to Bishop[51] John a copy of his *Regula Pastoralis* a few months after his elevation to the papacy.[52] That friendship, however, was strained two years later because of a dispute over the use of the pallium by Bishop John.

There appears to be no record as to the conferring of the pallium upon Bishop John by a previous Pope. Dudden is of the opinion that the bishop of Ravenna probably wore it by right: "In the sixth century in the East, it was worn indiscriminately by all bishops; in the West it was worn of right by only three, namely, the bishop of Rome, the bishop of Ostia as the usual consecrator of the Pope, and (it seems probable) by the bishop of Ravenna."[53] Since Pope John III conferred it upon Bishop Peter of Ravenna "as his predecessors had done," and since Gregory himself conferred the pallium upon John's successor in the see of Ravenna, Marinianus, in August of 596,[54] one must conclude that Bishop John had no special right to the honor of the pallium except that his predecessors had been granted it by the Pope.

Though not all of the documents concerning this controversy have been preserved, it is possible to reconstruct the whole story from the extant letters. "The order of the letters

---

[51] "The bishops of Ravenna are not called 'archbishops' in Gregory's letters, nor in the Roman Synod, a. 649. The title first appears in a document of the year 666 (*MGH, Script. Rer. Langobard.*, p. 350)."—Dudden, *Gregory the Great*, I, 434, note 3. It has been noted above, however, that the bishop of Ravenna was a metropolitan since the fifth century. Cf. *supra*, p. 110ff.

[52] Cf. *Ep.* i, 24a. Caspar considers it certain that Gregory dedicated the *Regula Pastoralis* to John of Constantinople and not, as Ewald (following Paul and John the Deacons) holds, to John of Ravenna. Cf. *Geschichte des Papsttums*, II, 366, note 2. Caspar's opinion is based on the statement of Isidore of Seville's *De viris illustribus*.

[53] *Gregory the Great*, I, 435.

[54] Cf. *Ep.* v, 61.

of Gregory and John concerning this matter, as is apparent from the words which follow and from *Epp.* iii, 66. 67, is this: Gregory first heard of John's acts from certain persons of Ravenna; he then gave, as we believe, an oral precept to John through Castorius, to whom Gregory addressed *Ep.* ix, 167: *Castorio Notario Nostro Ravennae*; there followed a letter of John of Ravenna, which is lost, but there was attached to it a privilege of Pope John III, which we will give as *Ep.* iii, 67; Gregory responded to John in the third paragraph of *Ep.* iii, 54; John replied to this letter in *Ep.* iii, 66."[55]

The first extant document, then, is the privilege granted by Pope John III (561-574) to Bishop Peter of Ravenna (569-578), preserved as *Ep.* iii, 67:

> Dilectissimo fratri Petro Johannes. Convenire novimus rationi, ut eos amictu pallii decoremus, quos in illis civitatibus divina inspirante misericordia sacerdotii honor inluminat, in quibus hoc etiam illis qui praeteritis temporibus fuere pontifices ab apostolica sede esse constat indultum. Ideoque caritati tuae usum pallii sicut decessores tui habuisse noscuntur praesenti auctoritate concedimus, atque ea omnia circa honoris tui privilegium volumus permanere, quae anterioribus temporibus ecclesiae tuae constat esse servatum, ut nihil prorsus de privilegiis eius doleas deminutum.[56]

In his reply to Bishop John of Ravenna, Gregory is careful not to act contrary to the privileges granted by his predecessors; it is his contention that Bishop John has, in his use of the pallium, gone beyond the limits granted his church by a former Pope. After chiding John rather gently for his unwillingness to receive humbly the Pope's first admonition (which, as noted above, is not extant), Gregory goes on to say:

> Mota autem nimis vestra fraternitas atque cum tumore cordis quasi satisfaciens, scripsit nobis, pallio te non nisi

[55] Ewald in note 2 ad *Ep.* iii, 54.

[56] Note the claim that Pope John makes that it was the Pope who had granted the pallium to the bishops of Ravenna, and that there is no reference to any imperial privilege.

post dimissos de secretario filios ecclesiae[67] et missarum tempore in laetaniis uti sollemnibus. Verbis aliquid te usurpasse contra generalis ecclesiae consuetudinem apertissima veritate professus es. Quomodo enim fieri potest, ut illud cineris atque cilicii tempore per plateas inter populorum strepitus agas licite, quod te agere in conventu pauperum, nobilium, et in secretario ecclesiae velut inlicitum excusasti? Illud tamen frater karissime tibi non putamus ignotum, quod prope de nullo metropolita in quibuslibet mundi partibus sit auditum, extra missarum tempus usum sibi pallii vendicasse. Et quod bene hanc consuetudinem generalis ecclesiae noveritis, vestris nobis manifestissime significastis epistolis, quibus praeceptum beatae memoriae decessoris nostri Johannis papae nobis in subditis transmisistis adnexum, continentem omnes consuetudines ex privilegio decessorum nostrorum concessas vobis ecclesiaeque vestrae debere servari. Confitemini igitur aliam esse generalis ecclesiae consuetudinem, postquam ea quae vos geritis, vobis ex privilegio vendicatis. Nulla ergo nobis in hac re ut arbitramur poterit remanere dubietas. Aut enim mos omnium metropolitarum etiam a tua est fraternitate servandus, aut si tuae ecclesiae aliquid specialiter dicis esse concessum, praeceptum a prioribus Romanae urbis pontificibus, quod

---

[67] "Secretarium ecclesiae—sacristy." —O'Donnell, *Vocabulary*, p. 26. In his descripion of the early church buildings, Eisenhofer states that two rooms were built at the eastern end of the church, in which were kept the sacred vessels and the necessary liturgical books, and in which the clergy later donned their vestments. Paulinus of Nola (†431) calls these rooms *secretaria*; later the terms *secretarium*, *sacrarium*, and *salutatorium* were used; still later the term *sacristia* also came into use. Cf. *Handbuch*, I, 355; also, Duchesne, *Origines*, pp. 172, 381.

Who are the "filii ecclesiae" who are dismissed? Garnier believed that they could have been: a) laymen of noble rank who came to pay their respects to the bishop before Mass; b) the clergy of the city not acting as ministers of the Mass; c) the *schola cantorum* which, after arranging the chants for the day, left the *secretarium* at a given signal and then proceeded to the altar before the bishop. He himself preferred the last-mentioned theory. Cf. Garnier, *De Usu Pallii*, p. 360; also Cabrol, *The Mass of the Western Rites* (Translated by C. M. Anthony, St. Louis: B. Herder Book Company, 1934), p. 227.

haec Ravennati ecclesiae sunt concessa, a vobis oportet ostendi. Quod si hoc non ostenditur, restat postquam talia agere neque consuetudine generali neque privilegio vendicas, ut usurpasse te comprobes quod fecisti....

Se ne forte putes, quia nos haec vobis scribentes quae pro fraterna sunt caritate neglesimus, scitote in nostro scrinio de privilegiis ecclesiae tuae subtiliter perquisitum. Et quidem quaedam inventa sunt, quae omnino possint fraternitatis tuae intentionibus obviare, nihil autem in quo de huiusmodi capitulis pars vestrae possit ecclesiae roborari....Ut enim ea quae superius dixi breviter colligam ammoneo, quatenus nisi decessorum meorum munificentia tibi haec per privilegium adtributa docueris, uti in plateis pallio ulterius non praesumas, ne non habere et ad missas incipias, quod audacter et in plateis usurpas. De secretario autem quod fraternitas tua resedisse cum pallio et filios ecclesiae suscepisse et fecit et excusavit, nunc interim nihil querimur, quia synodorum sententiam sequentes, minores culpas quae negantur ulcisci recusamus...[58]

Fortunately, Bishop John's answer to this letter is preserved. After stating that he received the Pope's letter "in which honey and stings were mingled," he continues:

Commemorastis igitur, quod ego novitatis ambitione pallii usum supra quam antecessoribus meis indultum fuerat usurpassem. Quam rem proprii domni mei conscientia, quae divina dextera regitur, nullo modo credere patiatur, nec opinionis incerto aures sacratissimas aperire....Et quibus excessibus ego sanctissimae illi sedi, quae universali ecclesiae iura sua transmittit, praesumpserim obviare, propter cuius conservandam auctoritatem, sicut Deo manifestum est, multorum contra me inimicorum graviter excitavi? Sed beatissimus domnus meus nihil me contra priscam consuetudinem estimet attemptasse, quod et a multis et prope ab omnibus civibus huius urbis, etiam inter gesta si adquievisset suprascriptus reverentissimus notarius, potuerat attestari; quo-

[58] *Ep.* iii, 54—July, 593.

niam iam de secretario descendentibus filiis ecclesiae et ingredientibus diaconibus ut mox procedatur, tunc primus diaconus espiscopo Ravennatis ecclesiae pallium consuevit induere; quod et in letaniis sollemnibus uti pariter consuevit....Nunc vero in Dei et in vestra est potestate quicquid veritate cognita fieri iusseritis, quoniam ego iussionibus apostolatus domni mei parere desiderans, quamvis antiqua consuetudo optinuit, usque ad secundam iussionem abstinere curavi.[59]

For a year there is silence; then in rapid succession Gregory wrote two letters[60] from which one can gather that the mild tone adopted by John in the letter quoted above was very misleading. For he continued his old usages, spoke disrespectfully of the Pope, and had others, even government officials, write to the Pope in his behalf. In his next letter, the Pope tells him that he has learned from Adeodatus, a former deacon of the church of Ravenna, that the bishops of that city only wore the pallium in the litanies on the feasts of St. John the Baptist, St. Peter the Apostle, and St. Apollinaris, patron of the church of Ravenna:

Cui quidem nequaquam credere debuimus, quia multi apud civitatem fraternitatis vestrae responsales saepius fuerunt, qui se fatentur tale aliquid numquam fuisse. Et hac de re multis potius credendum est quam uni pro sua ecclesia aliquid attestanti. Sed quia nos fraternitatem vestram contristari nolumus et petitionem filiorum nostrorum apud nos minime frustrari, usum pallii, donec suptilius veriusque aliquid cognoscamus, in letaniis sollemnibus, id est die natalicio beati Ioannis baptistae, beati Petri apostoli et beati Apollinaris martyris atque in ordinationis vestrae celebratione concedimus. In secretario vero secundum morem pristinum susceptis ac dimissis ecclesiae filiis induere vestra fraternitas pallium debeat atque ad missarum sollemnia ita proficisci et nihil sibi amplius ausu temerariae praesumptionis

[59] *Ep.* iii, 66. "Of uncertain date, but after July, 593."—Ewald, note ad *Ep.* iii, 66.

[60] *Epp.* v, 11. 15—Oct. and Nov., 594.

arrogare, ne dum in exteriori habitu inordinate aliquid arripitur, ordinare etiam quae licere poterant amittantur.[61]

A month later the Pope wrote another letter to John, a severe indictment of the latter's duplicity in that he wrote letters redolent of humility and willingness to obey, while in reality he continued his former practices and even ridiculed the Pope openly:

Primum me hoc contristat, quia mihi fraternitas tua duplici corde scribit et alia blandimenta in epistolis suis exhibet, alia in lingua sua saeculariter ostendit.... Ultimum vero est, quod tamen pondere elationis primum, quia de usu pallii extra ecclesiam, quod temporibus decessorum meorum facere numquam praesumpsit, numquam a decessoribus eius praesumptum est, sicut responsales nostri testantur, excepto si reliquiae conderentur,[62] quod tamen de reliquiis, unus tantummodo potuit inveniri, qui diceret—meis diebus in despectu meo cum summa audacia non solum faciebat, sed etiam frequentabat.... Et quidem ago omnipotenti Deo gratias, quia eo tempore quo ad me hoc pervenit, quod ad aures decessorum meorum numquam pervenerat, Langobardi inter me et Ravennatem civitatem positi fuerunt. Nam ostendere forsitan hominibus habui, quantum scio esse districtus.

Ne autem credas, quia ego ecclesiam tuam in aliquo gravari aut minui volo, recordare in missarum Romanarum sollemnibus, ubi Ravennas diaconus stabat, et require ubi hodie stat, et cognoscis quia Ravennatem ecclesiam honorare desidero. Sed ut quicumque quodlibet ex superbia arripiat, hoc ego tolerare non possum. Tamen hac de re iam diacono Constantinopolim scripsi ut per omnes, qui sub se etiam tricenos et quadragenos episcopos habent, requirere debeat. Et sicubi iste usus

---

[61] *Ep.* v, 11—Oct., 594.

[62] "*Excepto si reliquiae conderentur*, non nisi hoc loco occurrit."—Hartmann, note 1 ad *Ep.* v, 15.

est, ut in letaniis cum palliis ambulent, absit ut per me honor Ravennatis ecclesiae in aliquo inminui videatur.[63]

Gregory himself had been *apocrisiarius* at Constantinople from about 579 to 586. If the patriarch there had worn the pallium during litanies, Gregory would certainly have known of the custom, and he would not have had to ascertain if in *any* place such a custom existed. If it was so worn elsewhere, the Pope was prepared to allow Ravenna to keep the custom it claimed to have. As Ravenna was the home of the exarch, many of whose assistants must also have come from the East, Gregory may have had in mind to conform the use of the pallium at Ravenna to Eastern usage. From this inquiry, Thomassinus concludes that the usage in the East and the West at the time of Gregory must have been similar.[64] It has been noted above, however, that there is no definite knowledge that the Eastern bishops wore the omophorion outside of their churches. All one can say with assurance is that Gregory himself felt that the pallium should be used only in church and only during Mass, and that Ravenna had "proudly arrogated to herself certain privileges." Yet he wanted to be just, being prepared to allow Ravenna to continue its practices if a privilege to that effect could be shown, or if a precedent existed in the East.

The above-quoted letter closes with an eloquent appeal to Bishop John to reform his life and to eschew all duplicity, being mindful of the report he will one day have to make to his Judge. One may hope that this exhortation was not disregarded, for soon thereafter this very accounting was demanded of him—death overtook John of Ravenna on January 11, 595.[65]

After a lapse of six months, during which time Bishop Severus of Cervia ruled the church of Ravenna as visitor,[66] Marinianus, a former monk of St. Andrew's monastery in Rome, and formerly a fellow-monk of Gregory himself, was

---

[63] *Ep.* v, 15—Nov., 594.
[64] *Vetus et Nova Ecclesiae Disciplina*, Pars I, Lib. II, cap. 53.
[65] Hartmann, note 1 ad *Ep.* v, 21.
[66] Cf. *Ep.* v, 21—Feb., 595.

persuaded to accept the burden of the episcopacy at Ravenna; his first episcopal act was to sign the decrees of the Roman Synod of July 5, 595.[67] Apparently without any special request on the part of Marinianus, the Pope wrote to him in August of the same year:

> Apostolicae sedis benivolentia et antiquae consuetudinis ordine provocati fraternitati tuae, quam in Ravennati ecclesiae gubernationis suscepisse constat officium, pallii usum praevidimus concedendum. Quo non aliter uti memineris, nisi in propria tuae civitatis dimissis iam filiis ecclesiae, procedens a salutatorio[68] ad sacra missarum sollemnia celebranda; peractis vero missis id in salutatorio rursum curabis deponere. Extra ecclesiam vero non amplius illo tibi nisi quater in anno in letaniis quas ad decessorem tuum Iohannem expressimus uti permittimus....Omnia enim privilegia, quae tuae pridem concessa esse constat ecclesiae, nostra acutoritate firmamus et inlibata decernimus permanere.[69]

The new bishop seemed to be more amenable to the wishes of the Pope, for one nowhere reads that he disobeyed him. Yet he and other citizens of Ravenna, both ecclesiastical and lay, continued to beseech the Pope to restore what they claimed to be the ancient rights of the church of Ravenna. Two extant letters of Gregory to Castorius, the papal *apocrisiarius* at Ravenna, bid him find out from trustworthy persons under oath the exact custom in regard to the use of the pallium in litanies, for a certain Andrew claimed that former bishops used the pallium in all solemn litanies, which occurred almost daily.[70]

---

[67] Cf. *Ep.* v, 51; note 5, *ibid.*

[68] *"Salutatorium"*—audience chamber. Cf. O'Donnell, *Vocabulary*, p. 26. The writer, however, prefers to agree with Hartmann, who thinks that Gregory is here using a synonym for "*secretarium*," which he used in *Epp.* iii, 54 and v, 11. Cf. note 2 ad *Ep.* v, 61 and *supra*, page 117, note 57.

[69] *Ep.* v, 61. This letter follows very closely, except that the central portion is special for the church of Ravenna, the form which Gregory used for granting the pallium to the bishops of Sicily. Cf. *infra*, page 134.

[70] Cf. *Epp.* vi, 31—April, 596; ix, 167—June, 599.

With these two letters, the controversy comes to a close, or better, there is no further reference to it in the time of Gregory. But from the letters which are extant it is evident that, despite Ravenna's claim of special privileges, the Pope felt it was his right to confer the pallium upon the bishop of Ravenna, to see that it was used only at Mass and in the church or, by a special grant of the Pope, outside the church only during the more solemn litanies which the Pope specified.[71]

The history of the subsequent struggle between Rome and Ravenna after the time of Gregory the Great may be summarized as follows: Agnellus tells us that Bishop Maurus (642-671) "multis vicibus Constantinopolim attigit, ut ecclesiam suam ab iugo vel conditione Romanorum everteret." He adds that the bishop obtained his desire, quoting a section of the privileges obtained from Constans II in 666, who granted to Ravenna an autocephalous status.[72] At Maurus' death, his successor Reparatus (671-677) was consecrated at Ravenna by his own suffragans, and received the pallium from the emperor. The next bishop, Theodore (677-691), though consecrated at Ravenna, went to Rome for the Synod of 680 and "subjugavit se suamque ecclesiam sub Romano

[71] It may be noted here that Pope Honorius I (625-638) decreed that those metropolitans who wore the pallium in the streets or in litanies were to be deprived of its use. Cf. JE, 2030.

[72] *Liber Pontificalis Ecclesiae Ravennatis*, n. 110, *MGH*, *SS. Lang.*, p. 350f. "Privilegium Constantini, Eraclii imperatorum ad Maurum archiepiscopum Ravennatem...per presentem nostram piam iussionem SANCIMUS amplius securam atque liberam a omni superiori episcopali conditione manere et solum orationi vacare pro nostro exorando imperio et non subiacere pro quolibet modo patriarche antique urbis Rome, sed manere eam autocephalon et sanctam eius apostolicam ecclesiam cum omnibus sibi pertinentibus per diocesim et parochiis ordinatoribus...qui et a propriis consecratus episcopis, utens videlicet et decore palei, sicut nostre divinitatis sanctione superna inspiratione perlargitum est."—Quoted by Holder-Egger in note 7, p. 350, *MGH*, *SS. Lang.* The concession is recognized as genuine. Holder-Egger also notes that Bishop Maurus was on good terms with Rome in the early years of his episcopacy; though he himself could not attend the Roman synod of 649, he sent a very submissive excuse to the Pope and authorized delegates to represent him. Cf. *ibid.*, p. 349, note 4. Cf. also Gottlob, *Amtseid*, p. 21ff.

pontifice."[73] Damian, who ruled from 692-708 as successor of Theodore at Ravenna, was consecrated at Rome.[74]

From this brief account, it is evident that Rome did not recognize the emperor's right to approve the election at Ravenna or to grant the use of the pallium. That both Bishop Maurus and Emperor Constans II acted contrary to custom was admitted by later bishops of Ravenna when they again submitted to Rome. In the opinion of the writer, Maurus' reception of the pallium in no wise proves that its use was originally granted as an imperial privilege, as Duchesne would have it.[75] On the contrary, the entire controversy proves that this grant was an exceptional act on the part of the emperor, repudiated by the Pope, by later bishops of Ravenna, and by a later emperor. There is no reference whatsoever to an early grant of any privileges by Valentinian III. It is not surprising that Ravenna, as a metropolitan see and as the residence of the exarch, chafed at its status as a suffragan of Rome. Neither of the other two metropolitans in northern Italy were consecrated at Rome or obliged to attend the Roman Synods.[76] Why Ravenna was held to a more subordinate position is not known. It may be conjectured that the Popes, having

[73] Agnellus, *ibid.*, n. 115, p. 353f.; n. 117, p. 355; n. 124, p. 360. Cf. *Liber Pontificalis*, I, 348, where it is stated that Ravenna returned to submission under Pope Donus (676-678). A longer account of this submission to Rome is given in the life of Pope Leo II (682-683): "Huius temporibus percurrente *divale iussione* clementissimi principis restituta est ecclesia Ravennas sub ordinatione sedis apostolicae, ut defuncto archiepiscopo, qui electus fuerit, *iuxta antiquam consuetudinem* in civitate Romana veniat ordinandus. Hic fecit constitutum, qui archivo ecclesiae continetur, ut qui ordinatus fuerit archiepiscopus *nulla consuetudine pro usu pallii* aut diversis officiis ecclesiae persolvere debeat; sed nec Mauri quondam episcopi anniversitas aut agenda celebretur. Sed et typum autocephaliae quod sibi elicuerant, ad amputanda scandala sedis apostolice restituerunt."—*Liber Pontificalis*, I, 360. The italics are inserted by the writer.

[74] Agnellus, *ibid.*, n. 125, p. 360. Express mention of this consecration at Rome is made in the *Liber Pontificalis* in the *Vita* of Pope Sergius (687-701)—I, 376.

[75] *Origines*, p. 405.

[76] Pelagius I, between 558 and 560, granted the metropolitan of Milan the right to consecrate the newly-elected metropolitan of Aquileia, and vice versa. Cf. JK, 983.

had experience with the claims of Constantinople after it became the imperial residence, thought it wisest to keep Ravenna in a subordinate position from the first, though granting it the status of a metropolitan. Before the controversy over the pallium began, Gregory himself gave John of Ravenna a certain control over some of Rome's more distant suffragans who found it difficult to come to Rome.[77] Nevertheless, he kept close watch over Ravenna, and sought to stop all unlawful customs, as the controversy over the pallium has shown.

2. LETTERS GRANTING THE PALLIUM TO VARIOUS BISHOPS

Another group of letters was sent to the Bishop of Salona in Dalmatia.[78] The first three letters concern Bishop Natalis. The first is addressed to him personally, and rebukes him severely for having advanced his archdeacon Honoratus against his will to the priesthood, thus removing him from his position. The Pope orders Bishop Natalis to restore Honoratus to the position of archdeacon. "If you delay to do so, know that the use of the pallium, granted you by this see, is taken from you. And if after you have lost the use of the pallium you still persist in your pertinacity, know that you are deprived of the participation in the Body and Blood of the Lord."[79]

The second letter is addressed to all the bishops of Dalmatia. To them the Pope tells the story of Bishop Natalis and his archdeacon, and informs them of the penalties he threatened if the bishop did not amend. The third letter is addressed to Antoninus, subdeacon and rector of the patrimony in Dalmatia; again the story of the bishop is repeated, but here the Pope bids Antoninus to encourage the bishop to reform. If he should refuse, Antoninus is granted authority from the Apostolic See to inflict the penalties of deprivation of the pallium and even of excommunication.[80] One may presume

[77] Cf. *Ep.*, ii, 28; *supra*, p. 30, note 27.

[78] *Epp.* ii, 20. 21. 22; viii, 36. ix, 176. 234.

[79] *Ep.* ii, 20—March, 592.

[80] Cf. *Epp.* ii, 21. 22.

that these penalties were not inflicted, for in a letter to Bishop John of Ravenna the Pope tells him of his joy over Natalis' amendment;[81] a month later the Pope wrote to Bishop Natalis himself and promised that he would adjudicate the case between him and his archdeacon.[82]

The next three letters of this group[83] deal with the use of the pallium by Bishop Maximus of Salona, successor of Bishop Natalis, who died early in the year 593, for in March of that year the Pope wrote to Antoninus, rector of the patrimony in Dalmatia, to encourage the clergy and people to elect his successor.[84] It is not necessary to repeat here the whole story of the dispute regarding the election of Maximus. Suffice it to say that after six years of controversy, he was recognized by the Pope as Bishop. In his letter of July, 599,[85] Pope Gregory tells Maximus of his joy in receiving him back into communion with the Apostolic See upon his doing of penance; he bids him to "send someone to Rome who may, according to custom, receive the pallium for you." A month later, after he had been informed that Maximus had performed his penance, the Pope wrote directly to the Bishop:

> ...Itaque pallium ad sacra missarum sollemnia utendum ex more transmisimus, cuius vos volumus per omnia genium vindicare. Huius enim indumenti honor humilitas atque iustitia est. Tota ergo mente fraternitas vestra se exhibere festinet in prosperis humilem et in adversis, si quando eveniunt, cum iustitia erectam, amicam bonis, perversis contrariam. Nullius umquam faciem contra veritatem recipiens, nullius umquam faciem pro veritate loquentem premens, misericordiae operibus iuxta virtutem substantiae insistens et tamen insistere etiam

[81] Cf. *Ep.* ii, 45—July, 592.

[82] Cf. *Ep.* ii, 50—Aug., 592.

[83] *Epp.* viii, 36; ix, 176. 234—the former is not dated; the latter two were written in July and August of 599 respectively.

[84] *Ep.* iii, 22—March, 593. The election of Maximus is treated *supra*, pp. 49ff.

[85] *Ep.* ix, 176. Note that this letter was not sent directly to Maximus, but was to be given him after he had completed his penance. Cf. *Ep.* ix, 178.

contra virtutem cupiens, infirmis compatiens, benevolentibus congaudens, aliena damna propria deputans, de alienis gaudiis tamquam de propriis exultans, in corrigendis vitiis saeviens, in fovendis virtutibus auditorum animum demulcens, in ira iudicium sine ira tenens, in tranquillitate autem severitatis suae censuram non deserens; haec est, frater carissime, pallii accepti ratio; quam si sollicite servaveris, quod foris accepisse ostenderis, intus habes. . . .[86]

In this group of letters one notes that Pope Gregory threatened to revoke the grant of the pallium as a penance, that it is conceded to a metropolitan after he has been told to ask for it, and that it was to be used only during Mass. Only to Bishop Maximus does Gregory explain in such detail the virtues that are to adorn him who wears the pallium, though in the other concessions of the pallium Gregory as a rule stresses the fact that the pallium as an outer garment is to signify inner virtue.

The metropolitan John of Corinth requested the pallium from the Pope shortly after his installation in his see.[87] After bidding him to correct the evils of his predecessor and to temper severity with kindness, the Pope granted his request: "We have sent you the pallium, according to the request contained in your letter which I received through our brother and co-Bishop Andrew. You are to use it as your predecessors did in accord with the definite concessions of our predecessors." After exhorting the bishop to stamp out the heresy of simony, Gregory continued: "Your fraternity is aware that formerly the pallium was not given except for a price. But since this was very incongruous, we strictly forbade, in a synod held before the body of blessed Peter the Apostle, that anything be received for the pallium or for or-

---

[86] *Ep.* ix, 234—Aug., 599. Cf. also *Ep.* viii, 36: ". . .direxit pallium ad confirmationem eiusdem episcopi."

[87] Pope Gregory announced his elevation to the papacy to *Archbishop* Anastasius of Corinth in February, 591—*Ep.* i, 26. In *Ep.* v, 57, of July, 595, Gregory wrote to *Bishop* John of Corinth to tell him he was pleased at the masterful way in which a certain Bishop Secundinus conducted the trial of Archbishop Anastasius and deposed him.

dination..."[88] Apparently the bishops of John's province also requested the Pope to confer on him the pallium, for the next letter is written to all the bishops of the province of Helladia. Gregory recalls to their minds the case of Archbishop Anastasius, and prays that they will learn a lesson from his fall. Then he adds: "Besides, having received your letter through our brother and co-Bishop Andrew, be it known to you that we have sent the pallium to our brother, Bishop John of Corinth, whom you are to obey, since this is in accord with ancient custom and since his virtues invite your obedience...."[89]

It was seen above that several Bishops of Arles were made papal vicars, and were granted the use of the pallium.[90] Gregory followed the example of his predecessors, as is evident from the letters that concern the granting of the pallium to Vergil of Arles.[91] The first letter is addressed to Vergil, bishop of Arles. It thanks him for his letters to the Pope:

> Quod vero in eis epistolis iuxta antiquum morem usum pallii ac vices sedis apostolicae postulasti, absit, ne aut transitoriae potestatis culmen aut exterioris cultus ornamentum in vicibus nostris ac pallio quaesisse te suspicer. Sed quia cunctis liquet, unde in Galliarum regionibus fides sancta prodierit, cum priscam consuetudinem sedis apostolicae vestra fraternitas repetit, quid aliud quam bona suboles ad sinum matris recurrit? Libenti ergo animo postulata concedimus, ne aut vobis quicquam de debito honore subtrahere aut praecellentissimi filii nostri Childeberti regis petitionem contempsisse videamur.[92]

The second letter is addressed to King Childebert:

> ...Gratanter quae scripsistis accepimus et quae voluistis animo libenti concessimus; atque ideo fratri nostro Vergilio Arelatensis civitatis episcopo vices no-

[88] *Ep.* v, 62—Aug., 595. The reference is to the Roman Synod of July, 595, the acts of which are given as *Ep.* v, 57a.

[89] *Ep.* v, 63—Aug., 595.

[90] Cf. *supra*, p. 56.

[91] Cf. *Epp.* v, 58. 60; xi, 56a.

[92] *Ep.* v, 58.

stras iuxta antiquum morem et excellentiae vestrae desiderium Deo favente commisimus; cui etiam et pallii usum, sicut prisca habuit consuetudo, concessimus.[93]

Gregory clearly states that he made Vergil his vicar at the king's request, but that he himself conceded the pallium. Pelagius I (556-561) had spoken similarly to King Childebert regarding Sapaudus of Arles:

> Vices autem nostras praefato consacerdoti nostro Sapaudo secundum petitionem vestram direximus, usum pallii pariter concedentes; quia in scrinio ecclesiastico huiusmodi exempla repperimus, quibus ostenditur Arelatensibus episcopis a sanctae recordationis nostris haec fuisse conlata.[94]

A further reference to Gregory's concession of the pallium to his vicar at Arles is contained in the famous *Responsa* of Pope Gregory to Augustine of Canterbury.[95] When Augustine put the question, "How are we to deal with the bishops of Gaul and Britain?" he received this reply: "We gave you no authority over the bishops of Gaul, for from *ancient* times the bishops of Arles received the pallium from *our predecessors*; we ought by no means to deprive him of the authority he has received."[96]

Further light is thrown upon the use of the pallium in the group of letters dealing with the concession of it to the bishop of Autun.[97] The first letter of this series is written to Queen Brunichild. After praising her for her love and solicitude for the bishops and for her fear of God,[98] Gregory added:

> Susceptis itaque epistolis vestris, valde nobis excellentiae vestrae studium placuisse signamus atque fratri et coepiscopo nostro Syragio pallium dirigere secundum po-

[93] *Ep*. v, 60.

[94] JK, 945; *MGH*, *Epp*. iii, p. 75.

[95] Regarding the authenticity of these *Responsa*, cf. *supra*, p. 61, note 158.

[96] *Ep*. xi, 56a, n. vii. Italics inserted by the writer.

[97] Cf. *Epp*. viii, 4; ix, 213. 219. 222.

[98] For an explanation of Gregory's praise of this woman whose history is notorious, cf. Dudden, *Gregory the Great*, II, 70-72.

> stulationem vestram voluimus. Propter quod et serenissimi domni imperatoris, quantum nobis diaconus noster, qui apud eum responsa ecclesiae faciebat, innotuit, prona voluntas est et concedi hoc omnino desiderat,[99] atque multa de praedicto fratre nostro tam vobis, quam etiam aliis testificantibus ad nos bona perlata sunt. . . Sed res plurimae restiterunt, quae nos hoc interim facere minime permiserunt. Primum siquidem, quia is qui pallium ipsum venerat accepturus scismaticorum errore tenetur implicitus. Deinde quod non id ex vestra petitione, sed ex nobis transmissum voluistis intellegi. Extra hoc autem quia nec is qui eo uti desiderat directa ad nos hoc sibi largiri speciali petitione poposcerat et tantam causam nullo modo praebere sine eius postulatione debuimus, maxime quia et prisca consuetudo optinuit, ut honor pallii nisi exigentibus causarum meritis et fortiter postulanti dari non debeat. Nos tamen, ne vestrae excellentiae desiderium sub praetextu cuiusdam excusationis forsitan videremur velle differre, dilectissimo filio nostro Candido presbytero[100] pallium praevidimus dirigendum iniungentes ei, ut vice nostra congrua id debeat observatione tribuere. Unde necesse est, ut ex opere suprascriptus frater et co-episcopus noster Syagrius facta cum aliquantis suis episcopis[101] petitione hoc sperare atque eam praedicto debeat dare presbytero, quatenus digne eiusdem pallii usum cum Dei gratia valeat adipisci.[102]

A year and a half later the Pope, in a letter dealing with a synod that he has ordered to be called in Gaul, wrote to

---

[99] This reference to the emperor is considered *supra*, p. 102f.

[100] Rector of the Church's patrimony in Gaul. Cf. *Ep.* vi, 6.

[101] The words in themselves could be taken to indicate that the bishop of Autun was a metropolitan. But authors maintain that he was a simple bishop, which opinion is confirmed by the fact that Gregory gave the church of Autun a rank second to that of its metropolitan, the church of Lyons. Cf. *Ep.* ix, 222. But Bishop Syagrius was specially delegated by the Pope ("specialiter delegare curavimus"—*Ep.* ix, 213) to preside at a synod in Gaul to uproot simony and other evils. Cf. *Epp.* ix, 218. 219. 222.

[102] *Ep.* viii, 4.

Bishop Aregius of Gap: "We wish you to be present in the synod, which we have ordered to be called by Bishop Syagrius against simony, and to give to him the pallium we have sent, if he first promises to remove, through decrees of the synod, the evils from the Church."[103] Finally the Pope wrote to Bishop Syagrius directly, praising him for his works of charity and for his assistance to Augustine on his mission to England:

> Proinde secundum postulationis tuae desiderium pallii te usu, quod intra ecclesiam tuam habere debeas, ad sacra tantum missarum sollemnia celebranda Deo auctore praevidimus honorandum. Quod tamen ita tibi dandum esse decrevimus si prius per synodi definitionem emendari promiseris quae corrigenda mandavimus.... Cuius ne indumenti munificentiam nudam videamur quodam modo contulisse, hoc etiam pariter prospeximus concedendum, ut metropolis suo per omnia loco et honore servato ecclesia civitatis Augustodunis, cui omnipotens Deus praeesse te voluit, post Lugdunensem ecclesiam esse debeat et hunc sibi locum ac ordinem ex nostra auctoritatis indulgentia vindicare.[104]

Despite the foregoing clear enunciation of the custom that the pallium is to be asked for by the bishop himself, Gregory at various times dispensed with this rule. A noteworthy occasion was the granting of the pallium to Bishop John of Prima Justiniana, to whom as papal vicar it was granted by the Pope at the request of all the bishops of Illyricum when he confirmed the election and consecration of Bishop John: "....Proinde iuxta postulationis vestrae desiderium praedictum fratrem et coepiscopum nostrum in eo quo est sacerdotii ordine constitutus nostri assensus auctori-

[103] *Ep.* ix, 219—July, 599.

[104] *Ep.* ix, 222—July, 599. In this letter the Pope says nothing about a request of the emperor before the pallium was granted. Bishop Syagrius of Autun (561-600) was the first suffragan outside of the metropolitan rule of the Pope to receive the pallium.

tate firmamus ratamque nos eius consecrationem habere dirigentes pallium indicamus."[105]

The case of Andrew, metropolitan of Nicopolis in Epirus Vetus, is very similar to the preceding. For here also the Pope was advised of the election and consecration of Andrew by his suffragans only after those events had taken place. From the following words of Gregory's letter to the suffragan bishops of Nicopolis thanking them for the above-stated information, one may conjecture that they had requested the Pope to send Bishop Andrew the pallium: "Be it known to you that we have sent the pallium to our brother and co-Bishop Andrew, and that we have conceded all the privileges that our predecessors granted to his predecessors."[106]

Though it is not known definitely that Constantius of Milan requested the pallium, one may suppose that he did so in a letter sent to the Pope. In reply Gregory announced the grant of the pallium, after encouraging him to be a true shepherd of souls: "According to custom we have sent you the pallium for use at Mass only."[107]

A case exactly parallel to the one just described is that of Bishop Leander of Seville (584-601), since the Pope replied to a letter received from Leander, and sent him the pallium without any specific reference to a request for it. To King Reccared (586-601) Gregory simply announced, among other

---

[105] *Ep.* v, 10—Oct., 594. Cf. also *Ep.* v, 16. Thomassinus (1619-1695) offers the opinion that, since Bishop John's election and consecration were confirmed through the reception of the pallium, this is the first in a series of events leading up to the custom that archbishops are forbidden to exercise certain powers until they have received the pallium. Cf. *Vetus et Nova Ecclesiae Disciplina*, Pars I, lib. II, cap. 53; Grierson, "Rostagnus of Arles and the Pallium," *English Historical Review*, XLIX (1934), pp. 74-83; *Responsa Nicolai Papae I ad Consulta Bulgarorum*, n. LXXIII, *MGH*, Epistolarum Tomus VI, *Epistolae Karolini Aevi*, Tomus IV (Berolini: Apud Weidmannos, 1925), p. 593; *Caeremoniale Episcoporum*, Lib. I, Cap. XVI, num. 6; Canons 275, 276.

[106] *Ep.* vi, 7—Sept., 595. Thomassinus' conjecture (cf. preceding note) would seem to apply here also, since the Pope prefaces his statement about the concession of the pallium with an exhortation to the suffragans to be obedient to their metropolitan.

[107] *Ep.* iv, 1—Sept., 593.

things, the fact that the pallium had been conceded to Leander.[108]

In the letter to Leander it seems that the Pope refers to a custom in use at the present day, that of placing the palliums in a silver case in the "*confessio*" of St. Peter, whence they are taken as needed.[109] For the Pope says: "Praeterea ex *benedictione* beati Petri apostolorum principis pallium vobis transmisimus." Gregory uses the word *benedictio* with several different meanings, e.g., for blessing in *Ep.* vi, 28; for ordination in *Ep.* ix, 218; for relic in *Ep.* iv, 30; for gift in *Ep.* xiii, 28. In these and in other cases not listed, the context easily leads one to the correct meaning of the word. In the case under consideration, however, the word could mean "blessing," for palliums are blessed by the Pope. Mabillon (1632-1707) says: "Quod attinet ad pannos, qui super corpus beati Apostoli cum precibus et jejuniis inferebantur, *brandea* vocantur a Gregorio Magno. Eodem ritu pallia pro archiepiscopis sacrari mos erat, quae de corpore beati Petri sumta dicebantur.[110] An apodictic statement can hardly be made as to Gregory's meaning; yet to the writer it seems reasonable to consider Gregory's words as the foreshadowing of a practice in use today.

There are still other cases in which a request for the pallium does not seem to have been made; there are no records of such requests, and in the granting of the pallium Gregory does not refer to any previous letter received from the grantees. To this group belong the following: Augustine of Canterbury,[111] Donus of Messina,[112] John of Syracuse,[113] and John of Palermo.[114]

---

[108] Cf. *Epp.* ix, 227, 228. *Ep.* ix, 227a, is given by Hartmann as a letter of Reccared to Gregory, though the editor notes that Gams (1816-1892) and Mommsen (1817-1903) considered that this letter was composed by later writers from Gregory's own letter to the king. Caspar accepts the authenticity of *Ep.* ix, 227a; cf. *Geschichte des Papsttums*, II, 491, note 5.

[109] Cf. *Ep.* ix, 227; also Duchesne, *Origines*, p. 405; Eisenhofer, *Handbuch*, I, 458.

[110] *Museum Italicum* (2 vols., Paris. 1724), I, cxxxiii.

[111] Cf. *Ep.* xi, 39—June, 601.

[112] Cf. *Ep.* vi, 8—Sept., 595.

[113] Cf. *Ep.* vi, 18—Oct., 595.

[114] Cf. *Ep.* xiii, 40—July, 603.

Though the Pope seems to have granted the pallium to Augustine (for use at Mass only) without any previous request, he told him that in future the bishop of London (which city the Pope presumed to be Augustine's see) should be elected by his own suffragans, and should receive the pallium from the Apostolic See. In this same letter, Gregory instructed Augustine as to how the Church in England was to be organized. This letter has already been considered,[115] and it suffices to note here that the metropolitan of York was promised the pallium also if he were found worthy of it.

The letters to each of the three bishops, Donus of Messina, John of Syracuse and John of Palermo, which announced the granting of the pallium, were identical in form:

> Apostolicae sedis benivolentia et antiquae consuetudinis ordine provocati, fraternitati tuae, quam in Messanensi [Syracusana, Panormitana] ecclesia gubernationis officium constat suscepisse, pallii usum praevidimus concedendum illis videlicet temporibus atque eo ordine, quibus decessorem quoque tuum usum esse non ambigis, hoc nihilominus ammonentes, ut, sicut a nobis huius decoris usum ad sacerdotalis officii honorem accepisse te gaudes, ita etiam morum atque actuum probitate ad gloriam Christi susceptum adornare contendas officium. Sic enim alterno eris invicem decore conspicuus, si ad huius corporis habitum mentis quoque tuae bona concordent. Omnia etiam privilegia quae tuae pridem concessa esse constat ecclesiae, nostra auctoritate firmamus et inlibata decernimus permanere.[116]

3. LETTERS TO THE EX-PATRIARCH OF ANTIOCH

While Gregory was in Constantinople as *apocrisiarius* under Pope Pelagius II (579-590), he became a close friend to Bishop Anastasius, who had been deposed from the see of Antioch in the year 570, and resided in Constantinople there-

[115] Cf. *supra*, p. 62f.; also Haddan and Stubbs, *Councils and Ecclesiastical Documents Relating to Great Britain and Ireland* (3 vols. in 4, Oxford: Clarendon Press, 1869-1878), III, 319f.

[116] *Epp.* vi, 8. 18; xiii, 40. *Ep.* vi, 8 omits the last two sentences.

after.[117] A month after his elevation to the papacy, Gregory wrote to Bishop Anastasius, thanking him for his letter of congratulations and assuring him that he had strongly begged the emperor that, after his honor had been restored,[118] he should be permitted to come to Rome to live with the Pope.[119] For various reasons, however, this letter which Gregory says he had written to the emperor was never sent, as Gregory explains to Bishop Sebastian of Risano in Illyricum, whom he asks to contact Anastasius to ascertain the latter's mind regarding the concession of the pallium and permission to go to Rome.[120] Though Gregory considered the deposition of Anastasius null and void,[121] he did not, as far as is known, rebuke the emperor openly. Perhaps it was due to his influence that, when Bishop Gregory who had replaced Anastasius died in 593, Anastasius was reinstated in his former see.[122] Nothing further is said about the pallium, though the Pope sent Anastasius warmest congratulations on his reinstatement in his see, and continued to correspond with him in friendly terms.[123]

---

[117] Cf. Dudden, *Gregory The Great,* I, 155; II, 228f; Ewald's note 1 ad *Ep.* i, 7.

[118] "I.e., that the use of the pallium be restored to him, as is apparent from *Ep.* i, 27. For since his successor, Bishop Gregory, was appointed to the patriarchate of Antioch, Anastasius could not be restored to his see." —Ewald, note 4 ad *Ep.* i, 7.

[119] *Ep.* i, 7—Oct., 590.

[120] *Ep.* i, 27—Feb., 591. Even if Gregory had sent to the emperor the letter requesting the honor of the pallium to be restored to the deposed patriarch, the conclusion that the Popes were dependent upon the emperor in the granting of the pallium would not be justified—cf. *supra,* p. 102f. For it must be kept in mind that the Eastern Church was still in a position peculiarly subordinate to the emperor, and even Gregory was careful not to create any unnecessary friction between East and West.

[121] Cf. *Ep.* i, 25, addressed to Anastasius, *Patriarch* of Antioch: "I have sent to you, as also to the other patriarchs, a copy of my synodical letter (*Ep.* i, 24), for to me you are always that which you became by the grace of God, and not that which you seem to be because of the will of man."

[122] Cf. Hartmann's notes ad *Ep.* v, 41.

[123] Cf. *Ep.* v, 42—June, 595.

4. REFUSAL OF THE PALLIUM TO THE BISHOP OF VIENNE

There is only one letter extant in which Gregory refused to bestow the pallium upon a bishop who requested it. That letter was written to Bishop Desiderius of Vienne in Gaul:

> Fraternitatis vestrae desiderium Johannis regionarii relatione cognovimus; quod quidem libenter parati sumus implere, si diligenter fuerimus de his quae retulit informati. Inquit autem a vestra sibi relatum dilectione, quod ecclesiae vestrae quaedam olim privilegia ab apostolica sede concessa sint, atque usum pallii eius sacerdotes antiquitus habuisse. Quod quia vobis magnopere poscitis reformari, in ecclesiae nostrae scrinio requiri fecimus, et inveniri nil potuit. Sed quoniam quanto studiosius ista cupitis adipisci, tanto vos arbitramur esse sollicitos, in requirendis chartis ecclesiae vestrae vigilantius curam impendite et, si qua exinde scripta inveniri potuerint quae nos valeant informare, huc curae sit vestrae transmittere. Nam qui nova concedimus, vetera libentissime reparamus.[124]

This refusal may seem strange, but the explanation given by Dudden,[125] who finds the reason in Gregory's fear to incur the ill will of Brunichild who hated Desiderius for his outspoken condemnation of her incestuous marriage with Merovech, is contrary to what we know of Gregory's character and his love of right and justice. That he would stoop to give a false reason for refusing the pallium to get himself out of a difficult position, as Dudden suggests, is incredible. The real reason is, as Gregory indicates, that the bishop of Vienne no longer had a right to the pallium, since, at a time prior to the papacy of Gregory, the metropolitan see of the province of Vienne had been moved from Vienne to Arles when the Pretorian Prefect of Gaul changed his residence from Vienne to Arles.[126]

---

[124] *Ep.* ix, 220.

[125] *Gregory The Great,* II, 73.

[126] Cf. Hartmann's note 2 ad *Ep.* ix, 220.

5. REFERENCES TO NON-EPISCOPAL PALLIUMS

A deacon and two clerics of the church of Venafro sold, among other sacred vessels and ornaments, some palliums ("pallea maiora minora sex") to a Jew. Pope Gregory ordered that the Jew was to be forced to return the articles, and that the deacon and clerics were to be forced to do penance.[127] It is apparent from the footnotes of Ewald that the extant manuscripts of the register vary as to the number and size of the palliums sold. Why one church would have more than one pallium is difficult to say. One must conclude that the palliums sold were not episcopal palliums at all, but either diaconal *pallia linostima,* which Pope Sylvester ordered deacons to wear,[128] or linen altar cloths, also called *pallea* or *pallia.*[129]

With his friend, Eulogius of Alexandria, Gregory was ever on good terms. Hence it is not a matter of surprise that the Pope sent him various gifts. But there is matter for surprise in the following: "I have sent you as a gift from your beloved church of St. Peter six small Aquitanian palliums (sex minora Aquitanica pallia) and two handkerchiefs,"[130] for it is not known to what the Pope has reference. One thing only seems certain: he did not refer to the episcopal pallium, but to some sort of garment or scarf.

6. FORMULAS OF THE *LIBER DIURNUS* FOR GRANTING THE PALLIUM

Before summing up Gregory's regulations concerning the use of the pallium one may well consider the four formulas of the *Liber Diurnus* which were used for granting the pallium.[131] Garnier believed that formula 45 was formed from various letters of Gregory the Great: "Id fragmenta quaedam variis epistolis inserta produnt; id suadet stylus;. . .sua-

[127] Cf. *Ep.* i, 66—Aug., 591.

[128] Cf. *Liber Pontificalis,* I, 171.

[129] Cf. Baluzius' note ad Formulam XXII of the *Liber Diurnus,* ed. Rozière, p. 49.

[130] *Ep.* vii, 37—July, 597.

[131] Formulas 45 to 48: Sickel, *Liber Diurnus,* pp. 32-40; ed. Rozière, pp. 75-89. The formulas are entitled: 45, "De usu pallei;" 46, "Item aliud;" 47, "Item aliud;" 48, "Item aliud episcopis Siciliae."

dent et Gregorianae sententiae."[132] Baluzius however stated: "Ego vero arbitror illam aevo Gregorii posteriorem esse, cum nihil ex ea reperiatur in epistolis ab eo scriptis de usu pallii."[133] There is no doubt that the exhortation to the recipient of the pallium to wear it with honor is in harmony with the spirit of Gregory's letters. The most that can be said is that parts of some of Gregory's letters, particularly *Epp.* v, 16. 62; ix, 234, may have served as a model for part of this formula; the later composer, however, did not see fit to follow his model very closely, but freely enlarged upon the ideas contained in Gregory's letters.[134]

The second formula, 46, begins with a lengthy exhortation to the bishop to be a true shepherd of souls; there follows the mention that the pallium is sent according to custom, and the letter closes with an exhortation to root out the evils of simony. The composer of the first part of the formula freely enlarged upon Gregory's ideas, but the concluding section on the evils of simony is practically identical, word for word, with sections of the following letters of Gregory: *Ep.* v, 58, to Vergil of Arles; *Ep.* v, 62, to John of Corinth; *Ep.* v, 63, to all the bishops of Greece, and *Ep.* vi, 7, to all the bishops of Epirus Vetus.

It must be noted, however, that both formula 45 and formula 46 contain, closely connected with the concession of the pallium, the following statement: "Fidem autem quam in tuis epistolis breviter adscripsisti, licet latius explanare debueras, Redemptori tamen nostro gratias agimus, quod eam in ipsa etiam brevitate rectam esse cognovimus."[135] Garnier notes:

> Ex utraque constat: 1) fidem mitti solitam ab episcopis ad sedem apostolicam cum pallium scripto peterent; 2) utramque formulam pertinere ad episcopos, qui sedis apostolicae ordinationi non subiacent; hi enim et

---

[132] *Liber Diurnus*, ed. Rozière, p. 75.

[133] *Ibid.*, p. 76.

[134] A brief statement on the various opinions as to the origin and early use of the *Liber Diurnus* is given *supra*, p. 22, note 4.

[135] *Liber Diurnus*, ed. Rozière, pp. 79, 83. The statement of formula 46 is in its wording slightly different from that of formula 45.

> ordinabantur Romae, et fidem in ordinatione profitebantur; 3) ambas etiam paulo post synodum quintam esse compositas...; 4) utriusque auctorem aut informatorem potius esse Gregorium M.; nullus enim fuit curiosior fidei professionisque quintae synodi exactor.[136]

The writer disagrees with the latter two conclusions for the following reasons: 1) in none of Gregory's letters granting the pallium is there any similar reference to the faith of the recipient;[137] 2) Gregory certainly upheld the V General Council of 553, striving earnestly to heal the schism over the so-called Three Chapters, but he did not always think an open adherence to this Council to be expedient, nor did he demand an explicit statement of adherence to this Council from bishops who returned to the unity of the Church from schism.[138]

Formula 47 is much shorter than the first two, and begins immediately with the granting of the pallium. It is not similar to any of Gregory's letters. Garnier is of the opinion that this formula was used by Pope Symmachus in 501 when he sent the pallium to Theodore of Lorsch.[139] It has been noted above, however, that Pope Symachus' letter to Theodore of Lorsch is spurious.[140]

The last formula, 48, is without doubt taken from Gregory's letters: it is entitled, "Item aliud episcopis Siciliae," and is identical in form with the letters written by Gregory when he granted the pallium to the bishops of Messina, Syracuse and Palermo.[141] There is also no record of a concession of the pallium to a bishop of Sicily before the time of Gregory

---

[136] *Liber Diurnus*, ed. Rozière, p. 80.

[137] Cf. *supra*, p. 88ff.

[138] Cf. *Epp.* iv, 2. 3. 4. 33. 37; xii, 7. 13; also Fliche-Martin, *Histoire*, V, 45ff.

[139] Cf. *Liber Diurnus*, ed. Rozière, p. 85.

[140] Cf. *supra*, p. 105, note 18.

[141] Cf. *Epp.* vi, 8. 18; xiii, 40. *Ep.* vi, 8, however, omits the last two sentences—cf. *supra*, p. 134. Sickel admits that this formula was taken from Gregory's letters, but he adds that it was not right for the editors of the *Liber Diurnus* to correct the manuscripts by reference to Gregory's register. Cf. *Liber Diurnus*, p. lxxi. This latter opinion is in agreement with that expressed by Ewald, "Studien zur Ausgabe des Registers Gregors I.," *Neues Archiv*, III (1878), 552ff.

the Great. This same formula was likewise used by Gregory when he granted the pallium to Marinianus of Ravenna, except that the central portion was changed to provide for the special use of the pallium at Ravenna.[142]

Why does the *Liber Diurnus* contain a special formula to be used for granting the pallium to the bishops of Sicily? The only satisfactory answer seems to be that those who formed the *Liber Diurnus* put in this special formula since they found it used by Gregory three times for bishops of Sicily and once for Ravenna. A further question arises: why did Gregory use this special formula for Sicily? Pope Pelagius I (556-561) had interdicted the use of the pallium by Bishop Secundus of Taormina, but it is not known whence Bishop Secundus had this right.[143] Since Gregory permitted each of the bishops of Messina, Syracuse and Palermo to use the pallium "as your predecessor had done," one must conclude that the pallium was worn quite generally in Sicily, perhaps by all the bishops of the island. If that is true, why are there no records of previous papal grants to any Sicilian bishop? Is it possible that the use of the pallium may have been introduced into Sicily along with other eastern liturgical customs from Constantinople? From numerous letters of Gregory it is clearly evident that, in his time, the Church in Sicily was specially close to Rome. But it is possible that prior to his time eastern liturgical customs were introduced there.[144]

None of the formulas given in the *Liber Diurnus* for granting the pallium has any similarity to the papal letters conceding the use of the pallium before Gregory the Great.

SUMMARY

One may now sum up briefly Gregory's doctrine concerning the pallium and its use as contained in his letters: 1) It was conceded by the Pope for use at Mass only to the in-

---

[142] Cf. *Ep.* v, 61; *supra*, p. 122.

[143] JK, 1000. Cf. *supra*, p. 105, note 18.

[144] Cf. Eisenhofer, *Handbuch*, I, 30; Caspar, *Geschichte des Papsttums*, II, 412, note 10.

cumbents of the sees of London, Arles,[145] Seville, Milan, Autun, Salona, and Ravenna, though, until the records of previous grants and practices could be more definitely ascertained, the latter church was permitted to use it outside of Mass and *extra ceclesiam* during four specified litanies, and perhaps during the translation of relics. 2) It was granted for use according to the custom of their predecessors to the bishops of Messina, Syracuse, Palermo and Corinth. 3) In the concession of the pallium to the metropolitans of Prima Justiniana and Nicopolis no mention is made of the time when it may be used. 4) Though Gregory explicitly stated that the pallium had to be requested from the Pope by the recipient himself, it is known for certain that this was done only by the incumbents of the sees of Arles (for whom the king also made a request), Salona, Corinth, and Autun (after the queen had vainly requested it for him); it was requested for the metropolitan of Prima Justiniana by his suffragans, and probably also for the metropolitan of Nicopolis by his suffragans; one may conjecture that it was asked for by Leander of Seville and Constantius of Milan; it was apparently granted without any special request to the bishops of Ravenna, Messina, Syracuse, Palermo and to Augustine of Canterbury, though the future bishops of London and York (according to Gregory's plan of organization for the English Church) were to ask for it. 5) Perhaps in the case of Bishop Syragrius of Autun, Gregory asked the permission of the emperor, though he had in mind to request the emperor to restore the pallium to Anastasius of Antioch while he lived as ex-patriarch of that city. 6) The use of the pallium could be revoked as a penalty, as Gregory threatened to do to Bishop Natalis of Salona. 7) The Roman Synod of 595 legislated that no money was to be given for the grant of the pallium. 8) Only in one case did the Pope refuse to grant the pallium, though even then he was prepared to bestow it if a former concession of it could be proved.

---

[145] Three bishops of Arles were granted the pallium by predecessors of Gregory; in none of these earlier concessions does the phrase "for use at Mass only" occur. Cf. *supra*, p. 105.

Finally, the pallium was granted by Gregory to two papal vicars: those at Arles, and Prima Justiniana; to seven metropolitans: those at Ravenna, Salona, Milan, Corinth, Nicopolis, Canterbury and Seville;[146] and to four bishops: those at Syracuse, Messina, Palermo and Autun. All of these ecclesiastical dignitaries were under the jurisdiction of the Pope as patriarch of the West. Hence it is not possible to ascertain anything regarding the use of the pallium in the East from the letters of Gregory the Great, except the conjecture of Thomassinus that the usage in the East and the West was similar.[147] Hartmann emphasizes the fact that the phrase "for use at Mass only" does not occur in the letters granting the pallium to Eastern bishops, but only in those directed to bishops of the West. How is that statement to be understood? All of the bishops to whom Gregory granted the pallium were under his jurisdiction as patriarch of the West—hence all should be considered Western bishops, at least in that respect. The phrase "for use at Mass only" occurs in the letters to the bishops of London, Arles, Seville, Milan, Autun, Ravenna and Salona. Geographically considered, all these cities

---

[146] "Gregory sent to Leander...the pallium, giving him permission to wear it during Mass. Whether by this present Gregory meant to confer on Leander the vicariate of the Apostolic See in Spain is a disputed point. In his letter to Reccared, Gregory said that he was sending the pallium in conformity with 'ancient custom'; and Gams argues that there is here a reference to the Apostolic Vicariates conferred by Popes Simplicius and Hormisdas respectively on Zeno and Sallustius, archbishops of Seville. The argument, however, is not conclusive, and it is possible that the pallium in this case was nothing more than a mark of honor. Certainly during this period the decoration was not necessarily associated with the vicariate. We find, for instance, in Sicily that the pallium was given to the bishops of Syracuse, Messina and Palermo, while the vicariate was held only by the bishop of Syracuse."—Dudden, *Gregory the Great*, I, 412. The author should have added that Bishop Maximian of Syracuse was appointed vicar in Sicily in October, 591, *without* any mention of the pallium, and with the express statement that the vicariate was a personal privilege that did not adhere to the see of Syracuse (cf. *Ep.* ii, 8, and *supra*, p. 40) and that the pallium was granted to Maximian's successor in Syracuse, Bishop John, in October 595, *without* any mention of the vicariate (cf. *Ep.* vi, 18). The election of Bishop John and Gregory's intervention is considered *supra*, p. 41.

[147] Cf. *supra*, p. 121.

are definitely in the West, except Salona. But even this city, though it is on the eastern shore of the Adriatic Sea, was always considered a Western city; it certainly belonged to the patriarchate of the West. Gregory's letters, therefore, give us no definite information regarding the use of the pallium in the East.

GENERAL SUMMARY

In concluding a work of this nature one can but summarize in as few words as possible the important historical facts that have been presented at greater length in the preceding chapters and appendix.

In 590 the Church was divided into five patriarchates, those of the West, of Constantinople, of Alexandria, of Antioch, and of Jerusalem. Gregory's letters give evidence of the primacy of Rome in action at the end of the sixth century, even though his letters for the greater part and number treat of problems in the patriarchate of the West. The doctrine of the patriarchates began at the Council of Nicaea in 325 when Rome, Alexandria and Antioch were recognized as having special rights. Although the I Council of Constantinople in 381 gave to Constantinople a primacy of honor second to that of Rome, and although Rome never accepted the third canon of this Council, the bishops of Constantinople gradually extended their jurisdiction, and after the Acacian schism Rome no longer protested against Constantinople's usurpation of patriarchal jurisdiction and honors. Gregory listed the patriarch of Constantinople as first among the eastern patriarchs.

The Council of Nicaea also recognized the existence of ecclesiastical provinces under the jurisdiction of a metropolitan, though these arose at a later date in the West than in the East. At the end of the sixth century, however, they were well established all over the West, except in Britain and Ireland. In the former Gregory himself laid the foundations for a metropolitan organization in line with tradition, whereas he had no contact with the Church in the latter country.

It is not necessary to repeat even briefly the history of the various parts of the Western patriarchate, though it may be emphasized again that Eastern Illyricum was always part of the Western patriarchate, and that a papal vicar was established at Thessalonica by Pope Innocent I (401-417). The vicariate at Thessalonica continued up to and through the time of Gregory the Great without interruption except for a short period during the Acacian schism (484-519). Pope Vigilius (537-555) recognized the privileges of Prima Justiniana, created by Justinian in 535, and appointed the bishop thereof a papal vicar. Gregory the Great likewise recognized the special position of Prima Justiniana, but his letters indicate that the bishop thereof was not primate of all Eastern Illyricum, and that the bishop of Thessalonica held at least the first place in honor among the bishops of that province. It should be emphasized also that in Africa the metropolitan dignity was not attached to a fixed see, but was held by the oldest bishop of the province according to the time of his consecration. Gregory did not change this custom.

Gregory's letters treating of the election of bishops indicate that at the end of the sixth century bishops were elected by the clergy, aristocracy and people of the widowed diocese in most parts of the Western patriarchate, whereas his letters give little indication of the identity of the electors in the East. For elections within the metropolitan province of Rome, Gregory originated two form letters, one to the bishop visitor delegated to preside at the election, and the other to the inhabitants of the widowed diocese. In these form letters, which were not incorporated into the original *Liber Diurnus*, five rules were listed. It suffices to point out here that no simple, uniform list of canonical impediments seems to have existed; i.e., they were to be found at that time in the decretals of various Popes and in the decrees of the early Councils. It is probable that Gregory the Great made use of the *Collectio Dionysiana* for the canon law on episcopal elections; he did not make use of Roman law in those portions of his letters which deal with the election or qualification of a bishop, though in other instances he undoubtedly quoted from Justinian's legislation.

Each metropolitan had the right of approving the election of his suffragans and of consecrating those who were elected. Gregory frequently made use of this right over his suffragan sees, rejecting unworthy candidates, and, at times, designating a candidate whom he considered most qualified. With the exception of the metropolitan of Ravenna, whose election and consecration were regulated as though he were a suffragan bishop of Rome, other metropolitans were consecrated by their suffragans, though at Milan and at Salona the previous approval of the Pope was required. The Pope approved and ratified the election and consecration of the metropolitans of Prima Justiniana, Corinth and Nicopolis only after these events had taken place, and the approval and ratification were signified by the bestowal of the pallium. Gregory's letters give no indication whatsoever of any papal approval of the election of metropolitans in Spain, Gaul, or in Africa, or in the Eastern patriarchates.

Absolute ordinations were strictly forbidden by the Council of Chalcedon in 451. Although the contrary custom spread even after this prohibition, Gregory's letters contain no mention of absolute ordination. Nor do they contain any reference to the institute of rural bishops, which is first mentioned in the West in 439. His silence on this point seems to indicate that he was unaware of the institute, or at any rate unwilling to foster it.

The conjecture that Gregory the Great demanded from his suffragans at the time of their consecration an assurance of their orthodoxy of belief and of allegiance to the Holy See is probably correct, even though formulas 73 to 76 of the *Liber Diurnus* were formed only after Gregory the Great. For formula 6 of the *Liber Diurnus* dates back to a letter of Pope Gelasius I (492-496), and Gregory made use of and referred to this formula on several occasions. Therein various precepts are given to the bishop, and one may conclude that the bishop promised to obey these precepts before his consecration. That the promise was given under oath is a mere conjecture without foundation in Gregory's letters.

Although the transfer of bishops from one see to another was strictly forbidden by various Councils, Gregory's letters are evidence that these laws had no force whenever a bishop, for one reason or another, no longer had a diocese, e.g., if his episcopal city had been captured or devastated by the barbarians. If it appeared that a ruined city would be rebuilt, Gregory entrusted its care meanwhile to a neighboring bishop as visitor; but if it appeared that the city would not be rebuilt or would not regain its former size and importance, Gregory united it to some neighboring bishopric by means either of an *unio aeque principalis* or of an *unio minus principalis*. Formula 9 of the *Liber Diurnus* was probably formed from the letters of Gregory. Gregory's letters contain no provision for a *divisio* or *dismembratio* of existing dioceses, though in one instance Gregory probably removed a suffragan diocese from the jurisdiction of the schismatic metropolitan of Aquileia to place it under the jurisdiction of the metropolitan of Ravenna. This was only a temporary measure, as was also his placing of several of Rome's suffragans under the care of the metropolitan of Ravenna because of the difficulties of travel during the invasions—he did not, however, relinquish his rights as metropolitan over these sees, and accordingly reserved all grave cases to himself.

From its very origin the pallium was a liturgical vestment, and was most probably adopted in Rome from the Orient. In the East the pallium was worn by all bishops, but there is no definite evidence that these bishops wore it also when not engaged in liturgical functions *extra ecclesiam*. In the West the use of the pallium was from the beginning reserved to the Pope and to those bishops—with the possible exception of the bishops of Sicily—to whom its use was freely granted by the Pope without the necessity of requesting the emperor's permission. The writer rejects the theory of a special Gallican pallium worn by all the bishops of Gaul.

Gregory's letters indicate that Ravenna's claims to special privileges were unfounded; the privileges said to have been granted by Valentinian III are not authentic, though that emperor probably concurred with the Pope in raising Ravenna to the dignity of a metropolitan see. The general rules in the West at the end of the sixth century, as indicated in the letters of Gregory the Great, were: the pallium was granted by the Pope only upon request, and it was to be worn at Mass only. The pallium was not granted to all bishops. There is no record of any grant of the pallium to Bishop Maximian of Syracuse while he was papal vicar, nor of any grant to the papal vicar at Thessalonica. The absence of any record of the concession of the pallium to the latter may be explained by the fact that no episcopal election took place at Thessalonica during the pontificate of Gregory the Great. The successor of Bishop Maximian of Syracuse was granted the pallium, but there is no indication that he was also appointed papal vicar, and certainly there was no necessary connection at that time between the vicariate and the concession of the pallium.

The metropolitans to whom Gregory granted the pallium were all elected during his pontificate, with the exception of the metropolitan Leander of Seville. Particularly in the cases of the metropolitans of Prima Justiniana, Corinth, and Nicopolis, the concession of the pallium coincided with the papal approval of the bishop's election and consecration; to the other metropolitans, again with the exception of Leander of Seville, the pallium was granted shortly after their election and consecration. It is noteworthy that Gregory's letters record the granting of the pallium only to those metropolitans and bishops (excluding the grant of it to the papal vicar at Arles, the metropolitan at Seville, and the bishop of Autun) with whose election and consecration Gregory's letters deal. The converse is also true as regards metropolitans, but not true as regards bishops, i.e., Gregory's letters treat of the election of only those metropolitans to whom the pallium was granted, but they treat of the election of other bishops than those to whom he granted the pallium.

Formulas 45 to 48 of the *Liber Diurnus,* which treat of the granting of the pallium, are post-Gregorian. Of these, 48 was definitely formed from Gregory's letters, while only parts of formulas 45 and 46 were modelled upon Gregory's letters; there is no similarity between formula 47 and the letters of Pope Gregory the Great.

BIBLIOGRAPHY

I. SOURCES

Beda Venerabilis: see Plummer.

Bruns, Herm. Theod., *Canones Apostolorum et Conciliorum Saeculorum IV. V. VI. VII.*, 2 vols., Berolini, 1894.

Caeremoniale Episcoporum, Parisiis: Sumptibus A. Jouby, 1860.

Codex Iuris Canonici Pii X Pontificis Maximi iussu digestus Benedicti Papae XV auctoritate promulgatus, Romae: Typis Polyglottis Vaticanis, 1917.

Codex Theodosianus, ed. Th. Mommsen, Berolini: Apud Weidmannos, 1905.

Collectio Avellana: see Guenther.

Corpus Iuris Canonici, ed. Lipsiensis 2. post Aemilii Ludovici Richter curas . . . instruxit Aemilius Friedberg, 2 vols., Lipsiae, 1879-1881.

Corpus Iuris Civilis, Vol. II, *Codex Iustinianus* recognovit et retractavit Paulus Krueger, ed. stereotypa nona, Berolini: Apud Weidmannos, 1915.

Corpus Iuris Civilis, Vol. III, *Novellae* recognovit Rudolfus Schoell, absolvit Guglielmus Kroll, ed. stereotypa quinta, Berolini: Apud Weidmannos, 1928.

Deusdedit: see Wolf von Glanvell.

Dobschütz, Ernst von, *Das Decretum Gelasianum de libris recipiendis et non recipiendis in kritischem Text*—Texte und Untersuchungen zur Geschichte der altchristlichen Literatur, hrsg. v. Adolph Harnack und Carl Schmidt, XXXVIII, Leipzig: J. C. Hinrichs'sche Buchhandlung, 1912.

Doelger, Franz, *Regesten der Kaiserurkunden des oströmischen Reiches*—Corpus der griechischen Urkunden des Mittelalters und der neueren Zeit, hrsg. v. den Akademien der Wissenschaften in München und Wien, Reihe A. Abteilung I, 1. Teil, *Regesten von* 565-1025. München und Berlin: Verlag R. Oldenbourg, 1924.

Duchesne, Louis, *Le Liber Pontificalis*, 2 vols., Paris, 1886-1892.

Gramatica, L.-Galbiati, G., *Il Codice Ambrosiano del Liber Diurnus Romanorum Pontificum*, Analecta Ambrosiana, VII, Milano-Roma: Editori Alfieri & Lacroix, [1921].

Gasquet, Francis Aidan, *A Life of Pope St. Gregory the Great*, written by a monk of the monastery of Whitby circa 713; printed from MS. St. Gallen, 567, Westminster: Art and Book Company, 1904.

Greg. I: see *MGH*; *Sancti Gregorii* . . .

Greg. Turon.: See *MGH*, *SS. Merov.*

Grisar, Hartmann, "Die Gregorbiographie des Paulus Diaconus in ihrer ursprünglichen Gestalt," *Zeitschrift für katholische Theologie*, XI (1887), 158-173.

Guenther, Otto, *Epistulae Imperatorum Pontificum Aliorum inde ab a. CCCLXVII usque ad a. DLIII datae Avellana quae dicitur collectio*—Corpus Scriptorum Ecclesiasticorum Latinorum, XXXV, 1 vol. in 2, Vindobonae: F. Tempesky, 1895-1899.

Haddan, A. W.-Stubbs, W., *Councils and Ecclesiastical Documents Relating to Great Britain and Ireland*, 3 vols. in 4, Oxford: Clarendon Press, 1869-1878.

Hinschius, Paul, *Decretales Pseudo-Isidorianae*, Leipzig, 1863.

Jaffé, Philippus, *Regesta Pontificum Romanorum ab condita Ecclesia ad annum post Christum natum MCXCVIII*, 2. ed. correctam et auctam auspiciis Gulielmi Wattenbach curaverunt S. Loewenfeld, F. Kaltenbrunner, P. Ewald, 2 vols. in 1, Lipsiae, 1885-1888.

Kehr, Paulus Fridolinus, *Regesta Pontificum Romanorum, Italia Pontificia*, 8 vols. in 12, Berolini: Apud Weidmannos, 1906-1935.

Liber Diurnus: see Gramatica-Galbiati; Rozière; Sickel.

Liber Pontificalis: see Duchesne; *MGH*.

Loewenfeld, Samuel, *Epistolae Pontificum Romanorum ineditae ab a.* 493 *ad a.* 1198. Lipsiae: Veit et Comp., 1885.

Mansi, Ioannes Dominicus, *Sacrorum Conciliorum Nova et Amplissima Collectio*, 53 vols. in 60, Paris-Arnhem-Leipzig, 1901-1927.

Migne, Jacques Paul, *Patrologiae Cursus Completus, Series Graeca*, 161 vols., Parisiis, 1856-1866.

———*Patrologiae Cursus Completus, Series Latina*, 221 vols., Parisiis, 1844-1864.

Monumenta Germaniae Historica, Gestorum Pontificum Romanorum I, *Libri Pontificalis pars prior* (edidit Theodorus Mommsen), Berolini: Apud Weidmannos, 1898.

———Epistolarum Tomus I et II, *Gregorii I Papae Registrum Epistolarum* (ediderunt Paulus Ewald et Ludovicus Hartmann), Berolini: Apud Weidmannos, 1891-1899.

———Epistolarum Tomus III, *Epistolae Merovingici et Karolini Aevi*, Tomus I, Berolini: Apud Weidmannos, 1892.

———Epistolarum Tomus VI, *Epistolae Karolini Aevi*, Tomus IV, Berolini: Apud Weidmannos, 1925.

———Legum Sectio I, *Leges Nationum Germanicarum*, Tomus I, *Leges Visigothorum* (edidit Karolus Zeumer), Hannoverae et Lipsiae: Impensis Bibliopolii Hahniani, 1902.

———Legum Sectio II, *Capitularia*, Tomus I, *Capitularia Regum Francorum* (denuo edidit Alfredus Boretius), Hannoverae, 1883.

———Legum Sectio III, *Concilia*, Tomus I, *Concilia Aevi Merovingici* (recensuit Friedericus Maassen), Hannoverae, 1893.

———*Scriptores Rerum Langobardicarum et Italicarum Saec. VI-IX*, Hannoverae: Impensis Bibliopolii Hahniani, 1878.

———*Scriptorum Rerum Merovingicarum*, Tomus I, *Gregorii Turonensis Opera* (ediderunt W. Arndt et B. Krush), Hannoverae: Impensis Bibliopolii Hahniani, 1885.

Paulus Diaconus: see Grisar.

Plummer, Carolus, *Venerabilis Bedae Opera Historica*, 2 vols., Oxonii: E Typographeo Clarendoniano, 1896.

Quasten, Johannes, *Expositio antiquae liturgiae Gallicanae Germano Parisiensi ascripta*, Münster, 1934.

Rozière, Eugene de, *Liber Diurnus ou recueil des formules usitées par la chancellerie pontificale du Ve au Xie siècle*, Paris, 1869.

Sancti Gregorii Papae I. Cognomento Magni Opera Omnia, 17 vols., (ediderunt Benedictini ex Congregatione S. Mauri), Venetiis, 1768-1776.

Schroeder, Henry J., *Disciplinary Decrees of the General Councils, Text, Translation and Commentary*, St. Louis: Herder and Company, 1937.

Schwartz, Eduard, *Acta Conciliorum Oecumenicorum*, 4 vols. in 12 parts, Berolini et Lipsiae: Walter de Gruyter & Co., 1914-1936.

Sickel, Theodor, *Liber Diurnus Romanorum Pontificum*, Vindobonae, 1889.

Thiel, Andreas, *Epistolae Romanorum Pontificum genuinae a S. Hilario* (461-468) *usque ad Pelagium* (556-561), Brunsbergae, 1868.

Turner, Cuthbert H., *Ecclesiae Occidentalis Monumenta Iuris Antiquissimi, Canonum et Conciliorum Graecorum Interpretationes Latinae*, 2 vols. in 5 parts, Oxonii: E Typographeo Clarendoniano, 1899-1930.

Wolf von Glanvell, Victor, *Die Kanonessammlung des Kardinals Deusdedit*, Paderborn: Druck und Verlag von Ferdinand Schöningh, 1905.

II. REFERENCE WORKS

Abbott, Frank-Johnson, Allan, *Municipal Administration in the Roman Empire*, Princeton: Princeton University Press, 1926.

Barthel, Johannes Casparus, *Dissertatio Historico-Canonico-Publica de Pallio*, 2. ed., Herbipoli, 1753.

Batiffol, Pierre, *Cathedra Petri, Études d'histoire ancienne de l'Église*, Paris: Les éditions du Cerf, 1938.

———*Le siège apostolique*, 359-451, 2. ed., Paris: Librairie Victor Lecoffre, 1924.

———*Saint Gregory the Great* (Translated from the original French by John L. Stoddard), New York: Benziger Brothers, 1929.

Bingham, Joseph, *The Antiquities of the Christian Church*, 2 vols., London, 1865.

Bishop, Edmund, *Liturgica Historica*, Oxford: At the Clarendon Press, 1918.

Boak, Arthur, *A History of Rome to 565 A.D.*, 3. ed., New York: Macmillan Company, 1943.

Boüard, A. de, *Manuel de diplomatique française et pontificale*, Paris: Éditions Auguste Picard, 1929.

Boucharlat, A., *Les élections épiscopales sous les Mérovingiens*, Lyon: Imprimerie Waltener & Co., 1904.

Braun, Joseph, *Die liturgische Gewandung*, Freiburg im Breisgau: Herdersche Verlagsbuchhandlung, 1907.

Bresslau, Henry, *Handbuch der Urkundenlehre für Deutschland und Italien*, 2. ed., 2 vols., (2nd vol. re-edited by Hans-Walter Klewitz) Berlin-Leipzig: Walter de Gruyter & Co., 1912-1931.

Bury, J. B., *History of the Later Roman Empire*, revised edition, 2 vols., London: Macmillan and Company, Ltd., 1923.

Cabrol, Fernand-Leclercq, H., *Dictionnaire d'archéologie chrétienne et de liturgie*, 14 vols. in 27, Paris: Librairie Letouzey et Ané, 1907—.

Cabrol, Fernand, *The Mass of the Western Rites* (Translated by C. M. Anthony), St. Louis: B. Herder Book Company, 1934.

Cambridge Medieval History, 8 vols., New York: Macmillan Company, 1911-1936.

Caspar, Erich, *Geschichte des Papsttums von der Anfängen bis zur Höhe der Weltherrschaft*, 2 vols., Tübingen: Verlag von J.C.B. Mohr, 1930-1933.

Chapman, John, *Studies on the Early Papacy*, New York: Benziger Brothers, 1928.

Comyns, Joseph J., *Papal and Episcopal Administration of Church Property*, The Catholic University of America Canon Law Studies, n. 147, Washington, D. C.: The Catholic University of America Press, 1942.

Conrat, Max, *Geschichte der Quellen und Literature des römischen Rechts im früheren Mittelalter*, Leipzig: J. C. Hinrichs'sche Buchhandlung, 1891.

De Clercq, Carlo, *La législation religieuse franque de Clovis à Charlemagne*, Louvain: Bureaux du Recueil Bibliothèque de l'Université, 1936.

De Marca, Petrus, *De Concordia Sacerdotii et Imperii seu de Libertatibus Ecclesiae Gallicanae*, 8 books in 4 vols., Neapoli, 1771.

Diehl, Charles, *Études sur l'administration byzantine dans l'exarcat de Ravenne* 568-751, Paris, 1888.

————*L'Afrique byzantine, histoire de la domination byzantine en Afrique* 533-709, Paris: Ernest Leroux, Éditeur, 1896.

Du Cange, *Glossarium Mediae et Infimae Latinitatis* conditum a Carolo du Fresne Domino du Cange auctum a Monachis Ordinis S. Benedicti, editio nova a Leopold Favre, 10 vols., Paris: Librairie des sciences et des arts, 1927-1938.

Duchesne, Louis, *L'Église au VIe siècle*, Paris: E. de Boccard, 1925.

————*Mémoire sur l'origine des diocèses épiscopaux dans l'ancienne Gaule*, extrait des *Mémoires de la Société nationale des Antiquaires*, L (1890), Paris, 1890.

————*Origines du culte chrétien*, 5 ed., Paris: Anciennes Maisons Thorin et Frontemoing, 1920.

Dudden, F. Homes, *Gregory the Great, His Place in History and Thought*, 2 vols., London: Longmans, Green and Company, 1905.

Eisenhofer, Ludwig, *Handbuch der katholischen Liturgik*, 2 vols., Freiburg im Breisgau: Herder & Co., G.M.B.H. Verlagsbuchhandlung, 1932.

Findlay, Stephen W., *Canonical Norms Governing the Deposition and Degradation of Clerics*, The Catholic University of America Canon Law Studies, n. 130, Washington, D. C.: The Catholic University of America Press, 1941.

Fliche, Augustin-Martin, Victor, *Histoire de l'Église*, 7 vols., Paris: Bloud et Gay, 1935-1940.

Fuchs, Vinzenz, *Der Ordinationstitel von seiner Entstehung bis auf Innozenz III.*, Kanonistische Studien und Texte hrsg. v. A. M. Koeniger, Band IV, Bonn: Kurt Schroeder Verlag, 1930.

Garcia Villada, Zacarias, *Historia Eclesiástica de España*, 3 vols. in 5, Madrid: Libreria Fernando Fe, 1929-1936.

Garnier, Jean, *De usu pallii* (printed in Rozière's *Liber Diurnus ou recueil...*, Paris, 1869).

Gillmann, Franz, *Das Institut der Chorbischöfe im Orient, Historisch-kanonistische Studie*, Veröffentlichungen aus dem Kirchenhistorischen Seminar München, hrsg. von Alois Knöpfler, II Reihe, Nr. 1, München: Verlag der J. J. Lentner'schen Buchhandlung, 1903.

Gottlob, Theodor, *Der abendländische Chorepiskopat*, Kanonistische Studien und Texte, hrsg. von A. M. Koeniger, Band I, Bonn: Kurt Schroeder Verlag, 1928.

———*Der kirchliche Amtseid der Bischöfe*, Kanonistische Studien und Texte, hrsg von A. M. Koeniger, Band IX, Bonn: Ludwig Röhrscheid Verlag, 1936.

Grisar, Hartmann, *History of Rome and the Popes in the Middle Ages* (Authorized English Translation edited by Luigi Cappadelta), 3 vols., London: Kegan Paul, Trench, Trübner and Co., Ltd., 1911.

Hartmann, Ludo Moritz, *Geschichte Italiens im Mittelalter*, 4 vols., Stuttgart-Gotha: Friederich Andreas Perthes, 1900-1915, 1st vol. re-edited, 1923.

Hauck, Albert, *Kirchengeschichte Deutschlands*, Leipzig, 1887.

Hefele, Charles Joseph-Leclercq, H., *Histoire des Conciles*, 10 vols. in 19, Paris: Letouzey et Ané, 1907-1938.

Hinschius, Paul, *Das Kirchenrecht der Katholiken und Protestanten in Deutschland*, 6 vols., Berlin: Verlag von I. Guttentag, 1869-1897.

Hodgkin, Thomas, *Italy and Her Invaders*, 2 ed., 8 vols., Oxford: At the Clarendon Press, 1892-1899.

Höpfl, Hildebrandus-Gut, Benno, *Introductio Generalis in Sacram Scripturam*, 4. ed., Romae: Editiones Comm. A. Arnodo, 1940.

Howorth, Sir Henry H., *Saint Gregory the Great*, London: John Murray, 1912.

Kinnirey, Ann Julia, *The Late Latin Vocabulary of the Dialogues of St. Gregory the Great*, The Catholic University of America Studies in Medieval and Renaissance Latin, IV, Washington, D. C.: The Catholic University of America, 1935.

Kirsch, Johannes P.-Holnsteiner, Johannes-Veit, Ludwig, *Kirchengeschichte*, 4 vols., Freiburg im Breisgau: Herder und Companie, 1930-1933.

Knecht, August, *System des Justinianischen Kirchenvermögensrechtes*, Kirchenrechtliche Abhandlungen hrsg. v. Ulrich Stutz, Heft 22, Stuttgart: Verlag von Ferdinand Enke, 1905.

Kübler, Bernhard, *Geschichte des römischen Rechts*, Leipzig: A. Deickertsche Verlagsbuchhandlung Dr. Werner Scholl, 1925.

Lapide, Cornelius a, *Commentaria in omnes Sancti Pauli Epistolas* recognovit subjectisque notis illustravit, emendavit et ad praesentem sacrae scientiae statum adduxit Antonius Padovani, editio secunda stereotypa, 3 vols., Taurini: Ex officina Marii E. Marietti, 1934.

Loening, Edgar, *Geschichte des deutschen Kirchenrechts*, 2 vols., Strassburg, 1878.

Lot, Ferdinand, *The End of the Ancient World and the Beginnings of the Middle Ages*, New York: Alfred A. Knopf, 1931.

Maassen, Friedrich, *Der Primat des Bischofs von Rom und die alten Patriarchalkirchen*, Bonn: Henry & Cohen, 1853.

Mabillon, Jean, *Museum Italicum*, 2 vols., Paris, 1687-1689.

Mann, Horace K., *Lives of the Popes in the Early Middle Ages*, 18 vols in 19, St. Louis: B. Herder, 1902-1932.

Marriot, Wharton B., *Vestiarium Christianum*, London: Rivingstons, Waterloo Place, 1868.

O'Donnell, James Francis, *Vocabulary of the Letters of Saint Gregory the Great*, The Catholic University of America Studies in Mediaeval and Renaissance Latin, II, Washington, D. C.: The Catholic University of America, 1934.

O'Sullivan, Jeremiah-Burns, John, *Medieval Europe*, New York: F. S. Crofts & Co., 1943.

Palanque, Jean-Rémy, *Saint Ambroise et l'empire Romain*, Paris: E. de Boccard, Éditeur, 1933.

Pargoire, P. J., *L'Église byzantine de* 527 *à* 847, Paris: Librairie Victor Lecoffre, 1905.

Parsons, Anscar, *Canonical Elections*, The Catholic University of America Canon Law Studies, n. 118, Washington, D. C.: The Catholic University of America Press, 1939.

Pauly-Wissowa-Kroll, *Realencyclopädie der klassischen Altertumswissenschaft*, 26 vols. in 51 with 6 supplements, Stuttgart: J. B. Metzlersche Verlagsbuchhandlung, 1893—.

Peitz, Wilhelm M., *Das vorephesinische Symbol der Papstkanzlei*, Miscellanea Historiae Pontificiae, I, Romae: Typis Pontificiae Universitatis Gregorianae, 1939.

————*Das Register Gregors I.*, Ergänzungshefte zu den *Stimmen der Zeit*, zweite Reihe, Forschungen, 2. Heft, Freiburg im Breisgau, 1917.

Poole, Reginald, *Lectures on the History of the Papal Chancery*, Cambridge: At the University Press, 1915.

Sägmüller, J. B., *Lehrbuch des katholischen Kirchenrechts*, 4. ed., 1 vol. in 4 parts, Freiburg im Breisgau: Herder & Co., G.M.B.H. Verlagsbuchhandlung, 1925-1934.

Schmalzgrueber, Franciscus, *Ius Ecclesiasticum Universum*, 5 vols. in 12, Romae, 1843-1845.

Schröder, Richard-Künssberg, Eberhard Frh. v., *Lehrbuch der deutschen Rechtsgeschichte*, 7. ed., Berlin und Leipzig: Verlag Walter de Gruyter & Co., 1932.

Scott, Herbert S., *The Eastern Churches and the Papacy*, London: Sheed and Ward, 1928.

Silva-Tarouca, Carlo, *Nuovi studi sulle antiche lettere dei Papi*, Romae: Pontificia Università Gregoriana, 1932; reprint from *Gregorianum*, XII (1931), 3-56; 349-425; 547-598.

Snow, Abbot, *St. Gregory the Great*, 2. ed., by Roger Huddleston, New York: Benziger Brothers, 1924.

Spinka, Matthew, *A History of Christianity in the Balkans*, Chicago: The American Society of Church History, 1933.

Stein, Ernst, *Geschichte des spätrömischen Reiches*, Wien: Verlag von L. W. Seidel und Sohn, 1928.

Thomassinus, Ludovicus, *Vetus et Nova Ecclesiae Disciplina circa Beneficia et Beneficiarios*, Magontiaci, 1787.

Trombetta, Aloysius, *De Pallio Archiepiscopali*, Surrenti: Ex Typographia Hen. D. Onofrio, 1923.

Vacandard, E., *Études de critique et d'histoire religieuse*, 5. ed., Paris: Librairie Victor Lecoffre, 1913.

Vespasiani, Philippus, *De sacri pallii origine*, Romae: Typis S. C. de Propaganda Fide, 1856.

Walsh, John, *Mass and Vestments of the Catholic Church*, New York: Benziger Brothers, 1916.

Wisbaum, Wilhelm, *Die wichtigsten Richtungen und Ziele der Thätigkeit des Papstes Gregors des Grossen*, Köln, 1884.

Wurm, Hubert, *Studien und Texte zur Dekretalensammlung des Dionysius Exiguus*, Kanonistische Studien und Texte hrsg. v. A. M. Koeniger, Heft XVI, Bonn: Ludwig Röhrscheid Verlag, 1939.

Zeiller, Jacques, *L'empire romain et l'Église*, Paris: E. de Boccard, Éditeur, 1928.

Ziegler, Aloysius K., *Church and State in Visigothic Spain*, Washington, D. C.: Catholic University of America, 1930.

Zimmermann, Odo, *The Late Latin Vocabulary of the Variae of Cassiodorus*, The Catholic University of America Studies in Medieval and Renaissance Latin Language and Literature, XV, Washington, D. C.: The Catholic University of America Press, 1944.

III. ARTICLES

Anonymous, "Le 28e canon de Chalcédoine"—*Bessarione*, I (1897), 875-885.

Anonymous, "Rome et le 28e canon de Chalcédoine"—*Bessarione*, II (1897-1898), 215-224.

Baethgen, Friedrich, [Review of Caspar's *Geschichte des Papsttums*]—*Zeitschrift der Savigny-Stiftung für Rechtsgeschichte*, Kan. Abt., XXIV (1935), 344-354.

Batiffol, Pierre, "La prima cathedra episcopatus du concile d'Elvire"—*Journal of Theological Studies*, XXIII (1921-1922), 263-270.

———"Le *primae sedis episcopus* en Afrique"—*Revue des sciences religieuses*, III (1923), 425-432.

Blasel, Carl, "Die kirchlichen Zustände Italiens zur Zeit Gregors des Grossen"—*Archiv für katholisches Kirchenrecht*, LXXXIV (1904), 83-93; 225-243.

Bloksсha, Joseph "Die Altersvorschriften für die höheren Weihen im ersten Jahrtausend"—*Archiv für katholisches Kirchenrecht*, CXI (1931), 31-83.

Brandi, Karl, "Ravenna und Rom. Neue Beiträge zur Kenntnis der römisch-byzantinischen Urkunde"—*Archiv für Urkundenforschung*, IX (1926), 1-38.

Chapman, John, "On the *Decretum Gelasianum*"—*Revue bénédictine*, XXX (1913), 187-207; 315-333.

Conrat, Max-Kantorowicz, Hermann, "Römisches Recht im frühesten Mittelalter"—*Zeitschrift der Savigny-Stiftung für Rechtsgeschichte*, Rom. Abt., XXXIV (1913), 13-45.

Duchesne, Louis, "Le Liber Diurnus et les élections pontificales au VIIe siècle"—*Bibliothèque de l'École des Chartes*, LII (1891), 5-30; also reprinted separately, Paris, 1891.

———"L'Illyricum ecclésiastique"—*Byzantinische Zeitschrift*, I (1892), 531-550.

Ewald, Paul, "Studien zur Ausgabe des Registers Gregors I."—*Neues Archiv der Gesellschaft für ältere deutsche Geschichtskunde*, III (1878), 432-625.

———, "Zwei unedierte Briefe Gregors I."—*Neues Archiv der Gesellschaft für ältere deutsche Geschichtskunde*, VII (1881), 587-604.

Fabricius, Clara, "Die *Litterae Formatae* im Frühmittelalter"—*Archiv für Urkundenforschung*, IX (1926), 39-86; 168-194.

Fehr, J., "Der Primat des apostolischen Stuhles in der gallisch-fränkischen Kirche"—*Archiv für katholisches Kirchenrecht*, XIX (1868), 365-402.

Fiebiger, "Decurio"—Pauly-Wissowa-Kroll, *Realencyclopädie*, IV, 2319-2353.

Fischer, Balthasar, "Die Entwicklung des Instituts der Defensoren in der römischen Kirche"—*Ephemerides Liturgicae*, XLVIII (1934), 443-454.

Friedrich, J., "Ueber die Sammlung der Kirche von Thessalonich und das päpstliche Vicariat für Illyricum"—*Sitzungsberichte der philosophisch-philologischen und historischen Classe der königlich bayerischen Akademie der Wissenschaften zu München*, (1891), 771-887.

Grashof, Otto, "Die Gesetze der römischen Kaiser über die Verwaltung und Veräusserung des kirchlichen Vermögens"—*Archiv für katholisches Kirchenrecht*, XXXVI (1876), 193-214.

Grierson, Philip, "Rostagnus of Arles and the Pallium"—*English Historical Review*, XLIX (1934), 74-83.

Grisar, Hartmann, "Rom und die fränkische Kirche vornehmlich im sechsten Jahrhundert"—*Zeitschrift für katholische Theologie*, XIV 1890), 447-493.

Guenther, Otto, "Avellana-Studien"—*Sitzungsberichte der philosophisch-historischen Classe der kaiserlichen Akademie der Wissenschaften in Wien*, CXXXIV (1896), 1-134.

Hilling, Nikolaus, "Die Bedeutung der iurisdictio voluntaria und involuntaria im römischen Recht und im kanonischen Recht des Mittelalters und der Neuzeit"—*Archiv für katholisches Kirchenrecht*, CV (1925), 449-473; *ibid.*, CXVIII (1938), 165-170.

Honig, Richard M., "The So-Called 'Vicariate' of Illyricum"—*Anglican Theological Review*, XXVI (1944), 87-98.

Hülsen, "Curia"—Pauly-Wissowa-Kroll, *Realencyclopädie*, IV, 1815-1826.

Jüllicher, Adolph, "Die Synode von Elvira als Zeuge für den römischen Primat"—*Zeitschrift für Kirchengeschichte*, XLII (1923), 44-49.

Kerckhove, M. van de, "De notione iurisdictione in iure Romano"—*Jus Pontificium*, XVI (1936), 49-65.

Kleinschmidt, Beda, "Das bischöfliche Rationale und der 6. Kanon der Synode von Mâcon"—*Historisches Jahrbuch*, XXVII (1906), 799-803.

Kübler, B., "Ordo"—Pauly-Wissowa-Kroll, *Realencyclopädie*, XVIII, 930-934.

Kuttner, Stephan, " 'Cardinalis': The History of a Canonical Concept"—*Traditio*, III (1945), 129-214.

Le Bras, Gabriel, "Quantam partem habuerint Romani in Libris Canonum ante Decretum Gratiani confectis"—*Jus Pontificium*, XIII (1933), 237-240.

Leclercq, H., "Chorévêques"—*Dictionnaire d'archéologie chrétienne et de liturgie*, III, 1423-1452.

————, "Episcopat"—*DCAL*, V, 202-238.

————, "Espagne"—*DACL*, V, 407-523.

————, "Gallicane, Église"—*DACL*, VI, 310-471.

————, "Pallium"—*DACL*, XIII, 931-940.

————, "Patriarcat"—*DACL*, XIII, 2456-2487.

Müller, M., "Zur Frage nach der Echtheit und Abfassungszeit des Responsum b. Gregorii ad Augustinum Episcopum"—*Theologische Quartalschrift*, CXIII (1932), 94-118.

Nostiz-Rieneck, Robert von, "Die päpstlichen Urkunden für Thessalonike und deren Kritik durch Prof. Friedrich"—*Zeitschrift für katholische Theologie*, XXI (1897), 1-50.

Peitz, Wilhelm, "Liber Diurnus—Beiträge zur Kenntnis der ältesten päpstlichen Kanzlei vor Gregor dem Grossen"—*Sitzungsberichte-Akademie der Wissenschaften in Wien, Philosophisch-historische Klasse*, CLXXXV (1918), 1-144.

Posner, E., "Das Register Gregors I."—*Neues Archiv der Gesellschaft für ältere deutsche Geschichtskunde*, XLIII (1922), 243-315.

Piontek, Cyrillus, "De acephalis in iure canonico"—*Jus Pontificium*, XIII (1933), 25-41; XIV (1934), 194-215; 284-294.

Quasten, Johannes, "Oriental Influence in the Gallican Liturgy"—*Traditio*, I (1943), 55-78.

Santifaller, Leo, "Zum Liber Diurnus—Forschung"—*Historische Zeitschrift*, CLXI (1940), 532-538.

Schönfeld, Walter, "Die Xenodochien in Italien und Frankreich im frühen Mittelalter"—*Zeitschrift der Savigny-Stiftung für Rechtsgeschichte*, Kan. Abt., XII (1922), 1-54.

Schmidt, Herman J., "Die Kirche von Ravenna im Frühmittelalter, 540-967"—*Historisches Jahrbuch*, XXXIV (1913), 729-780.

Schmitz, Herman Jos., "Die Rechte der Metropoliten und Bischöfe in Gallien vom vierten bis sechsten Jahrhundert"—*Archiv für katholisches Kirchenrecht*, LXXII (1894), 3-49.

———, "Metropolitanverfassung und Provinzialsynode in Gallien während des fünften Jahrhunderts"—*Archiv für katholisches Kirchenrecht*, LVII (1887), 3-40.

Schneider, Philip, "Der kanonische Gehorsam"—*Archiv für katholisches Kirchenrecht*, LXXXII (1902), 290-324.

Seckel, E., [Review of Hartmann's *MGH* edition of the letters of Gregory the Great]—*Historische Zeitschrift*, LXXVI (1896), 110-112; *ibid.*, LXXIX (1897), 90-92; *ibid.*, LXXXVII (1901), 293-294.

Sickel, Theodor, "Prolegomena zum Liber Diurnus I"—No. VII in *Sitzungsberichte der philosophisch-historischen Classe der kaiserlichen Akademie der Wissenschaften in Wien*, CXVII (1889), 1-76; "Prolegomena zum Liber Diurnus II"—No. XIII *ibid.*, 1-94.

Steinacker, Harold, "Zum Liber Diurnus und zur Frage nach dem Ursprung der Frühminuskel," *Miscellanea Franceso Ehrle, Scritti di Storia e Paleografia*, IV (Studi e Testi XL), Romae: Biblioteca Apostolica Vaticana, 1924, 105-176.

Stein, Ernst, "La période byzantine de la papauté"—*Catholic Historical Review*, XXI (1935-1936), 129-163.

Streichhan, Fritz, "Die Anfänge der Vikariates von Thessalonich"—*Zeitschrift der Savigny-Stiftung für Rechtsgeschichte*, Kan. Abt., XII (1922), 330-384.

Sybel, Ludwig, "Zur Synode von Elvira"—*Zeitschrift für Kirchengeschichte*, XLII (1923), 243-247.

Syxtus, P., "Indumenta Sacra"—*Ephemerides Liturgicae*, XXIII (1909), 641-652; *ibid.*, XXIV (1910), 168-176.

Tangl, M., "Gregor-Register und Liber Diurnus"—*Neues Archiv der Gesellschaft für deutsche Geschichtskunde*, XLI (1917), 741-752.

Thurston, Herbert, "The Pallium"—*The Month*, LXXXV (1892), 305-325.

Vaes, M., "La papauté et l'église franque à l'époque de Grégoire le Grand"—*Revue d'histoire ecclésiastique*, VI (1905), 537-556; 755-784.

Walter, Ferdinand, "Ueber den Ursprung des erzbischöflichen Palliums"—*Archiv für katholisches Kirchenrecht*, VI (1863), 215.

Wasner, Franciscus, "De authenticitate 'Libelli Responsionum' B. Gregorii M. Papae ad S. Augustinum Angliae Apostolum Animadversiones"—*Jus Pontificium*, XVIII (1938-1939), 171-185; 293-299.

Wurm, Hubert, "Decretales selectae ex antiquissimis Romanorum Pontificum epistulis decretalibus"—*Apollinaris*, XII (1939), 40-93.

Zeiller, Jacques, "Le chorévêque Eugraphus—Note sur le chorépiscopat en occident au Ve siècle"—*Revue d'histoire ecclésiastique*, VII (1906), 27-32.

———, "Le montanisme a-t-il pénétré en Illyricum?"—*Revue d'histoire ecclésiastique*, XXX (1934), 847-851.

———"Les relations de l'ancienne église de Salone avec l'église romaine"—*Bessarione*, Series II, IV (1903), 235-248.

Ziegler, Aloysius K., "Pope Gelasius and His Teaching on the Relation of Church and State"—*Catholic Historical Review*, XXVII (1941-1942), 412-437.

IV. PERIODICALS

Anglican Theological Review, New York, 1918—

Apollinaris, Romae, 1928—

Archiv für katholisches Kirchenrecht, Innsbruck, 1857-1861; Mainz, 1862—

Archiv für Urkundenforschung, Leipzig, 1908-1935; superseded by *Deutsches Archiv für Geschichte des Mittelalters*, Hannoverae, 1937—

Bessarione, Rome, 1896—

Bibliothèque de l'École des Chartes, Paris, 1839—

Byzantinische Zeitschrift, Leipzig, 1892—

Catholic Historical Review, Washington, D. C., 1920—

English Historical Review, London, 1864—

Ephemerides Liturgicae, Romae, 1887—

Gregorianum, Romae, 1920—

Historisches Jahrbuch, Münster, 1864—

Historische Zeitschrift, München und Leipzig, 1824—

Journal of Theological Studies, London, 1899—

Jus Pontificium, Romae, 1921—

Month, The, London, 1864—

Neues Archiv der Gesellschaft für ältere deutsche Geschichtskunde, Hannoverae, 1876-1935; superseded by *Deutsches Archiv für Geschichte des Mittelalters*, Hannoverae, 1937—

Revue bénédictine, Abbaye de Maredsous, Belgium, 1884—

Revue d'histoire ecclésiastique, Louvain, 1900—

Revue des sciences religieuses, Paris, 1921—

Sitzungsberichte der philosophisch-historischen Classe der kaiserlichen Akademie der Wissenschaften, Wien, 1850—

Sitzungsberichte der philosophisch-philologischen und historischen Classe der königlich bayerischen Akademie der Wissenschaften zu München, München, 1861—

Theologische Quartalschrift, Tübingen, 1818—

Traditio, New York, 1943—

Zeitschrift der Savigny-Stiftung für Rechtsgeschichte, Kanonistische Abteilung, Weimar, 1911—; Romanistische Abteilung, Weimar, 1880—

Zeitschrift für katholische Theologie, Innsbruck, 1876—

Zeitschrift für Kirchengeschichte, Tübingen, 1876—

V. ABBREVIATIONS

AKK—*Archiv für katholisches Kirchenrecht*
Avellana—Guenther, *Epistulae Imperatorum Pontificum Aliorum...datae Avellana quae dicitur collectio*
CHR—*Catholic Historical Review*
CSEL—*Corpus Scriptorum Ecclesiasticorum Latinorum*
DACL—*Dictionnaire d'archéologie chrétienne et de liturgie*
Ep.—*Epistola*
Eph. Lit.—*Ephemerides Liturgicae*
Epp.—*Epistolae*
Italia Pontificia—Kehr, *Regesta Pontificum Romanorum, Italia Pontificia*
Jaffé—*Regesta Pontificum Romanorum*, 2. ed.
  JE—Jaffé, *Regesta Pontificum Romanorum*, ed. curavit Ewald
  JK—Jaffé, *Regesta Pontificum Romanorum*, ed. curavit Kaltenbrunner
  JL—Jaffé, *Regesta Pontificum Romanorum*, ed. curavit Loewenfeld
JTSt—*Journal of Theological Studies*
Mansi—*Sacrorum Conciliorum Nova et Amplissima Collectio*
MGH—*Monumenta Germaniae Historica*
Neues Archiv—*Neues Archiv der Gesellschaft für ältere deutsche Geschichtskunde*
PG—Migne, *Patrologiae Cursus Completus, Series Graeca*
PL—Migne, *Patrologiae Cursus Completus, Series Latina*
Regesten—Doelger, *Regesten der Kaiserurkunden des oströmischen Reiches*
Rev. béné.—*Revue bénédictine*
RHE—*Revue d'histoire ecclésiastique*
RSR—*Revue des sciences religieuses*
SS. Lang.—*Scriptores Rerum Langobardicarum et Italicarum Saec. VI-IX*
SS. Merov.—*Scriptorum Rerum Merovingicarum*
Turner—*Ecclesiae Occidentalis Monumenta Iuris Antiquissimi, Canonum et Conciliorum Graecorum Interpretationes Latinae*
ZKT—*Zeitschrift für katholische Theologie*
ZSS—*Zeitschrift der Savigny-Stiftung für Rechtsgeschichte*

INDEX I

PERSONS, PLACES AND THINGS

INDEX II

LETTERS OF GREGORY THE GREAT

(Bold face signifies direct quotation of some length.)

INDEX 3
PAPAL LETTERS

INDEX 4
COUNCILS AND LAWS

BIOGRAPHICAL NOTE

John Albert Eidenschink was born on August 9, 1914, at Detroit Lakes, Minnesota. After completing his elementary schooling in 1928 at Holy Rosary Parochial School in that city, he entered St. John's College Preparatory at Collegeville, Minnesota, graduating therefrom in 1931. In the fall of that year he began his college courses at St. John's University, and in 1933 he entered the novitiate of the Order of St. Benedict at St. John's Abbey and made profession of vows in 1935. In 1937 he received the degree of Bachelor of Arts from St. John's University, and thereafter entered upon his theological studies at St. John's Seminary. The summers of 1939 and 1940 were devoted to post-graduate studies in history at the Catholic University of America Summer Sessions in Dubuque, Iowa. In 1941 he was ordained to the priesthood, and in the following year he was sent by his Superior to the Catholic University of America, from which he received the Baccalaureate Degree in Canon Law in May, 1943, and the Licentiate Degree in May, 1944.

CANON LAW STUDIES *

1. FRERIKS, REV. CELESTINE A., C.PP.S., J.C.D., Religious Congregations in Their External Relations, 121 pp., 1916.
2. GALLIHER, REV. DANIEL M., O.P., J.C.D., Canonical Elections, 117 pp. 1917.
3. BORKOWSKI, REV. AURELIUS L., O.F.M., J.C.D., De Confraternitatibus Ecclesiasticis, 136 pp., 1918.
4. CASTILLO, REV. CAYO, J.C.D., Disertacion Historico-Canonica sobre la Potestad del Cabildo en Sede Vacante o Impedida del Vicario Capitular, 99 pp., 1919 (1918).
5. KUBELBECK, REV. WILLIAM J., S.T.B., J.C.D., The Sacred Penitentiaria and Its Relation to Faculties of Ordinaries and Priests, 129 pp., 1918.
6. PETROVITS, REV. JOSEPH, J.C., S.T.D., J.C.D., The New Church Law on Matrimony, X-461 pp., 1919.
7. HICKEY, REV. JOHN J., S.T.B., J.C.D., Irregularities and Simple Impediments in the New Code of Canon Law, 100 pp., 1920.
8. KLEKOTKA, REV. PETER J., S.T.B., J.C.D., Diocesan Consultors, 179 pp., 1920.
9. WANENMACHER, REV. FRANCIS, J.C.D., The Evidence in Ecclesiastical Procedure Affecting the Marriage Bond, 1920 (Printed 1935).
10. GOLDEN, REV. HENRY FRANCIS, J.C.D., Parochial Benefices in the New Code, IV-119 pp., 1921 (Printed 1925).
11. KOUDELKA, REV. CHARLES J., J.C.D., Pastors, Their Rights and Duties According to the New Code of Canon Law, 211 pp., 1921.
12. MELO, REV. ANTONIUS, O.F.M., J.C.D., De Exemptione Regularium, X-188 pp., 1921.
13. SCHAAF, REV. VALENTINE THEODORE, O.F.M., S.T.B., J.C.D., The Cloister, X-180 pp., 1921.
14. BURKE, REV. THOMAS JOSEPH, S.T.D., J.C.D., Competence in Ecclesiastical Tribunals, IV-117 pp., 1922.
15. LEECH, REV. GEORGE LEO, J.C.D., A Comparative Study of the Constitution "Apostolicae Sedis" and the "Codex Juris Canonici," 179 pp., 1922.
16. MOTRY, REV. HUBERT LOUIS, S.T.D., J.C.D., Diocesan Faculties According to the Code of Canon Law, II-167 pp., 1922.
17. MURPHY, REV. GEORGE LAWRENCE, J.C.D., Delinquencies and Penalties in the Administration and the Reception of the Sacraments, IV-121 pp., 1923.
18. O'REILLY, REV. JOHN ANTHONY, S.T.B., J.C.D., Ecclesiastical Sepulture in the New Code of Canon Law, II-129 pp., 1923.

* Below n. 100 only the following numbers are still available: Nos. 25, 57 and 75. Beginning with n. 100 only the following numbers are unavailable: Nos. 100-111 inclusive, 113 and 115-117 inclusive.

19. Michalicka, Rev. Wenceslas Cyrill, O.S.B., J.C.D., Judicial Procedure in Dismissal of Clerical Exempt Religious, 107 pp., 1923.
20. Dargin, Rev. Edward Vincent, S.T.B., J.C.D., Reserved Cases According to the Code of Canon Law, IV-103 pp., 1924.
21. Godfrey, Rev. John A., S.T.B., J.C.D., The Right of Patronage According to the Code of Canon Law, 153 pp., 1924.
22. Hagedorn, Rev. Francis Edward, J.C.D., General Legislation on Indulgences, II-154 pp., 1924.
23. King, Rev. James Ignatius, J.C.D., The Administration of the Sacraments to Dying Non-Catholics, V-141 pp., 1924.
24. Winslow, Rev. Francis Joseph, O.F.M., J.C.D., Vicars and Prefects Apostolic, IV-149 pp., 1924.
25. Correa, Rev. Jose Servelion, S.T.L., J.C.D., La Potestad Legislativa de la Iglesia Catolica, IV-127 pp., 1925.
26. Dugan, Rev. Henry Francis, A.M., J.C.D., The Judiciary Department of the Diocesan Curia, 87 pp., 1925.
27. Keller, Rev. Charles Frederick, S.T.B., J.C.D., Mass Stipends, 167 pp., 1925.
28. Paschang, Rev. John Linus, J.C.D., The Sacramentals According to the Code of Canon Law, 129 pp., 1925.
29. Piontek, Rev. Cyrillus, O.F.M., S.T.B., J.C.D., De Indulto Exclaustrationis necnon Saecularizationis, XIII-289 pp., 1925.
30. Kearney, Rev. Richard Joseph, S.T.B., J.C.D., Sponsors at Baptism According to the Code of Canon Law, IV-127 pp., 1925.
31. Bartlett, Rev. Chester Joseph, A.M., LL.B., J.C.D., The Tenure of Parochial Property in the United States of America, V-108 pp., 1926.
32. Kilker, Rev. Adrian Jerome, J.C.D., Extreme Unction, V-425 pp., 1926.
33. McCormick, Rev. Robert Emmett, J.C.D., Confessors of Religious, VIII-266 pp., 1926.
34. Miller, Rev. Newton Thomas, J.C.D., Founded Masses According to the Code of Canon Law, VII-93 pp., 1926.
35. Roelker, Rev. Edward G., S.T.D., J.C.D., Principles of Privilege According to the Code of Canon Law, XI-166 pp., 1926.
36. Bakalarczyk, Rev. Richardus, M.I.C., J.U.D., De Novitiatu, VIII-208 pp., 1927.
37. Pizzuti, Rev. Lawrence, O.F.M., J.U.L., De Parochis Religiosis, 1927. (Not Printed.)
38. Bliley, Rev. Nicholas Martin, O.S.B., J.C.D., Altars According to the Code of Canon Law, XIX-132 pp., 1927.
39. Brown, Mr. Brendan Francis, A.B., LL.M., J.U.D., The Canonical Juristic Personality with Special Reference to its Status in the United States of America, V-212 pp., 1927.
40. Cavanaugh, Rev. William Thomas, C.P., J.U.D., The Reservation of the Blessed Sacrament, VIII-101 pp., 1927.
41. Doheny, Rev. William J., C.S.C., A.B., J.U.D., Church Property: Modes of Acquisition, X-118 pp., 1927.

42. Feldhaus, Rev. Aloysius H., C.PP.S., J.C.D., Oratories, IX-141 pp., 1927.
43. Kelly, Rev. James Patrick, A.B., J.C.D., The Jurisdiction of the Simple Confessor, X-208 pp., 1927.
44. Neuberger, Rev. Nicholas J., J.C.D., Canon 6 or the Relation of the Codex Juris Canonici to the Preceding Legislation, V-95 pp., 1927.
45. O'Keefe, Rev. Gerald Michael, J.C.D., Matrimonial Dispensations, Powers of Bishops, Priests, and Confessors, VIII-232 pp., 1927.
46. Quigley, Rev. Joseph A. M., A.B., J.C.D., Condemned Societies, 139 pp. 1927.
47. Zaplotnik, Rev. Johannes Leo, J.C.D., De Vicariis Foraneis, X-142 pp., 1927.
48. Duskie, Rev. John Aloysius, A.B., J.C.D., The Canonical Status of the Orientals in the United States, VIII-196 pp., 1928.
49. Hyland, Rev. Francis Edward, J.C.D., Excommunication, Its Nature, Historical Development and Effects, VIII-181 pp., 1928.
50. Reinmann, Rev. Gerald Joseph, O.M.C., J.C.D., The Third Order Secular of Saint Francis, 201 pp., 1928.
51. Schenk, Rev. Francis J., J.C.D., The Matrimonial Impediments of Mixed Religion and Disparity of Cult, XVI-318 pp., 1929.
52. Coady, Rev. John Joseph, S.T.D., J.U.D., A.M., The Appointment of Pastors, VIII-150 pp., 1929.
53. Kay, Rev. Thomas Henry, J.C.D., Competence in Matrimonial Procedure, VIII-164 pp., 1929.
54. Turner, Rev. Sidney Joseph, C.P., J.U.D., The Vow of Poverty, XLIX-217 pp., 1929.
55. Kearney, Rev. Raymond A., A.B., S.T.D., J.C.D., The Principles of Delegation, VII-149 pp., 1929.
56. Conran, Rev. Edward James, A.B., J.C.D., The Interdict, V-163 pp., 1930.
57. O'Neill, Rev. William H., J.C.D., Papal Rescripts of Favor, VII-218 pp., 1930.
58. Bastnagel, Rev. Clement Vincent, J.U.D., The Appointment of Parochial Adjutants and Assistants, XV-257 pp., 1930.
59. Ferry, Rev. William A., A.B., J.C.D., Stole Fees, V-136 pp., 1930.
60. Costello, Rev. John Michael, A.B., J.C.D., Domicile and Quasi-Domicile, VII-201 pp., 1930.
61. Kremer, Rev. Michael Nicholas, A.B., S.T.B., J.C.D., Church Support in the United States, VI-136 pp., 1930.
62. Angulo, Rev. Luis, C.M., J.C.D., Legislation de la Iglesia sobre la intencion en la application de la Santa Misa, VII-104 pp., 1931.
63. Frey, Rev. Wolfgang Norbert, O.S.B., A.B., J.C.D., The Act of Religious Profession, VIII-174 pp., 1931.
64. Roberts, Rev. James Brendan, A.B., J.C.D., The Banns of Marriage, XIV-140 pp., 1931.
65. Ryder, Rev. Raymond Aloysius, A.B., J.C.D., Simony, IX-151 pp., 1931.

66. Campagna, Rev. Angelo, Ph.D., J.U.D., Il Vicario Generale del Vescovo, VII-205 pp., 1931.
67. Cox, Rev. Joseph Godfrey, A.B., J.C.D., The Administration of Seminaries, VI-124 pp., 1931.
68. Gregory, Rev. Donald J., J.U.D., The Pauline Privilege, XV-165 pp., 1931.
69. Donohue, Rev. John F., J.C.D., The Impediment of Crime, VII-110 pp., 1931.
70. Dooley, Rev. Eugene A., O.M.I., J.C.D., Church Law on Sacred Relics, IX-143 pp., 1931.
71. Orth, Rev. Clement Raymond, O.M.C., J.C.D., The Approbation of Religious Institutes, 171 pp., 1931.
72. Pernicone, Rev. Joseph M., A.B., J.C.D., The Ecclesiastical Prohibition of Books, XII-267 pp., 1932.
73. Clinton, Rev. Connell, A.B., J.C.D., The Paschal Precept, IX-108 pp., 1932.
74. Donnelly, Rev. Francis B., A.M., S.T.L., J.C.D., The Diocesan Synod, VIII-125 pp., 1932.
75. Torrente, Rev. Camilo, C.M.F., J.C.D., Las Processiones Sagradas, V-145 pp., 1932.
76. Murphy, Rev. Edwin J., C.PP.S., J.C.D., Suspension Ex Informata Conscientia, XI-122 pp., 1932.
77. MacKenzie, Rev. Eric F., A.M., S.T.L., J.C.D., The Delict of Heresy in its Commission, Penalization, Absolution, VII-124 pp., 1932.
78. Lyons, Rev. Avitus E., S.T.B., J.C.D., The Collegiate Tribunal of First Instance, XI-147 pp., 1932.
79. Connolly, Rev. Thomas A., J.C.D., Appeals, XI-195, pp., 1932.
80. Sangmeister, Rev. Joseph V., A.B., J.C.D., Force and Fear as Precluding Matrimonial Consent, V-211 pp., 1932.
81. Jaeger, Rev. Leo A., A.B., J.C.D., The Administration of Vacant and Quasi-Vacant Episcopal Sees in the United States, IX-229 pp., 1932.
82. Rimlinger, Rev. Herbert T., J.C.D., Error Invalidating Matrimonial Consent, VII-79, pp. 1932.
83. Barrett, Rev. John D. M., S.S., J.C.D., A Comparative Study of the Third Plenary Council of Baltimore and the Code, IX-221 pp., 1932.
84. Carberry, Rev. John J., Ph.D., S.T.D., J.C.D., The Juridical Form of Marriage, X-177 pp., 1934.
85. Dolan, Rev. John L., A.B., J.C.D., The Defensor Vinculi, XII-157 pp., 1934.
86. Hannan, Rev. Jerome D., A.M., S.T.D., LL.B., J.C.D., The Canon Law of Wills, IX-517 pp., 1934.
87. Lemieux, Rev. Delise A., A.M., J.C.D., The Sentence in Ecclesiastical Procedure, IX-131 pp., 1934.
88. O'Rourke, Rev. James J., A.B., J.C.D., Parish Registers, VII-109 pp., 1934.

89. Timlin, Rev. Bartholomew, O.F.M., A.M., J.C.D., Conditional Matrimonial Consent, X-381 pp., 1934.
90. Wahl, Rev. Francis X., A.B., J.C.D., The Matrimonial Impediments of Consanguinity and Affinity, VI-125 pp., 1934.
91. White, Rev. Robert J., A.B., LL.B., S.T.B., J.C.D., Canonical Ante-Nuptial Promises and the Civil Law, VI-152 pp., 1934.
92. Herrera, Rev. Antonio Parra, O.C.D., J.C.D., Legislacion Ecclesiastica sobra el Ayuno y la Abstinencia, XI-191 pp., 1935.
93. Kennedy, Rev. Edwin J., J.C.D., The Special Matrimonial Process in Cases of Evident Nullity, X-165 pp., 1935.
94. Manning, Rev. John J., A.B., J.C.D., Presumption of Law in Matrimonial Procedure, XI-111 pp., 1935.
95. Moeder, Rev. John M., J.C.D., The Proper Bishop for Ordination and Dimissorial Letters, VII-135 pp., 1935.
96. O'Mara, Rev. William A., A.B., J.C.D., Canonical Causes for Matrimonial Dispensations, IX-155 pp., 1935.
97. Reilly, Rev. Peter, J.C.D., Residence of Pastors, IX-81 pp., 1935.
98. Smith, Rev. Mariner T., O.P., S.T.Lr., J.C.D., The Penal Law for Religious, VIII-169 pp., 1935.
99. Whalen, Rev. Donald W., A.M., J.C.D., The Value of Testimonial Evidence in Matrimonial Procedure, XIII-297 pp., 1935.
100. Cleary, Rev. Joseph F., J.C.D., Canonical Limitations on the Alienation of Church Property, VIII-141 pp., 1936.
101. Glynn, Rev. John C., J.C.D., The Promoter of Justice, XX-337, pp. 1936.
102. Brennan, Rev. James H., S.S., M.A., S.T.B., J.C.D., The Simple Convalidation of Marriage, VI-135 pp., 1937.
103. Brunini, Rev. Joseph Bernard, J.C.D., The Clerical Obligations of Canons 139 and 142, X-121 pp., 1937.
104. Connor, Rev. Maurice, A.B., J.C.D., The Administrative Removal of Pastors, VIII-159 pp., 1937.
105. Guilfoyle, Rev. Merlin Joseph, J.C.D., Custom, XI-144 pp., 1937.
106. Hughes, Rev. James Austin, A.B., A.M., J.C.D., Witnesses in Criminal Trials of Clerics, IX-140 pp., 1937.
107. Jansen, Rev. Raymond J., A.B., S.T.L., J.C.D., Canonical Provisions for Catechetical Instruction, VII-153 pp., 1937.
108. Kealy, Rev. John James, A.B., J.C.D., The Introductory Libellus in Church Court Procedure, XI-121 pp., 1937.
109. McManus, Rev. James Edward, C.SS.R., J.C.D., The Administration of Temporal Goods in Religious Institutes, XVI-196 pp., 1937.
110. Moriarity, Rev. Eugene James, J.C.D., Oaths in Ecclesiastical Courts, X-115 pp., 1937.
111. Rainer, Rev. Eligius George, C.SS.R., J.C.D., Suspension of Clerics, XVII-249 pp., 1937.
112. Reilly, Rev. Thomas F., C.SS.R., J.C.D., Visitation of Religious, VI-195 pp., 1938.

113. Moriarity, Rev. Francis E., C.SS.R., J.C.D., The Extraordinary Absolution from Censures, XV-334 pp., 1938.
114. Connolly, Rev. Nicholas P., J.C.D., The Canonical Erection of Parishes, X-132 pp., 1938.
115. Donovan, Rev. James Joseph, J.C.D., The Pastor's Obligation in Prenuptial Investigation, XII-322 pp., 1938.
116. Harrigan, Rev. Robert J., M.A., S.T.B., J.C.D., The Radical Sanation of Invalid Marriages, VIII-208 pp., 1938.
117. Boffa, Rev. Conrad Humbert, J.C.D., Canonical Provisions for Catholic Schools, VII-211 pp., 1939.
118. Parsons, Rev. Anscar John, O.M.Cap., J.C.D., Canonical Elections, XII-236 pp., 1939.
119. Reilly, Rev. Edward Michael, A.B., J.C.D., The General Norms of Dispensation, XII-156 pp., 1939.
120. Ryan, Rev. Gerald Aloysius, A.B., J.C.D., Principles of Episcopal Jurisdiction, XII-172 pp., 1939.
121. Burton, Rev. Francis James, C.S.C., A.B., J.C.D., A Commentary on Canon 1125, X-222 pp., 1940.
122. Miaskiewicz, Rev. Francis Sigismund, J.C.D., Supplied Jurisdiction According to Canon 209, XII-340 pp., 1940.
123. Rice, Rev. Patrick William, A.B., J.C.D., Proof of Death in Prenuptial Investigation, VIII-156 pp., 1940.
124. Anglin, Rev. Thomas Francis, M.S., J.C.D., The Eucharistic Fast, VIII-183 pp., 1941.
125. Coleman, Rev. John Jerome, J.C.D., The Minister of Confirmation, VI-153 pp., 1941.
126. Downs, Rev. John Emmanuel, A.B., J.C.D., The Concept of Clerical Immunity, XI-163 pp., 1941.
127. Esswein, Rev. Anthony Albert, J.C.D., Extrajudicial Penal Powers of Ecclesiastical Superiors, X-144 pp., 1941.
128. Farrell, Rev. Benjamin Francis, M.A., S.T.L., J.C.D., The Rights and Duties of the Local Ordinary Regarding Congregations of Women Religious of Pontifical Approval, V-195 pp., 1941.
129. Feeney, Rev. Thomas John, A.B., S.T.L., J.C.D., Restitutio in Integrum, VI-169 pp., 1941.
130. Findlay, Rev. Stephen William, O.S.B., A.B., J.C.D., Canonical Norms Governing the Deposition and Degradation of Clerics, XVII-279 pp., 1941.
131. Goodwine, Rev. John, A.B., S.T.L., J.C.D., The Right of the Church to Acquire Property, VIII-119 pp., 1941.
132. Heston, Rev. Edward Louis, C.S.C., Ph.D., S.T.D., J.C.D., The Alienation of Church Property in the United States, XII-222 pp., 1941.
133. Hogan, Rev. James John, A.B., S.T.L., J.C.D., Judicial Advocates and Procurators, XIII-200 pp., 1941.
134. Kealy, Rev. Thomas M., A.B., Litt.B., J.C.D., Dowry of Women Religious, IX-152 pp., 1941.

135. Keene, Rev. Michael James, O.S.B., J.C.D., Religious Ordinaries and Canon 198, V-164 pp., 1942.
136. Kerin, Rev. Charles A., S.S., M.A., S.T.B., J.C.D., The Privation of Christian Burial, XVI-279 pp., 1941.
137. Louis, Rev. William Francis, M.A., J.C.D., Diocesan Archives, X-101 pp., 1941.
138. McDevitt, Rev. Gilbert Joseph, A.B., J.C.D., Legitimacy and Legitimation, X-247 pp., 1941.
139. McDonough, Rev. Thomas Joseph, A.B., J.C.D., Apostolic Administrators, X-217 pp., 1941.
140. Meier, Rev. Carl Anthony, A.B., J.C.D., Penal Administrative Procedure Against Negligent Pastors, XI-240 pp., 1941.
141. Schmidt, Rev. John Rogg, A.B., J.C.D., The Principles of Authentic Interpretation in Canon 17 of the Code of Canon Law, XII-331 pp., 1941.
142. Slafkosky, Rev. Andrew Leonard, A.B., J.C.D., The Canonical Episcopal Visitation of the Diocese, X-197 pp., 1941.
143. Swoboda, Rev. Innocent Robert, O.F.M., J.C.D., Ignorance in Relation to the Imputability of Delicts, IX-271 pp., 1941.
144. Dubé, Rev. Arthur Joseph, A.B., J.C.D., The General Principles for the Reckoning of Time in Canon Law, VIII-299 pp., 1941.
145. McBride, Rev. James T., A.B., J.C.D., Incardination and Excardination of Seculars, XX-585 pp., 1941.
146. Król, Rev. John T., J.C.D., The Defendant in Ecclesiastical Trials, XII-207 pp., 1942.
147. Comyns, Rev. Joseph J., C.SS.R., A.B., J.C.D., Papal and Episcopal Administration of Church Property, XIV-155 pp., 1942.
148. Barry, Rev. Garrett Francis, O.M.I., J.C.D., Violation of the Cloister, XII-260 pp., 1942.
149. Bolduc, Rev. Gatien, C.S.V., A.B., S.T.L., J.C.D., Les Études dans les Religions Cléricales, VIII-155 pp., 1942.
150. Boyle, Rev. David John, M.A., J.C.D., The Juridic Effects of Moral Certitude on Pre-Nuptial Guarantees, XII-188 pp., 1942.
151. Canavan, Rev. Walter Joseph, M.A., Litt.D., J.C.D., The Profession of Faith, XII-143 pp., 1942.
152. Desrochers, Rev. Bruno, A.B., Ph.L., S.T.B., J.C.D., Le Premier Concile Plénier de Québec et le Code de Droit Canonique, XIV-186 pp., 1942.
153. Dillon, Rev. Robert Edward, A.B., J.C.D., Common Law Marriage, X-148 pp., 1942.
154. Dodwell, Rev. Edward John, Ph.D., S.T.B., J.C.D., The Time and Place for the Celebration of Marriage, X-156 pp., 1942.
155. Donnellan, Rev. Thomas Andrew, A.B., J.C.D., The Obligation of the Missa pro Populo, VII-131 pp., 1942.
156. Eltz, Rev. Louis Anthony, A.B., J.C.D., Cooperation in Crime, XII-208 pp., 1942.

157. Gass, Rev. Sylvester Francis, M.A., J.C.D., Ecclesiastical Pensions, XI-206 pp., 1942.
158. Guiniven, Rev. John Joseph, C.SS.R., J.C.D., The Precept of Hearing Mass, XIV-188 pp., 1942.
159. Gulcynski, Rev. John Theophilus, J.C.D., The Desecration and Violation of Churches, X-126 pp., 1942.
160. Hammill, Rev. John Leo, M.A., J.C.D., The Obligations of the Traveler According to Canon 14, VIII-204 pp., 1942.
161. Haydt, Rev. John Joseph, A.B., J.C.D., Reserved Benefices, XI-148 pp., 1942.
162. Huser, Rev. Roger John, O.F.M., A.B., J.C.D., The Crime of Abortion in Canon Law, XII-187 pp., 1942.
163. Kearney, Rev. Francis Patrick, A.B., S.T.L., J.C.L., The Principles of Canon 1127.
164. Linahen, Rev. Leo James, S.T.L., J.C.D., De Absolutione Complicis In Peccato Turpi, 114 pp., 1942.
165. McCloskey, Rev. Joseph Aloysius, A.B., J.C.D., The Subject of Ecclesiastical Law According to Canon 12, XVII-246 pp., 1942.
166. O'Neill, Rev. Francis Joseph, C.SS.R., J.C.D., The Dismissal of Religious in Temporary Vows, XIII-220 pp., 1942.
167. Prince, Rev. John Edward, A.B., S.T.B., J.C.D., The Diocesan Chancellor, X-136 pp., 1942.
168. Riesner, Rev. Albert Joseph, C.SS.R., J.C.D., Apostates and Fugitives from Religious Institutes, IX-168 pp., 1942.
169. Stenger, Rev. Joseph Bernard, J.C.D., The Mortgaging of Church Property, 186 pp., 1942.
170. Waldron, Rev. Joseph Francis, A.B., J.C.D., The Minister of Baptism, XII-197 pp., 1942.
171. Willett, Rev. Robert Albert, J.C.D., The Probative Value of Documents in Ecclesiastical Trials, X-124 pp., 1942.
172. Woeber, Rev. Edward Martin, M.A., J.C.D., The Interpellations, XII-161 pp., 1942.
173. Benko, Rev. Matthew Aloysius, O.S.B., M.A., J.C.D., The Abbot *Nullius*, XVI-148 pp., 1943.
174. Christ, Rev. Joseph James, M.A., S.T.L., J.C.D., Dispensation from Vindicative Penalties, XIII-285 pp., 1943.
175. Clancy, Rev. Patrick M. J., O.P., A.B., S.T.Lr., J.C.D., The Local Religious Superior, X-229 pp., 1943.
176. Clarke, Rev. Thomas James, J.C.D., Parish Societies, XII-147 pp., 1943.
177. Connolly, Rev. John Patrick, S.T.L., J.C.D., Synodal Examiners, and Parish Priest Consultors, X-223 pp., 1943.
178. Drumm, Rev. William Martin, A.B., J.C.D., Hospital Chaplains, XII-175 pp., 1943.
179. Flanagan, Rev. Bernard Joseph, A.B., S.T.L., J.C.D., The Canonical Erection of Religious Houses, X-147 pp., 1943.

180. Kelleher, Rev. Stephen Joseph, A.B., S.T.B., J.C.D., Discussions with Non-Catholics: Canonical Legislation, X-93 pp., 1943.
181. Lewis, Rev. Gordian, C.P., J.C.D., Chapters in Religious Institutes, XII-169 pp., 1943.
182. Marx, Rev. Adolph, J.C.D., The Declaration of Nullity of Marriages Contracted Outside the Church, X-151 pp., 1943.
183. Matulenas, Rev. Raymond Anthony, O.S.B., A.B., J.C.D., Communication, a Source of Privileges, XII-225 pp., 1943.
184. O'Leary, Rev. Charles Gerard, C.SS.R., J.C.D., Religious Dismissed After Perpetual Profession, X-213 pp., 1943.
185. Power, Rev. Cornelius Michael, J.C.D., The Blessing of Cemeteries, XII-231 pp., 1943.
186. Shuhler, Rev. Ralph Vincent, O.S.A., J.C.D., Privileges of Religious to Absolve and Dispense, XII-195 pp., 1943.
187. Ziolkowski, Rev. Thaddeus Stanislaus, A.B., J.C.D., The Consecration and Blessing of Churches, XII-151 pp., 1943.
188. Heneghan, Rev. John Joseph, S.T.D., J.C.D., The Marriages of Unworthy Catholics: Canons 1065 and 1066, XVI-213 pp., 1944.
189. Carroll, Rev. Coleman Francis, M.A., S.T.L., J.C.L., Charitable Institutions.
190. Ciesluk, Rev. Joseph Edward, Ph.B., S.T.L., J.C.L., National Parishes in the United States.
191. Coburn, Rev. Vincent Paul, A.B., J.C.D., Marriages of Conscience, XII-172 pp., 1944.
192. Connors, Rev. Charles Paul, C.S.Sp., A.B., J.C.D., Extra-Judicial Procurators in the Code of Canon Law, X-94 pp., 1944.
193. Coyle, Rev. Paul Raymond, A.B., J.C.D., Judicial Exceptions. IX, 142 pp. 1944.
194. Fair, Rev. Bartholomew Francis, A.B., S.T.L., J.C.L., The Impediment of Abduction.
195. Gallagher, Rev. Thomas Raphael, O.P., A.B., S.T.Lr., J.C.D., The Examination of the Qualities of the Ordinand, X-166 pp., 1944.
196. Gannon, Rev. John Mark, S.T.L., J.C.D., The Interstices Required for the Promotion to Orders, VII-100 pp., 1944.
197. Goldsmith, Rev. J. William, B.C.S., S.T.L., J.C.D., The Competence of Church and State Over Marriage—Disputed Points, X-128 pp., 1944.
198. Goodwine, Rev. Joseph Gerard, A.B., S.T.B., J.C.D., The Reception of Converts, XIV-326 pp., 1944.
199. Kowalski, Rev. Romuald Eugene, O.F.M., A.B., J.C.D., Sustenance of Religious Houses of Regulars, X-174 pp., 1944.
200. McCoy, Rev. Alan Edward, O.F.M., J.C.D., Force and Fear in Relation to Delictual Imputability and Penal Responsibility, XII-160 pp., 1944.
201. McDevitt, Rev. Vincent John, Ph.B., S.T.L., J.C.L., Perjury.

202. Martin, Rev. Thomas Owen, Ph.D., S.T.D., J.C.D., Adverse Possession, Prescription and Limitation of Actions: The Canonical "Praescriptio," XX-208 pp., 1944.
203. Miklosovic, Rev. Paul John, A.B., J.C.L., Attempted Marriages and Their Consequent Juridic Effects.
204. Mundy, Rev. Thomas Maurice, A.B., S.T.L., J.C.L., The Union of Parishes.
205. O'Dea, Rev. John Coyle, A.B., J.C.D., The Matrimonial Impediment of Nonage, VIII-126 pp., 1944.
206. Olalia, Rev. Alexander Ayson, S.T.L., J.C.D., A Comparative Study of the Christian Constitution of States and the Constitution of the Philippine Commonwealth, XII-136 pp., 1944.
207. Poisson, Rev. Pierre-Marie, C.S.C., A.B., Ph.L., Th.L., J.C.L., Droits Patrimoniaux des Maisons et des Églises Religieuses.
208. Stadalnikas, Rev. Casimir Joseph, M.I.C., J.C.D., Reservation of Censures, X-141 pp., 1944.
209. Sullivan, Rev. Eugene Henry, S.T.L., J.C.D., Proof of the Reception of the Sacraments, X, 165 pp., 1944.
210. Vaughan, Rev. William Edward, J.C.D., Constitutions for Diocesan Courts, X-210 pp., 1944.
211. Paro, Rev. Gino, S.T.D., J.C.L., The Right of Apostolic Delegation.
212. Balzer, Rev. Ralph Francis, C.P., J.C.L., The Computation of Time in a Canonical Novitiate.
213. Dougherty, Rev. John Whelan, A.B., S.T.L., J.C.L., De Inquisitione Speciali.
214. Dziob, Rev. Michael Walter, J.C.L., The Sacred Congregation for the Oriental Church.
215. Eidenschink, Rev. John Albert, O.S.B., B.A., J.C.L., The Election of Bishops in the Letters of Gregory the Great.
216. Gill, Rev. Nicholas, C.P., J.C.L., The Spiritual Prefect in Clerical Religious Houses of Study.
217. Hynes, Rev. Harry Gerard, S.T.L., J.C.D., The Privileges of Cardinals, XII, 183 pp., 1945.
218. McDevitt, Rev. Gerald Vincent, S.T.L., J.C.L., The Renunciation of an Ecclesiastical Office.
219. Manning, Rev. Joseph Leroy, J.C.L., The Free Conferral of Offices.
220. Meyer, Rev. Louis G., O.S.B., S.T.B., J.C.L., Alms-gathering by Religious.
221. O'Donnell, Rev. Cletus Francis, M.A., J.C.L., The Marriages of Minors.
222. Prunskis, Rev. Joseph, J.C.L., Comparative Law, Ecclesiastical and Civil, in Lithuanian Concordat.
223. Sweeney, Rev. Francis Patrick, C.SS.R., J.C.L., The Reduction of Clerics to the Lay State.
224. Vogelpohl, Rev. Henry John, J.C.L., The Simple Impediments to Holy Orders.

www.ingramcontent.com/pod-product-compliance
Lightning Source LLC
LaVergne TN
LVHW050239080826
844660LV00012B/558

* 9 7 8 0 8 1 3 2 2 3 9 9 5 *